RAISING KIDS TO BE

BRAVE

SMART

& KIND

RAISING KIDS TO BE

BRAVE

SMART

& KIND

PARENTING WITH PURPOSE

PJ BRADY

Published and distributed by Merack Publishing.

Library of Congress Control Number: 2022916469

Brady, PJ

Raising Kids to be Brave, Smart and Kind: Parenting with Purpose

ISBN: 978-1-957048-73-4 Paperback

ISBN: 978-1-957048-74-1 eBook

ISBN: 978-1-957048-75-8 Hardcover

DEDICATION

To my dearests: Joey, Em and Alex,

You are going to be many things as you grow older. You are going to be someone's friend. You are going to be someone's partner. You might be someone's mother. You will be someone's happiness, joy, and comfort. You will also be someone's sadness, pain, and remorse. You are going to go through so many changes, and I hope you do. Some days you are going to feel like you are on top of the world, and other days you are going to completely fail.

On all of those days, remember that none of the above changes who you are to me. To me, you are the world. You are my courage, you are my thoughts, you are my kindness. You can fumble, you can fail, you can think that you aren't enough. Know that you are imperfect and worthy. Nothing in this book is an expectation of what you should or shouldn't become. These are my guideposts to help me be a better father, not for you to be a better daughter. You are already brave, smart and kind. Yes, you are.

Whoever you are to anyone else, you will always be the loves of my life and I am infinitely proud to be your Dad. Xoxo Always

To everyone else,

What you are about to read is an insight into my family's inner workings so that you may gain insight into your own. This book is meant to be thought-provoking and actionable for us as parents. As a father, I am terrified to let anyone read this. Why, you ask? Not all of my parenting examples are positive. For as much as I think about parenting, I fail at it too. And letting others read about, and hopefully learn from, your failures is pretty scary.

More importantly, I am opening my kids' lives to you as well. We have had plenty of family conversations about this book, and I need to ask you a huge favor. When it comes to my girls, please don't hold them to any brave, smart, kind standard you have in your mind. Don't make an assumption of what you THINK their brave, smart and kind should be in relation to your own. They are allowed to mess up in all the areas where others also mess up. Brave, smart, kind (BSK) isn't about being a perfect parent or a perfect child, but you'll understand that more as you read the book. Thank you and I hope you enjoy!

CONTENTS

PREFACE   1

SECTION ONE | PARENTING WITH PURPOSE

    CHAPTER 1 | REDEFINING BEAUTIFUL   15

    CHAPTER 2 | FORKS IN THE ROAD   29

    CHAPTER 3 | THE EXAMPLES WE SET   49

    CHAPTER 4 | THEIR INNER VOICES   71

SECTION TWO | DISCOVERY

    CHAPTER 5 | IT'S GRAVITY   85

    CHAPTER 6 | FUNDAMENTAL VALUES   111

    CHAPTER 7 | LET'S GET GEEKY   139

SECTION THREE | FRAMEWORK

    CHAPTER 8 | IT'S A JOURNEY   157

    CHAPTER 9 | RECIPROCITY AND EXTENSION   183

SECTION FOUR | JUMPING HURDLES

    SECTION FOUR | INTRODUCTION   219

CHAPTER 10 | THE STRUGGLE IS REAL   223

CHAPTER 11 | PARENTAL GATEKEEPING   241

CHAPTER 12 | FAILURE   261

SECTION FIVE | OK BUT HOW?

CHAPTER 13 | MUSCLE MEMORY   279

CHAPTER 14 | WHAT NEXT?   293

CONCLUSION   305

ACKNOWLEDGMENTS   309

ANNEX   313

ABOUT THE AUTHOR   325

PREFACE

WHAT THE BUBBLES!?!

I was interviewing a candidate several years ago for a management position at an entrepreneurial association. I threw my normal bevy of questions at them about how they maintain relationships with colleagues, what their leadership style is and how they handle conflict. In the first thirty minutes the candidate said that they "lead by example" at least half a dozen times. The last time they said it, I politely interrupted to tell them a story.

We were living in a village outside of Brussels, Belgium in 2017. At the time, the eldest of my three daughters, Alexandra, was seven years old, Emmeline had just turned five, and Josephine was a year old. While my wife was in the kitchen preparing dinner, the eldest two were at the table coloring. I asked, "Who wants to help me set the table?" and Alexandra being the helper that she normally is, got up and said, "Me me me, I wanna help!"

I smiled at her and said, "Thanks kiddo!" Emmeline just sat there coloring away in her own little world. "Emmeline sweetheart, would you like to help us set the table?" I repeated, hoping that she was going to volunteer for something that I was prepared to volun-tell her to do anyway. She just looked up at me and said, "No thanks." I thought to myself, "Well at least she was polite about it."

Alex started pouring drinks for everyone while I was bringing plates from the kitchen (*cue dramatic music*). As Alex was filling Emmeline's glass with water, her hand slipped. In slow motion, I saw one child focused on trying to stay in the lines in her coloring book, completely oblivious to the pending calamity. And I saw the other child's clumsy hands trying to get a grip on the bottle while the glass had already tipped too far for me to hope that this situation would have resolved itself. The water jumped out of the glass and SPLASH!!! The coloring book sat in a puddle of water and Alex wore a surprised but apologetic look on her face. Emmeline's jaw dropped, her brow furled, and her fists clenched at her side. My five year old looked up and yelled, "ALEX, WHAT THE HELL!!!"

My wife's head peeked out from the kitchen, and suddenly all eyes were on me—except for Emmeline's, which were still trying to burn a hole into Alexandra's soul. "Emmeline," I said, trying to keep from laughing at her inappropriate (yet mildly hilarious) language, "Sweetheart, you can't say 'what the hell'." Her face melted into innocence as she looked over to me and said, "Oh, I didn't know that, I am sorry daddy." Her eyes drill back at her sister and instead she said, "ALEX, WHAT THE FUCK!!!"

Oh boy.

All eyes were back on me. My voice raised, "EMMELINE, that is even worse! You can't say those words my love!" This time she was even more puzzled and said, "But Daddy, what AM I allowed to say?"

I tried to think of the first harmless word that came into my mind and I responded with, "Um… bubbles… say what the bubbles." Her eyes fix back on her sister and she shouts, "ALEX, WHAT THE BUBBLES!" She then turned back to me with eyebrows raised and a toothy grin, looking for approval. I nodded before walking away to laugh.

She was five years old when she first dropped the f-bomb. And we all know where she learned that language, right? Yes, your assumption is correct. She obviously learned it from her mother! Belgian women swear like sailors.

**Children are terrible at listening,
but they are incredible at mimicking.**

Ok ok, blame goes where blame is due. Admittedly, I am a native English-speaking father of these beautiful, amazing, exhaustingly devilish daughters, and I am also someone who can, on occasion, throw out an ill-timed swear word starting with "S" or "D" or "F" and ending with an exclamation point. In my defense, these words are not aimed at my children or at any one person in particular. I should also note that living in Europe, radio stations do not play the politically correct versions of songs and there aren't any bleeps. All the swear words are out in the open, and I don't exactly help the matter.

This means my children have a more advanced vocabulary that others could classify as "inappropriate" and each one is learning it a bit younger than the one before. As a mildly responsible parent, I've sat down and explained to them that these are not words they are allowed to use—and they test it. These are not nice words and they hurt people—and they test it. These are words that will get you in trouble—and they test it.

Here is the point. My daughters are intelligent young ladies. They speak Flemish, French and English, do well in school, are involved in after-school activities, AND they know how to swear because that is the example that I have set for them. The girls have since learned that if they just substitute non-offensive words in place of swear words they don't get in any real trouble. "What the bubbles? Dang it! Ah chips!" So I now try to follow their lead.

Kids don't do what we tell them to do, they do what they see us doing. If I don't eat healthily, my kids won't either. If I don't show an interest in sports, my kids won't either. If I don't treat people with respect, my kids won't either. The patterns go on and on. Kids with abusive parents are six times more likely to abuse their children, and it doesn't even need to be that extreme.[1] If you yell, if you get impatient, if you are easily distracted—they will be too. It reminds me of the idea that a parent spends the majority of their time arguing with a miniature version of themselves, which I find to be quite accurate in my home.

At the same time, there is hope. If we read books, our kids will read books. If we play games with them, they will learn to play games. If we are able to maintain composure in stressful moments, they will too—eventually at least.

---

1   Kaufman, J, Zigler E, "Do Abused Children Become Abusive Parents?" American Journal of Orthopsychiatry, April 1987, https://www.ojp.gov/ncjrs/virtual-library/abstracts/do-abused-children-become-abusive-parents.

SOME THINGS WE MODEL FOR KIDS:

- How we handle mistakes
- How we deal with frustrations
- How we solve problems
- How we take care of ourselves
- How we apologize and repair
- How we ask for help
- How we "speak up" for others and ourselves
- How we navigate conflict
- How we approach differences
- How we care for animals
- How we listen

It's completely irrelevant for us to say we "lead by example." We all lead by example. Leadership, at a minimum, implies followership. So whether we lead by good example or bad example, followers will see and hear what we do and will imitate the examples that we give them. This is true for leadership and this is especially true for parenting. The trick isn't to simply lead by example, the trick is to lead by GREAT example.

Most parents and teachers, or leaders and influencers, aren't going to argue that we lead by positive and negative examples, but how many of us look in the mirror when we find ourselves in difficult situations that we don't believe are of our own making? How many of us look outward to blame our kids, spouses, teachers, coaches, team, etc.? How many of us are making changes to the way we operate to reflect the changes we would like to see in our homes, or in the culture of our organizations? How many of us even know what to look for when we want to make a change in our lives? There has never been a framework to help us navigate successes and failures. If we don't have the ability to understand ourselves and our surroundings, then we are destined to make the same mistakes and pass unwanted patterns on to our children. That is where I hope this book can help.

Luckily, there is not only a framework that can help us navigate the treacherous terrain of parenting, but one that has been underlying the human condition for thousands of years. It has been observed, postulated, and assumed by leaders throughout history. It drives our successes, and it drives our failures. Yet, we have rarely (if ever) used it with the intention that it deserves, and it all lives in how we overcome challenges, how we think critically, and how we treat others and ourselves. This framework is at the root of how we live a values-based existence.

Values are the end-all be-all of human thought and action. Values drive our gut instinct. Values drive our conscious and subconscious thought. We view leaders through a values lens, whether that is to be authentic, inspirational, or hardworking. We want our political leaders to be values driven, to have integrity and be morally grounded. In my work, I have helped hundreds of people discover what their values are, and what I find is that the most pivotal period of values development happens at a young age. I began to wonder—why do we wait until people are in their thirties, forties, or fifties to ask what their values are? Why are full-grown adults only having this massively important conversation for the first time in their lives? Why are we not talking to kids about what values are? We should be able to use our own values with greater purpose to help kids understand this fundamental framework in the hope of creating future leaders—and generally incredible human beings.

In my world, I wanted to know how I could do that. What values could I use to help parent my children with greater purpose? One day I sat down and asked myself, "What am I tired of seeing in the world?"

I saw people using fear to control others. I saw people walking around like zombies, not thinking for themselves. I saw a lack of kindness in how we treat each other. It was a lack of these three characteristics—brave, smart and kind. I could have chosen a lot of different words to articulate my values, but I wanted to boil it down to the most basic concept of what I wanted to teach my girls so they felt beautiful.

Once I began viewing the world through a lens of brave, smart and kind (BSK for short), I began to see examples of these values everywhere I looked—history, literature, movies. It's truly undeniable once you see it. I wasn't trying to solve the world's problems. I just wanted to try to raise confident young ladies. What I found was that the Brave Smart Kind Framework I had developed for my kids was not only applicable in parenting, but also in leadership and in education.

QUICK AND EASY DOESN'T EXIST HERE

If you are looking for quick and easy, go somewhere else.

For any parents who are relieved that they have finally found a book to get their kids to listen to them, to do what they are told, to always be polite, get top grades, to overcome all obstacles, or to get them to be *<insert insurmountable expectation here>*, I am sorry to disappoint you.

This book is not a miracle cure for kids who misbehave (incorrectly implying there are some magical unicorn kids out there who DON'T misbehave). This is not some sort of Mary Poppins guide to parenting. Actually, now that I think about it, I am not sorry to disappoint you in the least. If you thought any book could do all that, then this situation might be worse off than we thought!

> *"The shortest distance between two points is a straight line."*
>
> **ARCHIMEDES CIRCA 250 BC**

I have always found the above quote troubling. It's accurate, sure, I just don't find it to be a useful piece of knowledge. Nothing against Archimedes, he was one of the greatest mathematicians of his time and for him this statement was an accurate way to explain geometric theories. But sometime over the past 2200 years, we have used it as a justification for quick and easy strategies and actions. In my opinion, it simply assumes too much.

The first assumption is that someone wants to take the shortest route because they feel it is the fastest. The older I get, the more I realize that the best moments in life are the ones that I want to slow down. I enjoy taking time to think, to reflect, to appreciate, to live whichever moment I am lucky enough to be experiencing.

The second assumption is that there aren't any roadblocks in our way. If you think that the fastest way across the Grand Canyon is straight, then by all means give it a shot. I'm going to find the path that doesn't lead me off a cliff.

I was sitting with Reid Hoffman, the Founder of LinkedIn, (I promise I won't name-drop any more in this book but for this story, it is relevant that my conversation was with him). I was telling him about a business idea that I had called, Massage by Referral, where people could find in-home masseuses through a referral system to take the creepiness out of inviting a stranger into your home to rub your body. I then told him that I couldn't do it because of state-regulations and certifications needed. He said something that I will never forget, "Hmmm good idea, you must not have wanted it bad enough." Not WANTED it?!?

I just told him that I COULDN'T! My first thought was that Reid Hoffman can be kind of an a-hole. (He is not, by the way. He is an incredibly thoughtful and generous person.) After getting over myself, I came around. He was absolutely right. Those roadblocks simply showed me how much I was willing (or unwilling) to do to get what I wanted. Had I sat with the challenge long enough, I could have found an answer. Lack of desire isn't the only type of blockage. Some roadblocks are meant to stop us for good reason, some test us. Some blockages are there for no reason at all, it's just circumstances, and we need to play the hand we are dealt. It doesn't make it right, it just makes it real.

If we imagine we are standing at point A and we want to get to point B, then the third assumption is that we know where point B stands—if it's standing still at all. (Hell, sometimes I'm standing at point A, and I don't even know where point A is.) There is plenty of self-discovery to do before you know exactly where you stand.

Parenting is aiming at moving targets. Just when you think you have something figured out (or sometimes when you are still sorting through), the original target is no longer relevant. Their fear of water disappears, they suddenly start failing addition and subtraction but ace multiplications, their teenage crush moves away, or their dream of being a marine biologist is no longer realistic for someone who fails biology (true story). You don't know why your kids are suddenly afraid/courageous, clear/clueless, or agreeable/frustrated. Parenting can be a messy, blurry, battlefield of a million moving parts. So yeah, your straight line might get you to a given place faster, but is that necessarily the place you were originally aiming for, or maybe you will end up at a place you THOUGHT was there, but isn't?

The reason I am making these points is because there are no shortcuts in this book. If you are looking to go from where you are right now, to raising kids to be brave, smart and kind, it's going to take some time. It will be an adventure and at the end, the shortest moments are probably going to be the moments you'll want to slow down. You will definitely hit roadblocks, because you are dealing with real life. How you decide to handle those roadblocks will tell you how much you want it, if you need to be tested, and some will just be there for no reason at all. And you will be aiming at moving targets. We don't always know what the destination is, sometimes we just need to take a step in the right direction and trust that we are making the best decision with the information and perspectives that we have. Hopefully, I can give you a little more information, a different perspective that can help you take those steps towards your destination. For me, my destination as a father is to raise my kids to be brave, smart and kind.

Parenting and teaching, like leading, is a long game and that is the one we are playing here. There are no short answers. You are not going to find one single tip that is going to take kids from crazy, rambunctious, nutjobs to well-behaved, polite, young ladies and gentlemen. Matter of fact, I actually love the crazy in my kids, it's what makes them interesting. I enjoy the politeness too, just know this just isn't the book that is going to Hogwarts your kid into the perfect child.

Everything in this book is about comprehension and action. It's about how we are able to make better, more positive decisions. That comes with knowledge, understanding the framework, adapting, failing, learning, and then doing it all over again. There are no straight lines here. There are curvy, angled, dotted, invisible, blurred lines. This book is here to help us navigate those parental complexities as best as we can with simple ideas on how to help us raise our kids with specific values.

It's also important to remember that we are only a fraction of what our children become. They will inherit some of your values because of the influence you have had on them. Is there anyone reading this book who was ONLY influenced by their parents? Of course not. We are influenced by so many other people and experiences in our lives— friends, teachers, coaches, other parents.

Part of my journey to realize the type of father I wanted to be was to see other fathers and to choose paths closer to theirs than perhaps that of my own father. It was me finding who I wanted to be and forging my own path. AND without knowing it, taking all that was good about my father and trying my best to emulate that.

My hope is that I can help my kids find their own brave, smart and kind values early on. Some of that will be from my influence. Some of it will be from their mother. A lot will be from the world around them. I have no doubt that they will need to navigate which values they find within and which they don't. I hope that as my family tree continues to branch, that the lessons my daughters are learning will get passed on to their children and so on. And who knows, maybe by parenting with greater purpose we will help our future generations live with greater purpose and spread that to others who may need it too.

SECTION ONE

PARENTING WITH PURPOSE

CHAPTER 1

REDEFINING BEAUTIFUL

I once asked leadership expert Warren Rustand about helping children find their purpose in life and this was his response.

"I always say follow your purpose with passion. Defining our purpose is really important. My purpose is to improve the human condition wherever I find it. When we share that with our children, they should be able to see that from our daily activities, and what we value. The best thing is to show them by our actions what our purpose is. If I stop to help a person who is homeless, our children can see I value that life, regardless of that person's condition, and that I have the means to help someone else. When our family prepares food and takes it down to the homeless shelter in our community, we take our whole family with us. We don't just drop off the food, but we serve it as well. And our children get to have talks with those who are there. They can see and feel an act of kindness, an act of generosity that their parents are demonstrating and leading them through. I have always believed with our children that how we act is more important than what we say. Our purpose comes alive through that which we do."

Warren has been living his life with this intent for years, his consistency in his purpose is amazing. He knows this better than anyone; he just has a much more poetic way to say it than I do.

I have always known I wanted to be a father. I never formally studied child psychology, I never intended to write a book on parenting. I did, however, study leadership. I have worked in the leadership arena for over fifteen years. Surprise! I'm not a parenting expert. Let's get that out of the way. I'm a leadership person who is also a full-time parent. However, there's such a strong, undeniable connection between leadership and parenting and I've been able to apply much of my professional knowledge to my role as a father. If you were expecting to hear from a PhD in parenting, I'm not your guy. This book is simply a collection of the thoughts and actions I've learned along the way to becoming a purposeful parent.

I have been fortunate enough to work for two leadership organizations since 1998. The first was an international leadership organization called Up with People (UWP). It sends college-aged students around the world to live in host families to do community service and perform musicals.

The second was a non-profit that engages leading entrepreneurs to learn and grow called The Entrepreneurs' Organization (EO). You'll see me reference both of them occasionally because of how much I learned and how they shaped me as a person.

The most impactful lessons I learned were in regard to leading others. At UWP, I was exposed to new countries and cultures. I was on the road for ten months of the year for two-and-a-half years, and approximately every four days we would change cities and host families. If you do the math, that exposed me to somewhere around 180 host families. That is 180 families, some with kids, some adopted, some living in poverty and willing to give you anything they had, some who were wealthy and shared their fortune with others. Not all of my experiences were good, and some were uncomfortable, but thankfully for me they were all safe. Moreover, it was an opportunity to learn through experience. It was in UWP where I held my first-ever managerial position, and I made A LOT of mistakes. Most I learned from and some I repeat.

At EO, I was part of a leadership-making machine. This is an incredible organization for helping business owners realize that if they can get their leadership right, then a lot of the other parts of their businesses and personal lives begin to work out as well. I lead a team that was responsible for all the entrepreneurial groups in Europe, the Middle East, Pakistan and Africa.

From 2005-2017, I did my best to learn from some of the best leaders in the world. I was able to travel to all of these locations and sit down with some very successful entrepreneurs to talk about leadership; talk about what they stood for, how they made decisions, how they motivated people, how they succeeded, and more importantly, how they failed. What I learned was that it came down to one very specific attribute: personal values.

> *"The leader's fundamental act is to induce people to be aware or conscious of what they feel—to feel their true needs so strongly, to define their values so meaningfully, that they can be moved to purposeful action."*
>
> **JAMES MCGREGOR BURNS**

Strong leaders have strong values. They know what they stand for, and that is how they intentionally live their lives.

As I was traveling the world, learning about leadership, facilitating leadership programs and sessions, I also became a father. Alexandra came into my world in 2010 and it was love at first sight—love and fear, let's not downplay that emotion. I was still working for EO in 2012 when Emmeline was born, and I was just about to wrap up my work there when Josephine was born in 2016. Sometime around 2014, I was a participant at EO's Leadership Academy and I met the incredible leadership expert previously mentioned, Warren Rustand. He was in his sixties when we met; a highly successful entrepreneur, with a background working for President Ford and a former professional basketball player. I walked into the Leadership Academy having significantly studied transformational vs. transactional leadership theory (more on my geeky side later) but I never related the transformational leadership skills specifically to values. It was Warren who got me to see the power in values, and in leading from values. As I was a young father, I saw a great opportunity to take what I was learning about being a leader and apply it to fatherhood.

When Alex was four and Emmeline was two, I started focusing on what type of women I'd like my daughters to become and what influence I had on that as a father. I started being more observant of the women around me. How they acted, what they said, and what they thought. It is amazing how much you see in the world when you open your eyes. What I saw was both inspirational AND terrifying! Paying better attention, I was inspired as I began to witness and hear many stories of courage, critical thinking and kindness. And it was terrifying because many women, in my world at least, are extremely critical of themselves. And they get SO much help in self-criticizing from society. Too fat, too skinny, too tall, too short, too bossy, not assertive enough, too fragile, too bitchy. This is not a women's empowerment book—there are others who are significantly more well-versed in the topic than I am—this is just to say that I noticed it. And something else I noticed was that a lot of women in my life didn't feel beautiful. And it broke my heart.

So, what do I want for my girls? I want them to grow up to be confident and happy. I want them to grow up and FEEL beautiful. But what the hell do I know about being a confident, happy, beautiful woman? Very little is the answer.

Moreover, what is my role in helping them get there and how was I going to do that? I might not know about being a confident, happy, beautiful woman, but I know about values. And what is my role? I am their father! That's who I am. And my role is to be their role model. I am going to be the support they need AND teach them what I can, so they can do what they need to on their own. As a father who also knows about values-based leadership, I decided to start there.

Fortunately, as I live in Belgium, I found myself with a very unique opportunity. My wife is Belgian and we live in the Flemish-speaking region in Belgium. That means that my children go to school in Dutch, they speak French with their mother, and I was the only person teaching them English resulting in their "advanced" vocabulary.

If I wanted my daughters to grow up feeling beautiful, I needed to define "beautiful" for them. This unique opportunity was how I was going to introduce values into my daughters' lives. The problem was how do you redefine a word that can mean so many things to so many people? I wish I could say that I gave it an abundance of thought, that I rigorously read through parenting books, behavioral psychology articles or even leadership theory. I did none of that. I simply asked myself, "What am I tired of in the world?"

My first thought was that I am tired of people using fear to control others. This answer probably came to me first because of how much I pay attention to the leadership and political scenes around the world, and even more so in the United States. I detest politically-swaying entertainment that disguises itself as "news." I'll refrain from going too far down that rabbit hole, but using fear to influence isn't a new concept. Yes it happens in politics, the "other side will ruin your life, vote-for-me" concept is getting old but it works. It also happens in the media, "catchy title of something terrible that will get you to click and get us more viewers = more advertising dollars" is a pretty lucrative marketing strategy. Looking back in history, many religions used fear to control people, and many rulers used religion to frighten subjects into subjugation. Look at how we use fear as a sales tactic. Most importantly, look at how we use fear to get children to do what we want them to do. That last statement deserves some time to digest. Think about how we, as parents, use fear in order to get a thought or action out of our children. Have you ever made your children scared of a consequence for you to get a desired outcome? An example would be, "Unless you want to get cavities, go brush your teeth!" Yes, I am guilty of the same. Now I don't want to negate fear. "No Fear" was a very popular bumper sticker in the nineties and pretty misguided. Fear exists and needs to be explored, understood and navigated. I simply don't want it to control me and I certainly don't want it to control my children. **I choose to teach my girls to be brave.**

My second thought was, I am tired of people walking around in front of their screens acting like zombies. You see more and more people digesting every bit of information without a second thought. We see cultural perspectives being taught as fact. (Please don't get me started on "alternative facts.") There are surefire ways to help our children navigate the misinformation that circulates. I don't need my daughters to be geniuses, I just want them to have the ability, tools, processes and language to think things through. I want my girls to be curious. I want them to seek out information. I want them to use their brains to be creative, or logical, or intelligent, so they can approach the world with critical thought. **I choose to teach my girls to be smart.**

My last thought may be unfair, but I am tired of seeing the lack of kindness in the world. The concept of kindness, or a lack of kindness, isn't the unfair part. The unfair part is that there is SO much kindness in the world, and yet we are drawn to unkind acts. I think unkindness is magnified for the same reason that fear is magnified. We hear stories of unkind people so often because those stories grab our attention. The reason it made it to my top three list was because for me "kind" is the value that has the least room for error. I have little tolerance for unkindness in my world, my parenting, and especially in my kids. Yet we are all guilty of it at some point. We act with judgement and defensiveness too quickly. We currently live in a time where it's easy to unleash our discomfort on others with anonymity online. It isn't that the world is less kind than it used to be, we have just created an environment where we witness it with more prevalence.

My affinity with kindness isn't just because I was given so many positive and negative examples as a child. When I was touring with Up with People and living with host families, I was welcomed into their homes, fed from their tables, given time to play with their kids, and introduced to neighbors and friends. I lived with 600 other UWP "students" over three years and heard incredible stories of kindness. I chose "kind" as a value because the worst situations in the world are where people lack compassion, empathy, goodwill, gratefulness, etc. And in the best of times, there is an abundance of those same characteristics. Those are lessons to be taught, and **I choose to teach my girls to be kind.**

As their father and primary source of the English language, I told my daughters that "beautiful" doesn't mean to be pretty. Pretty is something else, pretty is for things, pretty fades. Beautiful means three things and three things only: it means to be brave, to be smart, and to be kind. Just those three things. BEAUTIFUL is something you feel.

But, where did we start?

1.1 DEFINE BRAVE SMART KIND (BSK)

With Alexandra and Emmeline at the ages of four and two, I had to find ways to teach my daughters about being brave, smart and kind. The first thing we had to do was to define these words, and for young children I had to keep it introductory. So we said that:

- Brave is that it's ok to be afraid, but you need to make the right choice anyway.

- Smart is to think about something and make a good choice.

- Kind is to be nice to people.

This wasn't rocket science, just some basic concepts to help them understand these values.

1.2 DISPLAY BRAVE SMART KIND

If you are into advertising or marketing, then you know it takes a consumer approximately seven times to be reminded of your products before they actually register it. I wanted my girls to see it everywhere!

First I bought some paint from Ikea that lets you turn your wall into a chalkboard. And, as some people have told me, I can go overboard with certain ideas that I find exciting. I PAINTED EVERYWHERE! The hallway, office, kitchen, and my daughter's room. We actually had to repaint some walls with regular colors so that our home didn't look like a university lecture hall. (And by "we" I mean my wife. And by "had to" I mean that she did it when I wasn't home.)

On the walls, we started drawing pictures. I drew a lion's head to represent brave, I drew a light bulb to represent smart, and I drew two stick people with hearts, hugging each other to represent kindness. We also put up different quotes and sayings on the walls as reminders. If you remember the ages of the girls at this time, you'll note that they weren't at an age where they could read. The reminders weren't for them. The reminders were for my wife and I. This part is extremely important. We all need reminders. I need regular reminders. The glowing PTA parent needs reminders. The supermom who looks like she has all her shit together needs reminders. The wunderdad who is adored by all his friends needs reminders. If you really want me to shatter your world, your perfect grandma probably sucked as a mother sometimes too. Reminders are needed because with so much noise around us, we are easily distracted.

As time has gone on, we've changed the quotes and messages on our chalkboard walls. From when I first put the paint up, only one of the walls has the original message still written on it. The reminder is for my wife and I in the kitchen. It is a quote from clinical psychologist

Russell A. Barkley that says, "The kids that need the most love ask for it in the most unloving ways. Be patient." This saying has lasted the test of time because we need it pretty much every day! It not only speaks to the kindness and empathy that we need to show our kids, but also what we need to show each other.

Displaying values works. The messages need to be present in your child's eyes and ears. Find the books, find the movies, find the stories that resonate with children. BSK can be found everywhere.

I got so excited about how well the BSK stuff was working that I asked a graphic artist to design us a logo. We wanted to print some of our own swag as reminders. We got some shirts printed up and the girls proudly wore them out and about.

1.3 DISCUSS BRAVE SMART KIND

The last step is the bread and butter of BSK parenting, this is the part that makes the most significant and sincere difference in my relationships with my girls. We are able to discuss the hard stuff. Because we have put words around it and put definitions behind our values, we are able to talk about them regularly.

It first started when I would pick up the girls from school. As parents, our most relevant, encompassing, kind question that we ask (because we genuinely love our kids and want to know everything they have learned, and who they played with, and all their cares and concerns), preparing ourselves for them to share everything is, "Hey! How was your day?!?" To which they give an emphatic, if not indifferent response, "Fine," with an occasional addition of, "What are we having for dinner?"

Head, meet palm.

I decided one day that I was going to break up my destructive pattern of disappointment, so when my girls got in the car I changed my question to Alex. I said, "Hello sweetheart, who were you kind to today?" To which SHE responded, "Fine... Wait, what?"

Since that day, the first question I ask them when they get into the car has been either:

- Who were you kind to today?
- Did you make any smart choices?
- Did you do anything that scared you today, and what did you do about it?

At first, they had to think for a bit before giving me answers. I'd give them some time to think about it before they would struggle with a generic answer. Then the coolest thing started to happen. They started to give me stories BEFORE I asked the question. Then, in the natural order of the rest of my world, the girls would start to get into arguments about who would tell me their stories first.

Head, meet palm.

Honestly speaking, I'll take their fighting over indifference any day. The bigger part was that they started telling me things they never would have told me if I had just asked, "How was your day?"

The discussions started with an after-school story about Angela who fell and scraped her knee, and Alex helping her up or Emmeline who made the smart choice to walk away from some kids who were making fun of her. Then they started telling me about other things. They tell me about how they feel stupid because they aren't in a higher reading level. So we go back to the definition of smart, which doesn't mean to be intelligent, but does mean to make good choices. If you want to improve, the smart choice is to practice. They tell me that they are scared to talk to a friend who they were mean to the other day. So we go back to the definition and say that it is ok to be afraid, that you still need to do it anyway. They tell me about how someone else was mean to them. So we go back to the definition and talk about being nice to other people, and maybe they can forgive this person.

I can't emphasize enough that the definitions matter more than the words themselves.

> What brave means to you can be completely different than what it means to me, and that is ok. These are values, not commandments.

And when it comes to children, these are fundamental values that their future values will grow out of. What we are doing here is planting seeds that become roots, that grow into something much more beautiful.

What BSK has done is give us context for important conversations. For now my girls are telling me the schooltime stories of kids being nice or mean, of making smart or not-so-smart choices or being scared of what someone thinks of them, but those conversations are going to change.

What happens when "brave" means that they know they are making less money than their male counterparts at work and they need to confront their employer about it? They need to face down the fear of losing their job, of losing respect, of losing future opportunities for growth, being seen as a complainer or not being a team player.

What happens when "smart" means they realize they've engaged in some self-destructive behavior and they want to change but they don't know how? Do they need to sit with those thoughts? How can they learn to grow? Who are people they can approach? What are the steps to change?

What happens when "kind" means that they need to help a friend get away from an abusive relationship? Or heaven forbid, they need to get out of an abusive relationship themselves but they are afraid of abandoning someone else in need?

Whether they are five or fifty-five-years-old, these are the relevant conversations. Meaningful talks around very real issues that women, and people, struggle with on a regular basis. And we are just touching the tip of the iceberg here.

Note that I am not implementing BSK so I can have brave, smart, kind children. I am not that naïve. I am doing this because I hope they can get there one day. I am writing this for others because I hope they can get there too, and we all need some reminders along the way. I know that BSK is not some all-encompassing cure to all issues in the world. I am simply stating that when (not if) my daughters find themselves in these difficult situations, they will be able to recognize the issues, respond to what is going on around them, and recover to make decisions that will help them.

CHAPTER 1 TAKE HOME

- Write down what—beyond happiness—you want for your kids as they get older.
- Find a way to introduce values to your kids.
- Consider how you would define brave, smart and kind.
- Start writing down what you value around your house.
- Use values to begin talking with your kids about the easy stuff. Then when they are ready to talk about the hard stuff, they'll already have the language.

CHAPTER 2

FORKS IN THE ROAD

One of many difficulties a child struggles with is knowing what decision the "right" decision is. What does Mommy want me to do? What does Daddy want me to do? What will make people like me? What does a lemon taste like? What happens if I squeeze that lemon in my sister's eye? If I see the dog licking the floor, is it ok for me to do that too? If an adult yells, and gets what they want, shouldn't that work for me? How many times does it take jumping on Dad's groin before he thinks it's as funny as everyone else does?

Decisions, decisions! Well, if you ever have felt confused by the decision-making process that you have gone through as an adult, multiply that times 500 and take out logic, tact and consequence. Children learn lessons, much like everyone else, through experiential learning and failure. Their failure rate is just excruciatingly higher than most of ours.

The point is, choosing what is wrong or right, funny or annoying, playful or aggressive can be very hard for a child. Many of us have yet to perfect that skill, but when raising children how many chances do they get before a parent (who just put in a long work day with a micromanaging boss, is being told by their mother-in-law how perfect HER children were raised, and just stepped on their fourth LEGO of the day) says, "Enough is enough!" and dishes out the go-to punishment that has yet to work from the last hundred times it has been tried.

One of our primary roles as parents is to help our children make choices. Yeah, it doesn't sound like rocket science when we say it like that, but that doesn't mean it's any less difficult. In your mind and in mine, we know the exact choices that kids should make. Those choices are easy! As first-time parents, while our little ones' minds are still developing and struggling to find answers, it feels like we know all the answers to THEIR choices though we are struggling with our own choices. That is because our kids are experiencing things for the first time and are struggling through. As parents, we are experiencing things for the first time and struggling through. You know the answers to your kids' choices, because you have done it before. You know what lemon tastes like. They don't. And when your kid is crying their eyes out and you are holding on by a very thin string, you are experiencing that situation for the first time. You and your kids share the same frustrations.

If you are saying right now, I still don't know what to do after the second, tenth, or hundredth time my kid is crying their eyes out either—well, welcome to your adolescence of parenthood. You might not know how to handle a temper tantrum for a while, just like your kid won't know why they can't use a marker on the walls for a while. This is why people who have been around kids (like non-first-time parents, teachers, child care providers) aren't freaking out when a kid is crying. They have been there before and have more experience. I felt significantly more comfortable when my second child was freaking out than the first. I had done this before. It wasn't until my second presented me with NEW challenges, that I then felt like a first-time parent again.

We need to dig deeper and ask how and why those decisions were made, both for our children and from their perspectives. So get out your shovels! Here we go.

2.1 ALICE IN WONDERLAND

One of the things that values are able to give us, is guidance for our children to help in their ever-confusing world. My favorite illustration of this comes from *Alice in Wonderland*.

Alice is walking lost in the woods, strolling down a path. When she comes to a fork in the road she needs to decide which direction to choose. She becomes distressed and paralyzed. Just at that moment she sees a smile appear from thin air and the Cheshire cat presents himself to her.

Elated, she says, "I am so happy you are here, I am lost, and I don't know which choice to make. Can you help me?"

"Of course," replies the riddling cat, "Please tell me where you are going."

Alice thinks for a second and says, "Well, I don't know."

To which the cat wisely responds, "Then your choice doesn't matter."

> *"One day Alice came to a fork in the road and saw a Cheshire cat in a tree. 'Which road do I take?' she asked. 'Where do you want to go?' was his response. 'I don't know,' Alice answered. 'Then,' said the cat, 'it doesn't matter.'"*
>
> **LEWIS CARROLL,** *ALICE'S ADVENTURES IN WONDERLAND*

I love the simplicity and profundity in that answer. If you don't know where you want to go, choose any path, they will all get you there.

If you don't have a destination in mind, then how can you make any choice with intention? This is true for any decision in life, by the way, whether it is remodeling your home, creating your career path or nurturing a relationship. You need to have a destination in mind to make, what you believe to be, the best decisions to get there.

Now I can already hear people saying, "It's the journey that matters, not the destination." To that I say, you are half right. Both the journey AND the destination matter. How philosophical, right?!? Of course it is philosophical, right up until it isn't. Our destinations aren't physical places, they are our goals, our dreams, our desires, our late-night conversations that say, THIS is the person I want to be—and then taking action to become that person! THIS is the life I want to live— and then taking action to live that life! It's all philosophical until you take the action for it not to be.

And what actions are you supposed to take if you don't know what your "philosophical" destination is? My sister-in-law is a globe-trotting, journey-centric person. The destination for her means less than the journey she takes to get there. But part of her destination is to enjoy high-intensity adventures. If she is standing at a fork in the road, choosing between sitting at home or taking an exotic trip, nine out of ten times she'll choose the adventure because a journey can be a destination in its own right.

2.2 PURPOSE VERSUS CONSEQUENCE

Like it or not, the way we behave as parents has a huge impact on how our kids respond. Being the grown-up can be very hard! How we phrase things, the tone of voice we use, our body language and facial expressions set the tone for our interactions. We are teaching our children how to make requests, how to show respect and how to compromise. Sometimes, I do pretty well. Other times, I show up as less than my best self and that becomes a learning experience for both me and my girls.

As a parent, we are arguably the most influential people in our child's life, but we can't lead by force. We need to lead by influence. If you ever ask the question, "How can I get my kid to...?" then there are very few answers because trying to get kids to do what you want them to do is as futile as me trying to get that frickin' homemade slime stain off my couch (awesome present, Grandma!).

Now, don't get me wrong. You can absolutely get your kid to clean their room through some sort of reward system—or conversely through some sort of punishment system. My experience with those two concepts is they are mildly misleading. Do they get the job done? Sometimes, but we need to look at the purpose of our actions prior to the consequence of those actions.

We are able to address purpose better when we understand that all actions come from an emotion, and all emotions come from a need. If we are only addressing the actions of children, then they will continue to act in the same ways. Let's take an example of a child lashing out—hitting, biting, crying. If that action is hitting, then we quickly address that action by removing the child from the situation (time out) and/or some other sort of punishment so they learn that the consequence of their action is negative. Underneath that behavior however is an emotion—anger, sadness, loneliness. If we can identify the emotion, then we can see the need that emotion is looking to satisfy. Maybe it's a need for connection, for safety, or for a sense of control. When we deal with the emotions of children, they start to feel seen and heard. We start to earn their trust. If in addition, we can identify and work through the needs of the child, then we can create significant change in their emotions and actions.

P.S. This doesn't only apply to children.

The question I ask myself is, "What is the behavior I am trying to encourage in my child?" Am I trying to get them to clean their room, or am I trying to get them to do what they are told? One of them can be categorized by a positive action and the other is categorized as a dominance reaction. I don't want my child to be a "do-what-you-are-told" type of person. Should they do what others tell them to do? Yes, sometimes—assuming those actions have a purpose that makes sense. Should they do *everything* that others tell them to do? Absolutely not! I want my kids to grow up to think critically, to have their minds turned on, to ask questions and to make up their minds based on experience, knowledge, intuition, etc. THAT is how we have defined "smart." Think about it and make a good choice. So when it comes to cleaning their room, let's think about it. Is this a positive action or a dominance reaction? Positive reinforcement can actually work if the goal is to be smart.

CONVERSATION #1: THE POWER STRUGGLE

Me: Sweetheart, can you clean your room please?

Kid: Ugh, Daaaaddddd! It's so boring and I didn't even mess it all up!

Me: I don't care, clean it up.

Kid: Ugh, this is so unfair!

Me: Well, life isn't fair.

Kid: Yeah, yeah Dad, you say that all the time.

Me: Stop talking to me like that and just clean your room.

Kid: Why?

Me: Because I said so. Do it.

This differs from this conversation:

CONVERSATION #2: THE LOGICAL ARGUMENT

Me: Sweetheart, can you clean your room please?

Kid: Ugh, Daaaaddddd! It's so boring and I didn't even mess it all up!

Me: Why should you clean your room? What happens if you clean your room?

Kid: I don't know.

Me: Could you find your jacket this morning?

Kid: No.

Me: If your room was clean could you find your jacket?

Kid: Yes.

Me: So the smart choice would be to…

Kid: Yeah yeah, I get it Dad… I still don't want to clean my room.

Me: I know you don't and it still needs to get done.

Or this conversation:

CONVERSATION #3: POSITIVE REINFORCEMENT

Me: What happens if you clean your room?

Kid: I get my allowance <insert other reward here>.

Me: What happens if you don't clean your room?

Kid: I don't get my allowance <insert reward here>.

Me: So what do you think the smart thing to do would be?

Kid: Clean my room.

Me: You ARE a smart kid! And I love you.

Kid: Yeah, yeah Dad, you say that all the time.

Lessons from Conversation #1

The first lesson is that "life isn't fair." I would hazard a guess that most parents sincerely believe that life isn't always fair and it's a valuable lesson for kids to learn. And at the same time, what you have just taught them is that what they want isn't important, and even if they want something and don't get it, then they can go ahead and blame it on "life" as opposed to taking responsibility for why they didn't get it.

The next lesson is that life isn't fair AND that they need to obey. Now if one of your family values is obedience, then no need to read further.

Lessons from Conversation #2

The first lesson they may learn is, "Ugh, my Dad is super annoying." But they were always going to learn that lesson at some point! The next lesson is that, "While my Dad is annoying, he's not wrong." If we get into the habit of asking our kids "why" questions, they are going to get in the habit of asking themselves those same questions—which, in my opinion, is a great thing. The byproduct of asking themselves "why" questions is they will start asking YOU "why" questions, repeatedly if necessary. Be prepared for that. If you are looking to have smart kids, then encourage the questions. Critical thought doesn't exist without some form of curiosity.

Lessons from Conversation #3

I've heard mixed reviews on positively rewarding a child for chores they are supposed to do anyway. Personally, it has worked for us. Positive rewards give them a sense of accomplishment and create a longer-lasting conditioned response. We'll get into positive reinforcement in our leadership theory later, but the other lesson is just as important— they get in the habit of hearing you say that they are smart and that you love them. Please, I am begging you, do not discount this point. From a young age, reinforce every time that you notice your kids being brave, smart or kind. It happens all the time, even if we are programmed to look more for their faults than their victories. Look for the opportunities to tell them they are getting it right in a world that so regularly tells them they are getting it wrong.

And obviously each parent reading this knows that the scenarios I have outlined are just three of a thousand possible conversations, and we all know that each of those examples can go awry. Sometimes you just need to stay the course and keep your sights on your values. That conversation could go, and has gone on, for much longer! The end of it is, "What is the smart choice?" And the lesson that is emphasized throughout is to stop, think and make the smart choice. It is important to remember that there is a choice for them to make. I teach my kids that they always have choices AND that they may not like their options, but the choice is there.

Option 1: Clean your room and get what you want.

Option 2: Don't clean your room and don't get what you want.

Option 3: Yell at me and then you'll be sitting in your room until you clean it and you also won't get what you want.

Now look, as a faulted parent (which is as obvious as saying as a flightless turtle), I know that sometimes shit needs to get done and after repeatedly asking kindly, yelling will get that shit done faster! For instance, your mother-in-law is on her way over and for the love-of-all-things-holy she is bringing three bags of candy for the kids and they will be all hyped-up on sugar, riding the dog like a pony in twenty minutes and the last thing you need to hear her say is, "I told you, this is why kids need at least one parent to stay home."

So to avoid attempted assault charges, you just need your kids to pick up their bubbling room!!! (Ok breathe...) Raising your kids to be brave, smart and kind will NOT change that scenario. What it might do is give you context to have that conversation with your kids. What it might do is lead you to frame your thoughts, so you don't fly off the handle. What it most likely will do is help you keep your head on straight even when you feel you are the only person in your house holding on to even the slightest bit of sanity. Remember, raising kids with values is playing the long game where short-term victories are not guaranteed.

My wife and I see all our wonderful characteristics in our children at different times, and we also see our faults—most often we see the faults and credit their beauty to something or someone else.

I know that when it comes to temper, I have a long fuse but a big boom. I am a relatively patient person, AND when that patience runs out, the clouds turn dark and start to swirl, the ground cracks and from the fiery depths rises my hideous, "FOR THE LOVE OF ALL THINGS HOLY JUST PUT ON YOUR SHOES SO WE CAN WALK TO SCHOOL" monster. So, when my daughter gets frustrated at the end of her math assignment after we say "you still have one more page to do," I start to see HER clouds turn dark and start to swirl, the ground cracks and she loses her shit.

On one hand it's hard for me to get upset with her when I know exactly what she is feeling. On the other hand, my big BOOM is something I don't like about myself which means that I REALLY don't like seeing it in her. So it makes me react even stronger when she loses her temper and it often ends with something like—I don't know if you have ever seen the L.A. tornado scene in *The Day After Tomorrow* but if not, imagine when multiple storms combine to create one massive destructive force. Now, imagine that scene acting itself out between the living room, up the stairs, into her bedroom where she tried to slam the door only to find my boot stopping the force, before the epic staredown that I "win"—as if there are ever winners in this scenario.

How many times as a parent I wish I had a rewind button on conversations with my children…

Here is one of the places that values can help. What is the destination? If you don't know where you want to go, then how can you possibly know the right path to take? If the goal is always to "just get it done" then HOW you get it done doesn't matter. If how you get it done doesn't matter then why does raising your voice to your kids make you feel so bad about yourself? Why does it make them feel so bad about themselves too? The HOW is terribly important, and how you do things needs to be based on what your destination is. The HOW needs to be determined by your values.

If we want our kids not to let fear dictate their actions, then our choices need to acknowledge fear, as opposed to dismissing fear, and help give our kids the courage to do what is right.

If we want to raise our children to think critically, then our choices need to be considered and we need to encourage our kids to go through a thought process.

If we want to raise our children to treat themselves and others with respect, then our choices need to be respectful of ourselves and others.

So how do we do that?

The way to raise a child with values comes down to the difference between telling them what to do versus teaching them how to be. You can raise a child by teaching them the consequences of their actions or you can teach them to know the purpose of their actions, which then naturally HAVE consequences.

All actions have consequences, but children don't think in consequential terms, they think in short-term emotional, need-driven, instant-gratification terms. They have no concept of long-term purpose as a destination. *I am mad, so I will yell. I want a candy so I am going to take one—and if I don't get one, I will yell.*

And in all of our "adult wisdom" we discipline them by teaching them the consequences of their actions instead of asking them about the purpose of their actions.

Ever had this conversation?

Please go sit down.
Why?
Because I told you to sit down.
I don't want to sit down.
Then you'll be sitting in your room.

This is an oversimplified example, but it goes straight into "what will happen if you don't." What is missing from this conversation? We don't know why the kid was standing in the first place. What is the reason why they do what they do?

Purpose is their reason to make one decision over another, and we are able to give them purpose through values. We can use values to unscramble their minds, limiting input and putting them on the right track to make a good decision. And if/when they make the wrong choice, it gives you both a very easy way to discuss why the decision is wrong. And please don't misunderstand what I am saying. I absolutely believe that children need to understand "consequences of actions."

I was staying with a friend and his family when he got a text from his ex-wife saying that his fourteen-year-old son, Cal, cheated on a math exam by writing the answers on his arm. When the school sent the picture to my friend, you could see that Cal had indeed covered not only his whole forearm with equations, but he also wrote on his wrist, hand, and the inside and outside of each individual finger so that not even his long-sleeve shirt could cover it up. While my friend was naturally concerned that his quite intelligent son was cheating, he was even more concerned at how poorly he cheated! Of course, a teacher would see his fingers covered in equations. When he got home to talk to his son however, Cal explained that he hadn't written anything on his arm until the exam was over because they had to sit quietly and weren't permitted to have anything on their desk. So, he just started doodling math equations.

My friend was not sure what to believe, pulled between his son's innocence and his master cheating skills where he tried to cover up inconspicuous cheating by making it look TOO obvious. Either way, it was up to the school to decide if Cal had cheated and to dole out any punishment they felt necessary. My friend struggled as to whether the punishment from the school was going to match the perceived crime. As we spoke, our thoughts on the situation came to this conclusion: it didn't matter. If Cal got punished, he was either going to get punished for cheating OR he was going to be punished for not thinking, "Hmmm, if I write equations on my fingers, will that give the teacher the wrong idea?" In many real-life situations, intention doesn't negate consequence. Neither idea was "smart" and lessons would be learned either way.

This was very similar to me at the age of sixteen, sitting in Ms. Workens' history class. I sat next to an old metal fan, and while we were supposed to be reading, I was unassumingly flicking the cage around the fan and it would vibrate, making a funny noise. After a couple of flicks, Ms. Workens looked up at me and kindly told me not to touch it again. I looked up at her to acknowledge I heard her but because the fan cage was still vibrating, I put my hand on it to stop the sound. In her eyes, I was being a sarcastic little a-hole and I touched it just to challenge her authority, which earned me a one-way trip to detention that day. That was one of my first lessons in consequences of perceived actions compared to intentional actions. I have had to learn that lesson many times in life.

Kids need to have the realization about where their actions lead and who they affect—from family and friends, to society as a whole. And trust me, they DO learn consequences. Their developing brains are figuring out that each action has an equal and opposite reaction. Children run theory-testing experiments every waking minute of the day. What makes those conversations easier for you is the values you instill in them.

As parents, we also need to be aware of our own expectations for our kids. Are we creating situations where our children can learn to make their own choices within reasonable boundaries? We can't expect our children to go into the world fully prepared to make good decisions unless we provide a safe and risk-appropriate environment for them to practice making decisions. How can we communicate our expectations while also allowing our kids to maintain a sense of control and autonomy?

2.3 EXPECTATION SETTING

In my parenting experiments, I receive a lot of push back from my kids when I ask or tell them to do something they don't want to do. I guarantee this isn't news to any parent reading this book—or the parents not reading this book for that matter. If they are playing outside and I say, "Come in and take a bath," very rarely do I get an, "Ok Dad, on my way!" And when I do get a positive response, my immediate thought that is usually confirmed in the near future, is, "What are they setting me up for?"

What happens is that first they don't listen, then they negotiate, then they debate, then they argue, then they go off the deep end and melt down. It doesn't always go that far down the path of self-destruction. Depending on their mood that day—correction, their mood in that minute—they can choose to acquiesce at any of the above steps. For my girls, the average is somewhere between debate and argue, with the occasional meltdown.

I have since learned some tips and tricks to help them, and myself, not stray so far down the path and it requires a little advance thinking on my part.

In Las Vegas, one tactic that the blackjack dealers use to keep you in their casinos is by occasionally letting you win! True story, if someone is spending money at their tables and they see the player is on a cold streak, the dealer is allowed to "accidentally" not take the person's money away on a hand where they lost. They give this player a small victory to keep up their morale, make them feel like they are making some sort of progress. Now in the casino's case, it's ultimately used so the player stays and loses more money. In the case of our children, it's not that we want them to lose, we just don't want them to walk away feeling like they lose all the time. We want to give them small victories so that they stay motivated to keep trying.

Here's an example of the way that plays out in my parenting. Ten minutes before I call them in from playing outside, I tell them, "Girls, you have five minutes before it is time to come in!" Then they negotiate another five minutes and I "let" them win. A critic can say that I have now taught my daughters that what I say has room for questioning, room to negotiate, and that kids then question everything. Well, those critics are right—mostly. Yes, what I say has room for questions and sometimes room for negotiation. IF I approach them with something that needs to happen where there is no room for negotiation, then I tell them in advance as opposed to in the moment. In advance is where expectations are supposed to be set. Setting expectations in the moment of when you expect it typically ends in disappointment because it means that expectation hasn't been met AND the other side isn't prepared to meet that expectation immediately. Lose/lose.

2.4 DON'T TEACH KIDS TO BE ADULTS...

I occasionally hear myself say, "Alexandra, you are <insert number> years old, you should be able to <insert task> by now." Sometimes— ok often—I get exhausted as a parent. Usually, I am exhausted with my child in the moment, but afterwards, I am exhausted with myself. Why is that? Why do we have such great insight after the fact, when in the moment is where we can make the maximum impact. The statement is "raising kids is hard" but the hard part usually isn't the kids. Kids are easy, and we know exactly how we want to raise them. The hard part is us.

"Hard" is you, and "hard" is me, trying to teach our kids what we want them to learn, shielding them from our own personal baggage OR over-exposing them to our own personal baggage. It's us upholding the rules we have put down right up until we realize that maybe we laid down the wrong rules. It's emphasizing "consistency!" And then bending because we realize that kids are just kids and some of our greatest joys as children were when our parents bent the rules. It's saying in the same breath, "I am not going to make the same mistakes that my parents made," AND "Ugh, I am exactly like my parents," right as we are getting annoyed with our kids who are acting just like us! It's washing over the mistakes our parents made and giving them the benefit of the doubt because they were, "Doing the best that they could." and then getting disappointed in the evening when we think we didn't do the best that we could. "Hard" is us.

I don't know about you but I too often use myself and my experience as a measuring stick in regards to my children. Let me use some other words there to emphasize this point. Neglecting all wisdom, I use an adult measuring stick to judge my own children. I measure what they think, say and do at the ages of twelve, ten and six, based on my forty-five years of experience as a human being. And I get disappointed when they don't live up to those expectations. In the moment, I get disappointed in my kids, but at the end of the day, I get disappointed in myself. How unfair is this on so many levels?! For my kids, I have set unreasonable expectations and set them up to fail. As a parent, I am torturing myself thinking I have failed them, when they will probably look back and say, "Dad gave us his best." I guess the only thing to do is, well, my best.

2.5 HOW TO CHOOSE WITH PURPOSE

I feel that my daughters come to a fork in the road approximately every three point two seconds. Should I eat that broccoli or slide it off the table to the dog? Should I tell Mommy that I just wrote on the bathroom wall or try to hide it? Should I go brush my teeth or not? (By the way, that's not an option except in their own brain.)

But when they do come to that fork, we can always fit it into at least one of our three values. Is it a brave decision, is it a smart decision, and/or is it a kind decision?

Do they need to decide how to overcome a challenge? Talk about how your family defines brave. Talk about fear. Talk about perseverance, showing up, or risk. Talk about resilience. Talk about faith or conviction or exploration; whichever values you have defined to be brave.

Do they need to put some critical thought into a decision? Talk about how your family defines smart. Talk about seeking out information, knowledge, or wisdom. Talk about their goals and desires. Talk about perspectives. Talk about growth or reflection or awareness; whichever values you have defined to be smart.

Do they need to consider others and themselves in a decision? Talk about how your family defines kind. Talk about empathy. Talk about honesty. Talk about respect. Talk about credibility or patience or dignity; whichever values you have defined to be kind.

You are seeing the themes. The key ingredient in all of these is that you need to first talk about how your family defines how you overcome, how you think critically, and how you treat others and yourself. Brave, smart and kind mean nothing without those definitions. The easier we make the definitions as they are young, the better we are able to build on them as they get older.

CHAPTER 2 TAKE HOME

- Give clear purpose well in advance of clear consequences.
- Remember all actions come from an emotion, and all emotions come from a need.
- If you want to get to the root of the problem, you have to address the needs not the symptoms.
- Find times to let your kids win at the important stuff.
- Think about the baggage that you bring into parenting.
- Consider the unfair measuring stick that you use with your kids.

CHAPTER 3

THE EXAMPLES WE SET

How to Win Friends and Influence People by Dale Carnegie should be required reading for every human ever. This book has influenced me in countless ways because it is chock-full of incredible lessons in life and leadership that have gone on to become mainstream topics. Given that the book was written in 1936, the longevity of Carnegie's content is astounding. In the very first chapter he references a poem that was originally published in *People's Home Journal* and it hits me every single time I read it.

FATHER FORGETS

by W. Livingstone Larned

Listen, son: I am saying this as you lie asleep, one little paw crumpled under your cheek and the blond curls stickily wet on your damp forehead. I have stolen into your room alone. Just a few minutes ago, as I sat reading my paper in the library, a stifling wave of remorse swept over me. Guiltily I came to your bedside.

There are the things I was thinking, son: I had been cross to you. I scolded you as you were dressing for school because you gave your face merely a dab with a towel. I took you to task for not cleaning your shoes. I called out angrily when you threw some of your things on the floor.

At breakfast I found fault, too. You spilled things. You gulped down your food. You put your elbows on the table. You spread butter too thick on your bread. And as you started off to play and I made for my train, you turned and waved a hand and called, "Goodbye, Daddy!" and I frowned, and said in reply, "Hold your shoulders back!"

Then it began all over again in the late afternoon. As I came up the road I spied you, down on your knees, playing marbles. There were holes in your stockings. I humiliated you before your boyfriends by marching you ahead of me to the house. Stockings were expensive—and if you had to buy them you would be more careful! Imagine that, son, from a father!

Do you remember, later, when I was reading in the library, how you came in timidly, with a sort of hurt look in your eyes? When I glanced up over my paper, impatient at the interruption, you hesitated at the door. "What is it you want?" I snapped.

You said nothing, but ran across in one tempestuous plunge, and threw your arms around my neck and kissed me, and your small arms tightened with an affection that God had set blooming in your heart and which even neglect could not wither. And then you were gone, pattering up the stairs.

Well, son, it was shortly afterwards that my paper slipped from my hands and a terrible sickening fear came over me. What has habit been doing to me? The habit of finding fault, of reprimanding—this was my reward to you for being a boy. It was not that I did not love you; it was that I expected too much of youth. I was measuring you by the yardstick of my own years.

And there was so much that was good and fine and true in your character. The little heart of you was as big as the dawn itself over the wide hills. This was shown by your spontaneous impulse to rush in and kiss me goodnight. Nothing else matters tonight, son. I have come to your bedside in the darkness, and I have knelt there, ashamed!

It is feeble atonement; I know you would not understand these things if I told them to you during your waking hours. But tomorrow I will be a real daddy! I will chum with you, and suffer when you suffer, and laugh when you laugh. I will bite my tongue when impatient words come. I will keep saying as if it were a ritual: "He is nothing but a boy—a little boy!"

I am afraid I have visualised you as a man. Yet as I see you now, son, crumpled and weary in your cot, I see that you are still a baby. Yesterday you were in your mother's arms, your head on her shoulder. I have asked too much, too much.

This poem made such an impact on me that I printed it out and hung it on my office door. I read it regularly.

I can't teach my kids to "grow up," I can't teach them to be good adults. I can, however, show them what it looks like to listen with empathy when someone is speaking. I can show them what accountability is. I can show them what empowerment, communication, and mentorship look like. I can show them examples of what I believe courage is. I can show the benefits of being thoughtful. I can show them what kindness means to me and the importance of being kind to themselves.

I can't teach my kids to be adults, because quite frankly, I'm still learning what "being an adult" means.

Adulthood is simply the process of getting older, not better. There are plenty of misguided adults out there who just don't "get it." Even those who do well at "adulting" still frequently fail in life and, more impactfully, in parenting. I am, in part, a product of how I was raised and I'm still in the process of working through the impressions that were made on me. If I want to raise my own children with strong values, I need to examine the process I underwent growing up. I need to look at the shadows of my past to understand how they affect my present, thereby allowing me to parent with greater purpose.

3.1 THE FATHER I DON'T WANT TO BE

I was asked during a keynote, "As parents, how can we avoid handing down our negative values to our children?" My answer was, "We can't." I don't think it was the answer they were looking for. Let me explain.

My father was a good person. He was a kind man who looked out for others. He was emotional in showing love and was emotional in showing sadness and anger. He had his convictions, some right, some wrong. As he aged, I think many of those convictions softened. My father, however, wasn't present for the majority of my life. He traveled for weeks or months at a time for work when we lived together.

He was harder on my sister and I when we were younger, at least for what I can remember. My mom was much more empathetic. She showed her care through giving her time and listening. I don't remember much harshness from her even when we were getting punished. When my father was home, he had more old-school disciplinary tactics. I remember my parents arguing over appropriate punishments for not using table manners, lying, or general ridiculousness of kids.

My parents divorced when I was seven years old. My sister and I moved with our mom from California back to our old neighborhood in Florida where we had spent the majority of our lives up until that point. My father stayed in California. Soon after, he married the woman he'd been dating and though there was joint custody, I usually saw him just twice a year until I graduated from high school.

I don't know why, but sometime after I turned twenty-one, he stopped calling me on my birthday. After his second divorce in 2006, he started living alone. We didn't speak often, and it was always me who needed to initiate connection. When I would call him, he would be happy to hear my voice, but conversations never lasted long because he didn't have "anything important to talk about." As much as I tried to talk to him, I always felt "less-than" after our conversations. Even though I had been married for years, he often got my wife's name wrong and frustration would bubble up within me. My wife's nickname is "V," pronounced like the letter, short for Violaine. He always called her "Vi" like the beginning of the word Violet. It hurt when we spoke, but that wasn't a reason to stop all together.

One Christmas, my father sent gifts to all the girls, but on the labels he wrote the names Alexandra, Anastasia and Josephine. (My second daughter's name isn't Anastasia, it is Emmeline.) I cried when I saw that package on Christmas morning. If he had a mental health issue, it would've been more understandable, but there was no issue that we knew of. There could be hundreds of reasons for that mistake, but I never asked him about it and that part is on me.

The truth is that my dad just wasn't involved enough to know much about my family at all. I moved to Belgium about two years after his second divorce and lived there for another twelve years before he passed away. I tried to get him to come over and visit. Not knowing how much money he had to live off of, I offered to pay for his trip. He said he would make it here "soon," and maybe he believed that, but he never came over the fifteen years he could have.

For the handful of times my daughters met my father, I struggled when they would embrace him and tell me how wonderful he was.

I loved my dad, but I knew from an early age that I didn't want to be like him in most regards. I made the mistake of telling him that once. I didn't say it in anger but I did say it, in part, as a sort of defense mechanism when he wanted me to "decide what to do with my life." After Alexandra was born, I made the concerted effort to not become the father he was.

I was angry when he passed away in his sleep in 2020. I was angry that he left without saying goodbye. I was angry that he made, what appeared to be, such little effort to be part of my life and the lives of my girls—never having called any of my daughters on their twenty-two collective birthdays. I was angry when I found out how much money he actually had, and that he didn't use any of it to come and see us in Belgium. I was angry at myself for not making more effort to mend bridges, or to see him more often, or to find out why he did what he did. So you can see, I had (and have) some feelings to work through.

After he passed, I flew back to the U.S. to sort through his belongings with my family. My Dad was a minimalist, but he had saved some things he valued. He kept a bunch of Disney video tapes that he'd been collecting for over twenty years for the grandkids. He had a scotch collection that he gave to me and my brother-in-law. He kept forty-year-old speakers because they had a "pure sound." He also kept a lot of paperwork for some reason; phone bills, membership subscriptions, pamphlets. We found old letters between him and my Mom, both the loving kind and the hurtful kind. We found old letters he kept from my sister and I that we wrote after our parents divorced.

I opened one box of the stuff my Dad kept in the nightstand by his bed. There were the birth announcements for the girls, a recent envelope of pictures I had sent him, and some other keepsakes. Then I unfolded an old, weathered piece of paper. It had a poem on the inside:

FATHER FORGETS

by W. Livingstone Larned

Listen, son: I am saying this as you lie asleep, one little paw crumpled under your cheek and the blond curls stickily wet on your damp forehead. I have stolen into your room alone. Just a few minutes ago, as I sat reading my paper in the library, a stifling wave of remorse swept over me. Guiltily I came to your bedside...

I cried.

He never said it directly, but I know my father felt guilty about many parts of his life, perhaps he was ashamed and that is why he didn't address them. If nothing else, I imagine he had this poem close at hand for the same reasons that I do. We need the reminders. We carry baggage from our upbringings, and we want to protect our children from the worst parts of us. We feel remorse when we don't live up to our own expectations or promises our past selves made to our future selves. We make mistakes.

I know there are parts of my judgement of my father that are unfair and misplaced. I know the real answer here is to reserve judgement completely, however difficult to do. I can't blame him for all the negative characteristics of fatherhood without acknowledgement of me becoming who I am. Unpacking the "father I am" because of the "father he wasn't" would take an entirely different book and a whole lot of therapy. I am not going to do that here.

I am a good person. I am a kind man who looks out for others. I am emotional in showing love as well as in sadness and anger. I have my convictions, some right, some wrong. AND I am present in my daughters' lives. I make it a point to be involved. I communicate with them. I will not let the important things go unsaid and I will show them, and teach them as much as I can. And I'll both succeed and fail at all of those things in certain moments. As they get older, I will call them on their birthdays and visit them as often as I am able.

The point I would like to make is, at some point in our lives, we need to accept the good characteristics that our parents gave us and we need to be able to accept and change how we want to be different. And guess what, our children will do the same. The answer to, "How can we avoid handing our negative values down to our children?" is still, "We can't," because with our positive values, come our negative values. We don't get to give one without the other because in their acceptance of our values, they will also fail because of those exact same values.

> But what our kids CAN do, and what we can help them to do, is to understand the values, talk about our failures and let them make their own choices about who they want to become.

3.2 MORAL BARGAINING

In *How to Win Friends and Influence People*, Dale Carnegie writes a chapter called "How to Get Cooperation." He shares a story about Adolf Seltz, a sales manager in an auto showroom who was attempting to motivate what he described as a "discouraged and disorganized group of salespeople." Calling a sales meeting, he urged his people to tell him exactly what they expected from him. As they spoke, he wrote their ideas on the blackboard. He then said, "I'll give you all these qualities you expect from me. Now I want you to tell me what I have a right to expect from you." The replies came quick and fast:

loyalty, honesty, initiative, optimism, teamwork, eight hours a day of enthusiastic work. The meeting ended with a new courage and new inspiration. One salesperson volunteered to work fourteen hours a day, and Mr. Seltz reported that the increase of sales was phenomenal. "The people had made a sort of moral bargain with me, and as long as I lived up to my part, they were determined to live up to theirs."

Carnegie used moral bargaining as a way to use your values to nurture a relationship. If you use the language of BSK in moral bargaining, you are able to set the boundaries for how you will act brave, smart and kind AND what your expectation is of your children to do the same. This only works if you first define what brave, smart and kind mean to you and your family.

If your children are at an age when they can understand expectations, ask the question, "What is the type of parent you want me to be?" See what they say, see what you can agree to and what you can't. If your kids are younger, you can start by telling them all of the things you love about them, and some of the things that are hard, such as when they don't listen or when they start yelling. Then ask them to tell you what they love about you, and then get ready to ask the question of what makes them upset. In both cases, get specific in your expectations and allow them to be specific in theirs. Talk specifically about how you want to talk about fear and failure. Talk about how you think things through together instead of simply giving each other answers. Most importantly, talk about how you want to treat each other. Work hard in your communication so that IF you are doing something that isn't brave, smart or kind you kids know how to tell you about it.

Here's an example. Since my girls were infants, we talked about accepting fear and failure. They know that if they mess up, they need to be honest with me about it. My expectation of them is honesty. In return, what they can expect from me is empathy and understanding.

That was one of the deals I struck with my girls. They give me truth, I give them understanding. That doesn't mean there aren't consequences, it just means my anger won't be one of them. For now, we have a pretty truthful relationship. It's to be determined whether that holds up through adolescence, but it is at least a good place to start.

When Alex was eleven, I asked her to write down an example of bravery. This is what she said, "Brave is that if you are scared of something that you still do it, overcoming your fears. If you do something wrong and you are scared to tell your parents, just try to tell them. It is not going to help if you don't and if they are going to get mad you can't do anything about it."

I'd like to think that understanding of bravery has come from our moral bargain. She has had a safe place to mess up because she knows exactly what to expect out of me. That started with her just understanding fear. It was nurtured to make her feel like honesty was a way to overcome your fears.

Moral bargaining is NOT about winning an argument with your child. Matter of fact, how often does any adult "win" an argument with their child? Think even further, how often do any of us ever "win" an argument with anyone ever? Typically, one of two things happen when we argue with someone. Either we make such good points that the other person feels terrible OR the other person makes such good points that we feel terrible OR no one is willing or able to bend to the point that they say they were wrong. Admitting we are wrong in what we believe to be true is a humbling experience that many adults are unwilling to have, yet we constantly expect that of our kids. "You are wrong and here's why. You can't do that and here is why. You should do something else and here is why."

One reason that yelling doesn't work is well summarized by Dr. Laura Markham, Ph.D., a clinical psychologist and author of *Peaceful Parent, Happy Kids: How to Stop Yelling and Start Connecting.*

"Yelling is about releasing anger; it's not an effective way to change behavior," says Dr. Markham. When children are scared, they go into fight-or-flight mode and the learning parts of their brains shut down. The fight-or-flight response is a physiological reaction that happens when we are experiencing something our brain perceives as threatening. Our children cannot learn when we are yelling at them because their brain tells them the person yelling at them is a threat and that action shuts down the parts of the brain that aren't dedicated to protecting them. Dr. Markham says, "Peaceful and calm communication helps a child feel safe and makes them more receptive to the lesson we're teaching."

What does that mean to me? It means if I am in the argument stage with my children, I have already lost the battle. Much like Adolf Seltz, we need to make a moral bargain with our children before we are able to set or follow up on any expectations. We need to be able to tell them in many ways (both verbally and nonverbally), here is what you can count on with me as your parent; unconditional love, dedication, trust, etc. Then we need to back it up repeatedly. At the same time, we ask them what we have the right to expect from them and then have to be prepared for them to not be able to hold up their end of the bargain, and be ok with that. Keep giving them what they can count on you for, and what happens is that they will, at the very least, try to keep up their end as we continue to recognize and acknowledge when they do it well.

So let's summarize…

How to lose in Moral Bargaining:

- Get in an argument with your kids

- Yell at your kids

- Condescend to your kids

- Tell them one thing and do another

How to win with Moral Bargaining:

- Set expectations repeatedly, start by asking them what they expect from you

- Listen as often as you can—even if you already know that you will disagree—kids want to be heard

- Ask questions

- Calm your brain, keep their brains turned on

3.3 BAD ASSES AND SAFETY

It's so frustrating when your kids don't listen to you! Anyone else struggle with this? It is a regularity in our home. Sometimes I verbalize that irritation, sometimes I just let it go because I would rather just avoid the fight that I know is coming.

Like our *Alice in Wonderland* analogy where Alice gets lost in the woods and comes to a fork in the road, our kids get lost, as we all do, but with more frequency. The values of BSK help kids find their destination and then give them practice in making their own choices. This part is very important—they are making their own choices. But there is an additional point that has caught me off guard when it comes to our family disputes.

I remember back when my daughters were nine, seven and three; we had a good share of disagreements in our home. Alexandra is ridiculously kind and sincerely wants to have a harmonious family, so much that she is easily thrown into tears and anger when that harmony is out of whack. She also hates to fail, even in the slightest way and she easily gets down on herself. Emmeline is crafty. By that I mean she not only loves crafts, but even more so, is quick as a whip, and processes thoughts and actions extremely fast. It is both her strength and her undoing many days because she is still young and Mom and Dad can still outsmart her, for now. Josephine has no fears—except for Ursula the Sea Witch but honestly who isn't afraid of her, she's terrifying. No, Josephine has no problem showing her sisters who is boss and that has also rubbed off on her communication with me. I was walking up the stairs the other day as she was coming down and I smiled and said, "Hey Joey!" The look that I received could have put me six feet under. With a furled brow, pursed lips she says, "NO DADDY!!!... no." I capitalize the first part because she screamed it, the lower case "no" was what she whispered as I walked past. When I got to the top of the stairs, I had the great idea to look back and say, "I love you sweetheart." She was still staring at me and didn't blink or respond. She did however hold out her thumb and pull it across her throat in a cutting motion. Seriously, my child gave me a death threat at the age of three!

Here is a good time to let everyone know that we do have SOME normal interactions and instances in the house with laughter and kindness. Yesterday the older girls sat at the table practicing their spelling as I dictated (butchered) their Dutch vocabulary words to them. Joey was coloring next to them and the rest of the night was bath time, stories and songs.

Good nights happen, I just want more of them. While I realize that not every night will be like that, I get frustrated when the girls talk back, when they yell at us, when they fight, etc. I was stressed one day because it was one of those nights where they were all in that mode and my wife said to me, "Well you always wanted them to be a bit bad-ass." The comment did not do anything to ease my mental state, or at least not immediately.

The next day I was thinking in the shower—where the best thinking gets done—and I had a lot of pieces fall into place for my own sanity. My wife was right. I do want my kids to be a bit bad-ass. I talk to them about not being paralyzed by fear. I teach them that they need to think before they act, to know their destination before choosing their path. Most importantly I teach them about compassion, empathy and being kind to not only other people, but also to themselves, that it is ok to fail. I am teaching them to be brave, smart and kind, I am NOT teaching them to be obedient. That point deserves to be repeated. Nowhere, in any of the values that I am defining, displaying or discussing with my children, do I teach them obedience (compliance with an order, request, or law or submission to another's authority).

It's true! The times we get in fights are when they don't listen, when they disagree, when they feel like something isn't fair and they have the courage, thought, and self-care to speak up about it. I look at the number of arguments that I have gotten into with my kids BECAUSE they are acting brave, smart and kind; even if it's in their own heads. I have had forty-five years to figure this stuff out and I still get it wrong on a regular basis. They are just at the beginning of this journey, and sometimes they are living up to the values in their own ways and fighting for things they believe in AND getting in trouble for it!

How frustrating it must be for them to get in arguments when they feel they are living up to the values I reinforce with them every single day.

What I am coming to terms with is that my kids will not listen to me for the sake of listening. I have not taught them patriarchal respect. "Because I told you so," is a phrase that has very little success in our home, and I am grateful for that. If you want obedient children, then stay away from brave, smart and kind.

I have taught my kids that when they come to a fork in the road that their destination is to make the right choice even when it is hard, to think about why they are doing something before they do it, to be thoughtful of others and of themselves—to be brave, to be smart and to be kind. And when that comes across as disobedience, well, "Just do what you're told" is not the way I want my young ladies to operate in this world. The problem I am having is that sometimes I get lost and afraid, and they are picking up the BSK faster than I am, I can do better.

Now that we have established that obedience is not one of the values, we need to recognize the times our children get in trouble for not being obedient and ask why it happens. That lack of obedience often comes because children and adults have a different level of measurement when it comes to doing what they are told. Let's do an exercise to see where the fights come from.

Some causes of fights in the Brady home:

- Challenges they can't overcome

    o When they don't control their choices

    o When fear of failure paralyzes them

    o Circular failure with no apparent progress

- Things that make them feel stupid

- o Math homework

- o Making mental connections

- o Inability to communicate

- o Not being understood

- Things when they feel hurt

  - o Something isn't fair

  - o Someone not listening

  - o Someone not watching

A key to living BSK is to identify how to overcome your fears. Please note that this doesn't say to not be afraid. The faster you come to terms with the fact that fear is a natural emotion, the faster you can overcome it.

If you are fearful, then it's very difficult to make smart choices or to be kind to others. It isn't impossible, but if you are afraid it's easier to lie, it's easier to cheat, it's easier to make whatever choice makes you feel safe. Overcoming that fear is the first step to the other values. If you get past the fear part, you are able to look at your actions with intention. Think before you act and make the right choices for the right reasons. Only after you think critically in whatever fashion applies to you, then you can truly help others AND yourself.

3.4 METHODS CONTRADICTING VALUES

There are some values that we can very easily confuse or dilute when trying to instill them in our children. This doesn't come with any negative intention, quite the opposite. We want to have "good" kids. Now that definition of "good kids" can change from parent to parent, but I promise you, people are not out there trying to create little a-holes. Our kids just act like little a-holes because of OTHER kids and OTHER parents—right? Obviously I am joking, no one else has turned your kids into a-holes. Your kids are little a-holes because of you. One of the things that living in Belgian culture has taught me is confrontational truth. How is it working?

I am MOSTLY joking. Of course we all want to raise good kids. Most people aim to raise polite, respectful, kind children—yet there is a problem in how we raise our kids which leads to contradiction of the values we want to teach our children and the values we are using to teach. Would an example help here? The most obvious one that I can think of in my own upbringing is that if I hit my sister, I would get a spanking. I don't have a degree in behavioral psychology, but teaching someone to not hit by hitting them seems counterproductive. Let's look at some other tools we use to teach kids good behavior.

What happens when a child is making a bad choice? We give them the right choice and then tell them what they need to do. We use obedience when kids fail in thinking for themselves. When I was young, my dad often said, "Stop crying or I'll give you something to cry about." We want a child to be brave, so we scare them into a desired reaction.

There are some other examples of methods contradicting results.

- Yelling at a child, "Be quiet!"
- Taking a toy away from them when they won't share.
- Dominating a child who is bullying another child.
- Making a child feel bad when they are making someone else feel bad.

Brave, smart and kind are only three values that serve as a foundation for thousands of others. What are the specific values that you are parenting through?

What perceived values are you sending with your actions?

- Discipline
- Obedience
- Prudence
- Caution

Compared to the values you ask for?

- Kindness
- Politeness
- Understanding

One takeaway that you can implement from this book is to see if your reaction to your child reaffirms their original action.

3.5 CONTRADICTING WORDS

Yet, it's so easy to contradict the message we want to send with our actions.

It was probably 2018 when I sat down with the girls one day to reinforce the message, "Don't talk to strangers, stranger danger," and all of that stuff. We talked about what they should do if they are approached by someone they don't know, the importance of walking together or with a friend, and to listen to their gut if they think something is wrong. That same morning as we went for a walk, someone passed us on our street and I said, "Good morning," and the stranger gave me an equally friendly greeting in return. The girls looked up to me to ask me who that was, and I said, "I don't know, I was just being kind." I looked down at some pretty confused faces.

For adults, we know that not every stranger means danger. We are able to spot when we might be in trouble but we are also terrified of the image of a kidnapper in a van luring our children away with candy and puppies. So, what we do is go to the safe extreme of telling our kids that they shouldn't talk to people they don't know. What terrible advice is that? Firstly, they aren't going to adhere to it because kids are incredibly innocent, social and forgetful beings. And secondly, if they do listen to that advice, it means that we scared the crap out of them by saying that if they talk to strangers, they are going to get kidnapped. Statistically speaking, people who hurt children are typically people that they know already so "stranger danger" is actually very misleading. According to the National Center for Missing and Exploited Children, only 1% of missing children cases are committed by non-family members. "Stranger danger" implies kids can openly trust someone that they have been introduced to.

The contradictions we present our children are numerous AND we typically don't do it consciously. I too have yelled at my kids, "STOP YELLING!!!" Our accidental hypocrisy is as ineffective for our short-term results as it is for our long-term results. Not only is that child unlikely to stop yelling, we just threw more gasoline on the fire which most likely will end with more yelling, stomping, grumpiness, pouting, and perhaps a slammed door. (And our kids might do some of that too!) In the long-term, we are setting examples for our children to follow. The worst part is that we rarely think about it like that.

CHAPTER 3 TAKE HOME

- Think about what situations truly scare you. Ask yourself why.
- Write out the type of parent you want to be. Be as specific as you can.
- Write out the type of parent your kids want you to be. Be more specific.
- Are you in the habit of finding fault? Pay attention to this when you interact with your kids.
- Remember back to the promises your past self made to your future self. See if you can fulfill them.
- What do you DO that contradicts what you say? Ask your loved ones to call you out on it. (Scary, I know.)

CHAPTER 4

THEIR INNER VOICES

I recently saw a post on social media that spoke about how our kids see us. It spoke about yelling at your kids to get them in bed and then wondering why they aren't sleeping well. And likewise, what happens when we yell at our kids to get them out the door to school and then hope they have a nice day. We as parents become the inner voice for our kids. What a powerful thought that the inner voice of a child in their most vulnerable and impactful moments is YOU. And how easy it is for us to become their inner critic.

If we show them courage, then we become the voice of bravery in their heads.

If we show them critical thought, then we become the voice of smart in their heads.

If we show them kindness, then we become the voice of kind in their heads.

YOU become their courage…

YOU become their thoughts…

YOU become their kindness…

AND it works in the negative too…

If we are driven by fear, then we will become the voice of fear and self-doubt in their heads.

If we are apathetic in thought, then we become the voice of detachment in their heads.

If we disregard others' feelings, then we become the voice of indifference in their heads.

YOU become their fear…

YOU become their detachment…

YOU become their indifference…

Now before we start to think our children are doomed because WE have fear, make dumb choices, and aren't volunteering at the soup kitchen over the holidays—or ever—let's gain some perspective.

We need to understand that we will become many voices in our children's heads. They will look to us for comfort when we aren't there. They also may make decisions very specifically because they DON'T want to be like us at a certain moment of their lives.

When I was about to become a father for the first time, my mom gave me a short book of quotes on fatherhood. Out of all of them, one touched me more than the rest. It said, "Make your choices, live your life so that when your children picture the word integrity, they picture you." Now I fail at this, time and time again. Over and over I do or say things that do NOT align with that idea. But I know it, and I think of it. Only after realizing can I apologize, or encourage, or support (or whatever action needs to happen) so that I continue to live up to that picture of integrity. Am I teaching them that they have to be perfect? Not in the least. We talk about failure, how to accept it and move on. What I am teaching them is that integrity is saying you are wrong when you are wrong, it's brave. Integrity is being able to shift your own thinking and being mindful of others, it's smart. Integrity is lifting someone up when they have fallen, because that is the right thing to do, it's kind.

Want to know if it's working? We were watching a movie called *Onward* about two young men who are trying to use magic to have one more day with their late father. The youngest brother, played by Tom Holland, is trying to cast the spell to bring his father back and the eldest brother, played by Chris Pratt, looks over to him and says, "You can DO this." Emmeline turned back to look at me with her thoughtful caring eyes and with a smile said, "Dad, he sounds like you." I hope that is a voice that gets stuck in her head in her hardest times. The inner voice of belief, confidence in herself, that says no matter what, you can do this.

If we know that we become that voice in their heads, then we have one of two choices. We can continue to act in whatever way we were taught to, OR we can act with a bit more intention and decide which voice we want to be. I promise you, your kids are listening. They don't only hear what you say to them, they also hear what you say to yourself and what you say about others when they aren't looking. Do you tell yourself you can do it, or do you tell yourself that you can't? Do you believe in others, or do you doubt them? Do you use self-loving words when talking about your character, your actions, your looks; or do you criticize yourself regularly? THAT becomes their inner voice too.

The trick here is that I can't tell you what voice to become for your children. You need to find your own authentic voice. It helps me to find my voice when I know what I specifically stand for, my values. That is the easiest way to raise our kids because it takes the very least energy for us to be the most authentic version of ourselves. Once we find that most authentic self, then we can start parenting from it. Then we can start working from it. Then we can start leading from it. Then we can start speaking from it.

4.1 BE INTENTIONAL

Have you ever stepped on one of your kid's toys? I'm not talking about the nice soft stuffed animal. I am talking about the jagged, hard plastic, feels-like-you-punctured-the-sole-of-your-foot toys. It happens consistently in my world, yet I have inconsistent reactions. Sometimes I yell out, "What the BUBBLES!" Other times, I take a breath and keep rolling along with whatever my purpose is in that moment. Each time when I don't let it get to me, I think back to the fable about what we put in our cups.

The story goes like this: An unassuming person was walking along with a cup of coffee when someone accidentally bumped into them and they spilled their coffee on the floor. The question is then asked, "Why did they spill coffee?" The natural answer is because someone bumped into them, but that isn't the answer. They spilled coffee because coffee was what was in their cup. If they had milk in their cup they would have spilled milk. It obviously speaks to the concept that when we are tested, whatever we have inside of us comes out. If we have frustration, and we get bumped into and we let it bother us, we have a harder time letting it go. If we have kindness, when we get bumped into, we make sure the other person is ok, we say, "No big deal," with a smile and we keep going without giving it another thought. If we have the energy to keep our positive selves present in our day then the positivity will continue to spill over.

If we aren't living as our positive selves because of either hardship or ignorance, then we have less energy to keep ourselves positive. Then when we are bumped into, we dive into the dark side of our values even without knowing it. We become the "negative" self where honest becomes rude, intelligent becomes egotistical, and kindness becomes painfully apologetic.

Living by your values takes the least amount of your energy. It takes a great deal of energy to work against your nature. Once you align with your values, then you live with more authenticity. That authenticity allows you to live with greater intention and freedom.

If you are constantly fighting with yourself, if you contradict what you say, if you can't make decisions, if you second guess, if you feel like you are tearing yourself apart, if you ever think, "THIS isn't me!"—then you are struggling with your values. It feels like you are failing over and over again.

Think back to your school days and what happened if you kept failing the same test. Did you jump right back in the test, or do you go back and study? Did you get someone to help you? Did you prepare yourself before retaking the test, or did you guess what the answers were and HOPED that you got it right? Life is not a multiple choice test. If you don't know the answer you can't just choose "C"—stop guessing at your life. Don't live it by accident, live it with purpose.

4.2 CREATE A SAFE ENVIRONMENT

I remember back in 2019, Alex was eight years old and we were about to go in for a parent-teacher meeting. At the time, Alex was growing up to be the sweet young lady that she is. She was always wanting to help and sincerely caring about other people. Like me, she is the one that cries in the movies if something sad happens or someone gets hurt. She was absolutely torn up one day when she and I went on a walk and went past a herd of sheep. One of them was coughing really hard and Alex couldn't stand to see it in pain. (By the way, we had no idea if there was any pain, it just sounded like it had smoked ten packs a day for the past couple decades.) Alex tried to help by feeding it grass, but she walked away in tears.

Being the sensitive person she is, if something doesn't go Alex's way, she has a short fuse and a very strong, projecting voice. That has led to some all-out insanity, temper tantrums, and bouts of anger. Her twos were ok, her four to fives were much harder, six and seven were manageable, but at eight she had some monster moments.

My wife and I went to this parent-teacher meeting and Alex had been having some really hard days at home that week. I dreaded hearing how that had carried over to school. I wasn't so concerned with her teacher's perception of Alex as much as I was concerned with her teacher's perception of us as parents! No one wants to have the kid in class who whines or throws temper tantrums. It's not like we don't know that these are natural parts of childhood, but even worse is for the outside world to know where the kids get it from! (Like teachers don't know that anyway.)

We walked to the classroom and the teacher ushered us to a desk where we sat down in seats three times smaller than my own ass. As I strained my quad muscle trying to balance myself on one butt cheek, the teacher said, "I would like to let you know that Alexandra has been such a joy to have in the class. She can work on her listening skills, but she is always in a good mood and she is such a polite young lady." With my eyes squinted and my head cocked to the side I tried to remember if Belgian teachers were known for their sarcasm. My wife obviously knew the answer to that question and smiled, acknowledging how great it was to hear that Alexandra was doing so well. I now focused my disbelief back at my wife and in my head said, "WHAT?! Are we all talking about the same kid? She has been an absolute monster at home and we are getting the reports of how great she is at school. This is BULLSHIT!"

I told the teacher what we were struggling with at home, and she said, "Yeah that happens a lot when kids feel very comfortable at home." *Excuse me, what's that now? She feels comfortable at home, so she acts like an a-hole?* As a matter of fact, that is exactly what can happen at that age. It means that Alexandra feels safe. Think about it, we can be the same. When we are at work, or out in a social environment, we are much less likely to show our negative traits. We try to act a little more politely, try to maintain a healthy mode of communication, and try to be aware of the people around us.

At home, we are able to let loose a bit more. We care less about how we are perceived and don't feel the need to be on our best behavior. Now look, I am a huge supporter of being authentic, and sometimes that is admitting that we aren't the exact same person outside of the house that we are inside of the house. No judgement, it's just what happens. I am more patient as a father because I don't want to embarrass my kids or myself and lose my shit in front of other people. (I don't want to lose my shit in front of my kids either; but statistically speaking, they are around me more often and are most likely the instigators of me losing my shit in the first place.) Why do I let them see me lose my shit? Because I know that they'll still love me. Because I know they will see the best of me, and they will see the worst of me. Because I know that I can sit down with them and apologize and explain. My children have seen me fail, and I am very thankful for that. I feel safe around them. And they feel safe around me.

The reason that Alexandra lost her cool at home every day for several weeks and the teacher didn't witness any of her breakdowns was because she felt safe. That safety means that when she is around us, she doesn't have to hold back anything. She can scream and we'll still love her. She can fight and we'll still love her. She can pick on her sisters, cry over not wanting to do math, get mad because she has to clear the table—all because she is at home, with people that she fully trusts. I know that it's so hard to deal with complaining, crying, screaming kids but if a child is upset, the opposite reaction isn't a well-behaved child. The opposite is a silent child who is holding in a whole lot of emotion. Yes, vocalized frustration is difficult, but silent frustration is dangerous.

I was talking to a parent about the concept of safety being the reason kids act up at home and they challenged me, asking if some dose of fear or not feeling safe is a good thing for balanced values. I think that fear is a healthy emotion to feel. Bravery isn't the absence of fear, it is the ability to get past it, to "out-smart" and "out-kind" that fear. The recognition and understanding of fear is what helps you overcome it.

4.3 NOT USING FEAR TO CONTROL

It might be easy to say that kids who act up at home because they don't feel fear in the house but act respectfully outside of their home, aren't acting with courage or authenticity at all. If they act respectfully out of fear of judgement, yet act disrespectfully when that fear is gone, they are caving in to external pressures.

Look, I want my kids to act respectfully for the right reasons too, but remember the goal here isn't to have respectful kids. The goal here is to make sure they feel safe enough to have healthy conflict, to teach them open communication skills, and to give them a place to express themselves. If the goal is simply to have kids who do what you tell them, then there is easy justification to strike the fear of God in them so they behave as well at home as they do at school. This is a common mistake that parents make—sorry, let me rephrase that. This is a common mistake that I also make. I see faster action when they are scared, but that doesn't fit my long-term goals. I want my kids to give me their best side, but more importantly for them to feel safe and be real.

When my kids aren't listening, when I've had a bad day, when the stress is high in the house, when I have an argument with my wife, when we are all stuck together in the same space for several months on end because of the COVID-19—these are times when I mistakenly, and oftentimes regrettably, strike fear into my children.

Here is what happens when I use fear to control behavior

1. They stop coming to me.
2. They keep secrets.
3. They are afraid to discuss their failures.
4. They keep their problems locked inside.
5. They turn to other people for advice.
6. They learn that if you want to control people, you just need to make them afraid.
7. They start yelling at other people.
8. They feel worse about themselves.

Yes, I might get the screaming, sarcastic, moaning child but I also get the trusting, courageous, bold, honest, confident, creative, loving child. I fear silence in my children much more than I fear unruliness.

I repeat this statement to remind myself regularly.

The trouble is that fear-based parenting is so effective from a short-term perspective that it easily hides itself under the guise of discipline. Discipline, this is a loaded word. Let's unpack that for a second to understand its power.

There are two definitions of discipline. One definition describes discipline as "self-control," or development of self-control through training and exercises. This is also how we talk about discipline in habit-forming. This is where the positive values of brave, smart and kind need to operate. The more habits we can develop around courage, critical thought and kindness, the more disciplined we become in our values.

The other definition describes discipline as "punishment" or to punish/penalize for the sake of enforcing obedience and perfecting moral character. This is where brave, smart and kind go downhill—quickly. It's this definition that some adults use to try to get the results of the first definition. They confuse punishment with reinforcing positive discipline. They use punishment to reinforce their notion of self-control. Most likely because that is how their own parents did it and said something along the lines of, "You need to be respectful," as they were spanking them. "You need to learn how to listen," as their children are trying to communicate something that they don't know how to say. "You need to understand the consequences of your actions," while the parent is oblivious to the consequences that occur by punishing a child.

The first understanding of discipline is talking about having a respectful, healthy dose of self-control. That comes with training, with education, with understanding, with the knowledge and know-how.

This understanding of discipline is an extremely healthy value to have and where we use brave, smart and kind.

CHAPTER 4 TAKE HOME

- Think about what you want your kids' inner voice to say to them… then say that to them regularly.
- Think about what you DON'T want their inner voice to say to them… stop saying those things immediately.
- Define what integrity means to you.
- Consider what you "spill" most often, negativity or positivity.
- Do you allow your kids to feel their negative emotions or do you reprimand them?
- Think about which definition of discipline you use more often than the other. Is it working?

SECTION TWO

DISCOVERY

CHAPTER 5

IT'S GRAVITY

Do you know what happens when the brain processes emotions?

In an article submitted to the journal *Frontiers in Psychology*, the authors wrote, "Emotion has a substantial influence on the cognitive processes in humans, including perception, attention, learning, memory, reasoning, and problem-solving. Emotion has a particularly strong influence on attention, especially modulating the selectivity of attention as well as motivating action and behavior."[2]

Summarized, this says that emotion influences thought which then turns into action and behavior.

I am ok with the idea that the end goal of parenting and leadership is to motivate action and behavior. And in all cases that will come from the perception, attention, memory, learning, reasoning and problem-solving skills that we are able to enact in our children and in those who follow us.

---

2 Tyng, Chai M., "The Influences of Emotion on Learning and Memory," PubMed Central, August 24, 2017, https://www.ncbi.nlm.nih.gov/pmc/articles/PMC5573739/.

Molecular biologist John Medina explains the phenomenon in his book *Brain Rules*, "When the brain detects an emotionally charged event, the amygdala releases dopamine into the system. Because dopamine greatly aids memory and information processing, you could say it creates a Post-It note that reads, 'Remember this.'"

This is why we remember significant events. We remember falling in love and heartbreak. We remember births and deaths. This is why (age permitting) you can probably remember where you were on September 11, 2001, what you were doing and who you were with, yet you can't remember September 11, 2021. That day in 2001 created a lot of emotion and a lot of dopamine. It placed a Post-It in your memory of the details of that day. 2021 was more recent by 20 years, and yet you most likely don't remember it unless you have a significant emotion tied to that day.

Why is this relevant to raising brave, smart and kind kids?

If we are able to tie emotions to values, then what we are able to do is to affect the perception, attention, learning, memory, reason and problem-solving of our children. If we aren't able to tap into those emotions, the memories don't last as long. It becomes much more difficult to raise them with any sort of intention or purpose.

Once we recognize the three foundational values of brave, smart and kind, then we are able to recognize those values in memorable moments. There are two sides to that coin. The first is to see it in places where it already exists. The second is to create experiences where we can teach and experience those values.

The first place I noticed that evoking emotions helped in establishing values with my kids was with storytelling.

5.1 BSK STORIES

WIZARD OF OZ

It wasn't long after I started talking to the girls about BSK when I sat down to watch the classic movie channel. On that specific evening, one of the movies that scared the crap out of me as a child came on, *The Wizard of Oz*. I don't remember how old I was when I first watched it, but I do remember that I was terrified of the cackling, vengeful, green Wicked Witch of the West flying in on her broom, spewing dark smoke. And if she wasn't scary enough, her "muscles" in the movie were flying apes that tore people limb from limb. Seriously, Dorothy's dream world was pretty jacked up. However, it led to some significant lessons.

We all know that Dorothy gets sucked up in a tornado and lands in Oz to the delight of some very small, sugar-addicted, singing and dancing friends. She is lost in a fantasy world and has to follow a path to find her way out. As Dorothy and her dog Toto are following the yellow brick road to the Emerald City to find The Wizard, they come to a fork in the road and don't know which way to go.

Dorothy is talking to Toto wondering which path to choose when she hears a voice from the fields. As she wanders over to see where it came from, she finds a very confused scarecrow who is attempting to give her directions but admits he's not sure because he doesn't have a brain. Dorothy asks him how he can talk if he doesn't have a brain and then he gives a wonderful response, "I don't know, but some people without brains do an awful lot of talking, don't they?"

As she helps him down, he confesses that he isn't a very good scarecrow. No one is afraid of him and they just laugh. He thinks he is a complete failure because he doesn't have a brain. Well, isn't that a common feeling? The Scarecrow wants to be SMART.

Later in the woods, they join up with a rusted tin man who got caught out in the rain while chopping wood. After getting oiled up, he is grateful but feels incomplete telling them he is hollow without a heart. "I'd be tender—I'd be gentle and awful sentimental, regarding love and art. I'd be friends with the sparrows and the boys who shoot the arrows, if I only had a heart." The Tinman wants to be KIND.

As they get deeper into the forest, they are attacked by a lion who comes across as a bully but turns into a complete scaredy-cat when Dorothy smacks him for chasing Toto. This cowardly lion joins the crew on their journey because he wants The Wizard to give him courage. The Lion wants to be BRAVE.

It simply is not enough to notice the patterns of BSK, they need to be relevant and applicable.

The Scarecrow feels like a failure because he doesn't feel smart. The Tinman feels hollow without a heart. The Lion puts on an act when he is scared.

How many times do we feel "less than" because we don't think we are smart enough? How many times do we feel empty without connection to others? How many times do we put on a strong face when we are completely terrified? We are all the Scarecrow, Tinman, and Lion.

As I was watching this movie, I did my first mental double-take, thinking what a coincidence that RIGHT after I defined beautiful as being brave, smart and kind, I would find the same message here. As it turned out this was simply the first of many reassurances from the universe that how I had started to define "beautiful" for my girls was the right path to choose.

HARRY POTTER

Did *The Wizard of Oz* reference pique some interest? It is one thing to see BSK in a single movie, but what about arguably the most popular characters of a generation? For those who haven't read or seen Harry Potter, there are some spoilers ahead (AND it's never too late to pick up the series!).

Let's start with the four houses and how J.K. Rowling describes them as the sorting hat sings in the first book:

Gryffindor: "Where dwell the **brave** at heart, their daring, nerve and chivalry set Gryffindors apart."

Hufflepuff: "Where they are just and **loyal**, those patient Hufflepuffs are true and unafraid to toil."

Ravenclaw: "Or yet in **wise** old Ravenclaw, if you've a ready mind, where those of wit and learning, will always find their kind."

Slytherin: "Those cunning folk use any means to achieve their ends."

Not to spoil the stories, but we all know that 99% of Slytherins are the over-ambitious who turn bad. The other three houses are literally split into BRAVE, SMART and KIND!

A deeper look at the three main characters actually shows that while they all showed courage, critical thought and kindness, each of them were developed (though perhaps not intentionally) around one of the foundational values.

Harry was not only forced into facing his fears, he got so accustomed to it that he often did it without thinking he needed Hermione to help him think things through. And near the end, his bravery almost killed him. He needed Ron to say, "You don't have to do it alone, mate." His courage and his ability to overcome his challenges was his defining value.

Hermione, honestly the one who saved the day more often than not, was by far the smartest. It wasn't just book-smarts, she made connections where others couldn't. In the beginning she started as an insufferable know-it-all and she would tend to overthink the problem. It wasn't until she faced her fears and learned to treat others as equals that she became such a hero.

Ron, the loyal friend. Not the sharpest tool in the shed, not particularly brave, but he was always there. Frankly speaking, he was my least favorite character in the books right up until the last book after he ran away and how he found his way back.

What I love about these stories is that they all had the brave, smart, kind characteristics in varying amounts, but by the end of the story, it was the BSK demons they had to face AND that Harry, Hermione, and Ron's reliance on each other was what made them triumph.

Read the books again, or watch the films, and see how the characters develop. Notice the brave, smart and kind parts. Notice, especially in the last book, when they are all tested and how they fail and succeed. If you are looking for an entrypoint to talk about BSK with your kids, Harry Potter is an incredible place to start.

PICK ANYTHING

In *Toy Story 3*, Andy is giving his toys away and this is how he describes Woody, "He's been my pal as long as I can remember. He's **brave**, like a cowboy should be, and **kind** and **smart**."

In the movie *Home*, Jim Parsons' alien character says, "But then I met a human person and she is not like you said. She is **brave** and **smart** and **cares** about other humans persons."

Throwback to one of my favorite childhood cartoons, *The Teenage Mutant Ninja Turtles*. Raphael was the **brave** one, Donatello was the **smart** one, Michelangelo was the **kind** one and Leonardo was the leader to bring them together.

Go through any story with your kids, and you can point out the brave, smart and kind stuff.

- *Frozen*: Sisters brave (**brave**) the unknown, to find the truth (**smart**), to look after each other (**kind**).

- *Big Hero Six*: Courageous adventure (**brave**) with some uber-smart kids (**smart**) to avenge their friend and help his little brother (**kind**).

- *The Lion King*: Monkey brings Simba wisdom/perspective (**smart**) and gets support from his friends (**kind**) to face his fear of being rejected by his family and defeat Scar (**brave**).

- *How to Train Your Dragon*: Hiccup shows compassion for a Toothless (**kind**), studies all about dragons (**smart**), learns to be brave like a Viking (**brave**).

Not into kids movies?

Look at the three main characters in Marvel's Avengers. Thor is the fearless one who jumps into any fight without thinking, Tony Stark is the one who will out-smart opponents and doesn't play well with others, and Steve Rogers is the one who always puts people first, "a good man." **Brave, Smart, Kind.**

The beauty of BSK is that it applies to all stories; it is actually the brave, smart and kind part of the stories that make them worth telling.

It was about this moment that I started thinking to myself, "Wow PJ, you are kinda pushing it and just finding examples to make this BSK stuff fit." But here is the thing. When those popped up, I wasn't even looking. They just started to reaffirm the message.

They ALL work, and not just the popular ones. I was watching a really bad horror flick the other day called *Fear Street*. The kid was describing two friends and said the first one was "funny and brave," and the second friend was—do I even need to tell you? I knew the script before it was revealed. Of course, the second one he says, "was smart and kind."

These are the messages that we have been digesting our entire lives. These are messages our children are digesting every day and we don't even notice. The language has already been set up for you to build off of. If you don't like your kids watching too many movies and you are more into books, go ahead and look at the popular authors.

J.K. Rowling and *Harry Potter*, C.S. Lewis and *The Lion, The Witch and the Wardrobe*, E.B. White and *Charlotte's Web*, J.R.R. Tolkien and *The Lord of the Rings* (really it's anyone else who goes by initials).

I could go on with these lists, but I don't need to. It's not just that there are lessons in values in these stories, there are lessons in values everywhere you look. It's the patterns that we are looking for to find a common language so we can raise children with intention. It is to find common language so that schools and parents can reinforce the same messages.

It is finding the common language so that when children are struggling, we are able to meet them on their level, make sure they feel understood, and create connections that carry through adolescence into adulthood.

When I started to notice these patterns, I instinctively tried to negate them. I would say things like, "These are too easy. OF COURSE you are going to find them everywhere in Disney. That is their formula for telling stories." You might be saying, "All of the examples you are referencing are fiction." (With the exception of J.K. Rowling who is secretly working for the Ministry of Magic responsible for Muggle relations so she wrote the books as a way to gauge Muggle interest to decide if the Magical and Muggle worlds could coexist.)

Sorry back on point… "PJ, these are all fiction, not based on real-life situations that we are confronted with."

Except that they aren't. After noticing the patterns in storytelling, I tried to find any non-fictional examples. And guess what! It also wasn't very hard.

HEART, MIND AND SOUL

Perhaps one of the reasons that brave, smart and kind sounds so universal and encompassing is because there have been so many teachings rooted in the heart, mind and soul. When we give those nouns corresponding adjectives in describing people, what do we say? We describe them as having a kind heart, a smart mind and a brave soul. Sometimes we switch it up and say they have a brave heart, a smart mind and a kind soul, but the brave, smart and kind are always there. Now, I am definitely not an etymologist, however, the frequency in which BSK shows up in any form of teaching, parenting, leadership, storytelling (across eras), languages, cultures, and religions shows us their significance.

5.2 THE HISTORY OF BSK

From a historical standpoint, we can start by looking back to 500 B.C. to Chinese antiquity. Confucius was a philosopher who shaped China and East Asia through his teachings. He said, "Wisdom, compassion, and courage are the three universally recognized moral qualities of men." Wisdom was his smart, compassion was his kind, and courage was his brave. That was more than 2500 years ago.

Not long after Confucius died, we can travel West to witness the foundation of Stoicism, an ancient Greek philosophy based on four virtues that were derived from the teaching of Plato that he outlined in Republic IV in early 400 BC.

- Courage
- Wisdom
- Justice
- Temperance

Courage is brave, wisdom is smart, and justice (or treating people justly) is kind. The last one, temperance, is not taking any virtue to an extreme, it is finding a balance. We'll get more into how that applies to BSK when we talk about reciprocity.

The Stoics believed that unhappiness and evil are the results of a person's ignorance of their purpose in the world. Being unkind is a result of being unaware of one's own universal reason. The natural solution to evil and unhappiness is the practice of Stoic philosophy.

I have been helping people find their values for years. It wasn't until I discovered that all values are either brave, smart and/or kind that it made sense. Looking at BSK through Stoicism, they talk about it in the same way, meaning if you don't know what your values are, then they are much more likely to send you down the wrong path. If you aren't aware of who you are, and what you specifically stand for, then the only way to come back is to see how you fit into the reason of nature, and then see how you can self-correct.

Religion

If you know your history of religion and Greek philosophy, you'll also know that Aristotle, a student of Plato, had significant influence on both Christianity and Islam. Medieval Chistians called him "The Philosopher" and medieval Muslim scholars knew him as "The First Teacher." He is also known to many as the "Father of Logic" as he was the first known man to do a formal study on the subject of logic. From Aristotle, Catholics adopted the four cardinal virtues which are known to be the basis for Chrisitan morality.

- Prudence (described as wisdom)
- Justice (described as fairness)
- Fortitude (described as courage)
- Temperance (described as restraint)

Those came from Greek antiquity.

There are also hints throughout history that point to the Stoics as having a great influence on the teachings of Jesus himself which are built into Christianity. If you look at the Holy Trinity, of the Father, Son and Holy Spirit, it has been argued that it came from the Greeks who recognized the unity of the mind, heart and soul. The Holy Spirit is the faith and strength to overcome. The Father is all-knowing and wise. The Son teaches love. Brave. Smart. Kind. Much like many Christian traditions, in order to build a more influential church and win over followers, they adopted thoughts and significant dates such that beliefs could be more easily explained and accepted.

In Islam, they speak of the soul having three components: the spirit, mind and the self.[3] The spirit is how God lives through people and gives them strength or the ability to live. The mind is how we collect and process information. The self is how we treat ourselves and others. Brave. Smart. Kind.

Know that I am more of a spiritual person than a believer in any singular religion. I was raised in a Christian family but the presence of brave, smart and kind values are woven into all religious parables. Take a look at how kindness, i.e. the "Golden Rule," has origins from around the globe.[4]

Confucianism: "What you do not want done to yourself, do not do to others."

Buddhism: "Hurt not others with that which pains you."

Islam: "No one is a believer until he loves for his neighbor what he loves for himself."

---

3 El-Najjar, Hassan Ali, "Spirit, Soul, Mind, Self, and Happiness, from an Islamic Perspective," Al-Jazeerah, July 7, 2020, http://www.aljazeerah.info/Islamic%20 Editorials/2007/November/Spirit,%20Soul,%20Mind,%20Self,%20and%20 Happiness,%20from%20an%20Islamic%20Perspective%20By%20Hassan%20Ali%20El-Najjar.htm.

4 Maxwell, John, "The 5 Levels of Leadership," Center Street, 2021, 109.

Judaism: "What is hateful to you, do not do to your fellow man. This is the entire Law, the rest is commentary."

Christianity: "Whatever you want men to do to you, do also to them."

Hinduism: "This is the sum of duty; naught unto others what you would not have them do unto you."

Jainism: "A man should wander about treating all creatures as he himself would be treated."

Baha'i: "And if thine eyes be turned towards justice, choose thou for thy neighbour that which thou choosest for thyself."

Yoruba Proverb: "One going to take a pointed stick to pinch a baby bird should first try it on himself to feel how it hurts."

Language

There are multiple words across languages that mean heart-mind such as "xin" in Chinese and "qalb" in Arabic. I think my favorite is the word "kokoro." It is Japanese and is mentioned in ancient text to mean heart, mind and spirit, and specifically implies their interconnectivity.

There is an entry for kokoro in a dictionary of classic Japanese words:

"Originally, kokoro referred to the beat of the heart, which was considered to be the essential organ of life and the source of all activities. By extension, kokoro refers to all human activities affecting the outside world through intention, emotion, and intellect."

According to this, Kokoro has three basic meanings: the heart and its functions; mind and its functions; and center, or essence. Heart is kind or how we interact with people/emotions, mind is smart and where we process information and decision-making, and center is brave or how we show up and overcome from our core.

Kokoro seems very similar to the Sanskrit word for heart, "hrid or hrdayam." This can be translated into heart, mind and/or soul.

In Latin, there was a word that took on the meaning of brave, smart and kind combined. It was "courage." In *Gifts of Imperfection*, Brené Brown talks about the root of courage being "cor"—or heart in Latin. Brown writes that the original definition of the word courage was to, "Speak one's mind by telling all one's heart." Bravery came from the ability to tap into your heart and mind.

Leadership

For those who study leadership and/or history. How can we not view leaders through the lens of brave, smart and kind when they have given us every opportunity to do so?

Nelson Mandela, for me, is arguably the most impressive leader in history. Read about his life, find his stories, find his quotes:

Brave

- "I learned that courage was not the absence of fear, but the triumph over it. The brave man is not he who does not feel afraid, but he who conquers that fear."
- "It always seems impossible until it's done."
- "A winner is a dreamer who never gives up."

Smart

- "Fools multiply when wise men are silent."

- "The power of education extends beyond the development of skills we need for economic success. It can contribute to nation-building and reconciliation."

- "Education is the most powerful weapon which you can use to change the world."

Kind

- "There can be no greater gift than that of giving one's time and energy to help others without expecting anything in return."

- "What counts in life is not the mere fact that we've lived. It is what difference we've made to the lives of others that will determine the significance of the life we lead."

- "To deny people their human rights is to challenge their very humanity."

And those that show how values work together:

- "A good head and a good heart are always a formidable combination."

- "Forgiveness liberates the soul. It removes fear."

- "A good leader can engage in a debate frankly and thoroughly, knowing that at the end he and the other side must be closer, and thus emerge stronger."

Honestly, if you need motivation, inspiration and classic examples in brave, smart, kind, read about Mandela. How he was able to overcome his imprisonment and show compassion for those who locked him up is beyond any other stories that I have heard outside of religion. The value he placed on expanding his mind was insane. He would smuggle books into prison to continue his education. I'd have to write a whole other book to do a deep dive on Mandela's brave, smart and kind.

Another legend is Mahatma Gandhi. All of Gandhi's values and principles are related to BSK, but his first value specifically is the unity and integrity of the body, mind and soul. Yes, the body isn't the heart, but when we define "kind" it is how we treat others and how we treat ourselves. Gandhi saw the body as a vessel to carry out the actions both externally and internally (that is to say how we treat others and how we treat ourselves).

We can look at any leader in history and break down their success (and their failures) into how they were brave, smart and kind. Abraham Lincoln, Martin Luther King Jr., Malala Yousafzai, Muhammad Yunus, etc.

In Brené Brown's *Dare to Lead*, she did research with leaders who, when asked what needs to change in leadership to face the future challenges, said a resounding, "we need braver leaders and more courageous cultures." But when they dove deeper into WHY there was a need for braver leadership, she notes that the answers, "Weren't intuitively connected to courage. Leaders talked about everything from critical thinking and the ability to synthesize and analyze information to building trust, rethinking educational systems, inspiring innovation, finding common political ground amid growing polarization, making tough decisions, and the importance of empathy and relationship-building in the context of machine learning and artificial intelligence."

If you read that message again, when people are describing why they need BRAVE leadership, they describe:

SMART

- Critical thinking
- Synthesize and analyze information

- Rethinking education systems
- Inspiring Innovation
- Machine learning
- Artificial intelligence

KIND

- Building trust
- Finding common ground
- Importance of empathy
- Relationship building

They are literally outlining the three foundational values of brave, smart and kind in single finding. They just aren't labeling them as such.

5.3 CONNECTING DOTS

Here's the thing: I didn't discover brave, smart and kind any more than Europeans "discovered" America or Sir Issac Newton "discovered" gravity. America and gravity were always there, just as these values have been. I just discovered BSK in my own world and am beginning to understand how it fits into society.

There have been many words throughout history and across various cultures and languages that show the connectivity of these values. Confucius spoke of courage, wisdom and compassion in 500 B.C. Stoics wrote about courage, wisdom, justice and temperance in 300 B.C. Christians started making the BSK connections in 100 A.D. People who have shaped the world have been leading with them and redefining them in every courageous, thoughtful and kind way. And all along these journeys the brave, smart and kind values have shown up in just about every instance we can imagine. I think it is as good a time as any to start recognizing these foundational values and their importance in raising children.

For someone who prides himself in intention, I didn't choose to raise my girls with these values because of their rich historical relevance or their presence in stories. I chose those values with intention and their abundance in society was a complete coincidence. I either stumbled upon, or was programmed to see their significance. It wasn't until after watching *The Wizard of Oz* and seeing "brave, smart and kind" come up in their characters that I began to notice these values in other places. Now that I have seen them so often, I can't unsee them.

Historically or philosophically speaking, I am really ok if people find some flaws in how I have connected the dots of BSK throughout time periods, cultures and religions. I don't think that part matters much. What is much more relevant to me is the undeniability of the patterns and history of values. If we can package all of this up and apply it to parenting and raising our kids to be brave, smart and kind, then we have discovered something that frames decisions and helps to give us direction.

Personally, BSK has given me a way to connect with my little girls that I didn't have before. That, to me, makes this message timeless. And the BSK message could have stopped right there with my kiddos, but much like gravity, once it was noticed it became undeniable in the eyes of others as well.

It Caught on Quickly

I was going around the world talking about values AND implementing the BSK values in my home when something unexpected began to occur.

I was doing a workshop called Leading with Values. This involves going into companies or large events and explaining the importance of having personal values and then I run a series of exercises that allow people to walk out of the room with their own well-defined values. Because of the powerful stories with my daughters, I typically introduce the session with our family values and how I was raising the girls. If I speak for ninety minutes, this may take ten minutes of the presentation. I will introduce the girls, talk about the three Ds—how we define, display, and discuss the values. After this, I dive into the meat of personal values. After the sessions are done, I stick around and talk to some of the participants about their values.

When I look back to when I started these sessions, the passionate interest in the session would come from parents who would ask me more about the BSK stuff. I enjoy a good conversation, so we would share battle stories of parenthood and I would talk more about values as it relates to children and we would then part ways.

My network of people, while quite global, isn't that big. I bump into people all the time who had taken part in a workshop and they would say, "Hey, I loved your BSK workshop; I told my spouse about it and we are implementing them in our home with our kids and it's going great!" The first time someone came up to me I thought, "Wow! That is amazing, but wait, that wasn't what the workshop was about!" I mean it's great to help people find their own values, but one guy came up and said, "Is it ok if we just steal yours?" And I said yeah of course, if they work for other people, who am I to argue?

One audience member who started to implement this was an entrepreneur in Belgium named Miten Shah, Founder of Lifare.com. Miten was at a session I did outside of Antwerp and we instantly connected. I saw him a couple months after the presentation. He told me how much he loved the values and that he had put a board up in his house where each family member could give a sticker each day to someone else in the family who had done something brave, smart or kind. He said his kids give him a lot of the smart stickers, but not many of the kind ones! But don't let him fool you, he is an incredibly kind man. Miten actually wrote an article in *Forbes* talking about how he is putting BSK into his home. One of the quotes from Miten was:

> "Discovering BSK is like discovering gravity, you always follow its rules but you don't know its power until something as simple as an apple falls on your head and changes your world and makes you understand the universe."

We're going to come back to the importance of this quote in a bit. I quickly realized that people were responding to BSK with enthusiasm. I decided to share this idea with a wider audience to see who else it might resonate with.

I took the BSK concept to Facebook Live, to share with my "closest" 2000 friends how I use values to raise my girls. I got some likes, got some shares and then I just left it alone. A couple months later I got a message in my inbox from an old high-school friend from Jamestown, NY who I hadn't heard from in over twenty years. Her name is Michelle Sabol and she wrote to me to say that she has been using BSK with both her son and with her class. Michelle is a first grade teacher at Sol Feinstone Elementary in Newton, Pennsylvania.

Now in my mind, she was contacting me because she and I had both been doing BSK stuff and she was just saying how cool it is that we coincidentally are teaching the same values. So I replied to say, "what a coincidence! We are both using brave, smart and kind!" I started asking her questions about how she came up with BSK, what her experience had been with it, how long she'd been doing it and what the results had been—to which she said, "Um, I started it after seeing your video."

Head meets palm...

I like to think that I am a mildly insightful guy, but I smack myself in the head a lot. This was so cool! I have had people take my BSK message to heart, and having those "aha" moments out of an audience is one of the best feelings for speakers. Getting someone to implement those ideas in their classroom and tell you how it's impacting the lives of all of those kids is incredible. Michelle also shared that before she saw my video she was losing a lot of her motivation to teach. She'd been doing it for a long time, but the job had lost some of its luster. With the rigidity of the educational system and teachers having fewer resources and higher demand for good test results, it's no wonder that the profession has taken a beating over the last twenty years. One of the beautiful parts of BSK is that it's not a curriculum, it is a mentality and an easy way to streamline the language that we use in schools with the language we use in homes. It gave Michelle a new way to re-energize herself, shape how she is able to move the needle as a teacher and the flexibility to be creative and more meaningful in her work.

After Michelle started implementing in her class, she began speaking with other teachers about the impact BSK was having on her teaching, her students and their parents. It began to spread. She then approached her principal who decided to adopt a Brave, Smart, Kind theme for the entire elementary school. Then Michelle's neighbor, a teacher from a neighboring school heard about it as well along with more teachers from her school, teachers from NY and Colorado and Florida, and hopefully some who haven't contacted me yet, began to implement their own BSK practices. BSK is such a simple, memorable concept to understand and apply and it can address some very deep, complex issues. It IS like gravity!

What started out as a way to redefine the word "beautiful" for my daughters has turned out to be what many families and teachers have been searching for. It's not just relevant for me, it's relevant for everyone—parents, educators, leaders—and even more so, it is a way for all of the players to get on the same page.

At first I wondered why BSK caught on so quickly. I thought it was because of how simple it was and because it's easy to remember in sets of three. Maybe it reminded people of what they are also tired of in the world; people using fear to control, the lack of people using critical thought, or the sincere need for more kindness in the world. I slowly began to realize that it caught on because it feels like a truth re-discovered, something that's always been present, but needed to be dusted off and renewed. I think the reason BSK resonates with so many people is because it gives them a better understanding of what they observe. When we start to observe our own thoughts and our own behavior (not to mention the behavior of others), through the brave, smart, kind lens, then it starts to make sense. Once it makes sense, then we give it more recognition, and we give it more power. And once we figure out the patterns, we get to use it with greater meaning and intention.

5.4 WHAT WE PAY ATTENTION TO MATTERS

In *Daring Greatly*, Brené Brown illustrates the importance of purpose. "The real question for parents should be 'Are you engaged? Are you paying attention?' If so, plan to make lots of mistakes and bad decisions. Imperfect parenting moments turn into gifts as our children watch us try to figure out what went wrong and how we can do better next time. The mandate is not to be perfect and raise happy children. Perfection doesn't exist and I've found that what makes children happy doesn't always prepare them to be courageous adults. The same is true for schools. I haven't encountered a single problem that isn't attributed to some combination of parental, teacher, admin, and/or student disengagement and the clash of competing stakeholders vying to define **one purpose.**"

What Michelle (and other teachers and parents) found was that BSK is a way to achieve this one purpose, and once you are aligned with those ideas you are able to spread them quite easily among stakeholders.

When I started going to schools to ask people what brave, smart and kind meant to them, you know what I found out? Kids LOVE to tell their stories! Who knew?!? If you're a teacher reading this book you are probably thinking, "Um, we knew. We do that all the time." Some parents however struggle at allowing their kids to open up.

Give children the opportunity to talk about themselves and their successes, instead of pointing out the things they can work on. When you do this, you will find they will jump over fences to do more things INTENTIONALLY, just so they have something to talk to you about. They want your praise, they want to impress you, they want your approval. Most importantly they want to FEEL important, and you have the power to make them feel that.

Kids notice when you are listening and when you aren't. Here is a story Michelle shared with me to illustrate an example of this.

"I was driving Chase to baseball practice on a rainy, stormy night and it was hard to see. Chase was nine years old. We usually discuss his school days on our car rides to practice. It didn't happen on this particular night as we were distracted with the rain and traffic. On the car ride home, we were equally distracted and didn't talk much. As soon as we got home, Chase jumped in the shower, and I sat in a chair and caught up with emails on my phone. When he got out of the shower and dressed, he jumped up on my lap and was in my face with mom,

mom, mom... clearly wanting my attention. I redirected him and asked for a couple minutes, then he said in a very stern voice... How were you brave, smart, or kind today?

Although I had been asking him these questions daily, he hadn't asked me. He clearly knew this is how I would start our nightly conversations to get as much detail as I could out of his days. It always worked. On this night, he clearly knew it would work on me. I dropped my phone immediately and with a teary-eyed grin, told him all about my day and he told me all about his. BSK wins again! This time he used it to his advantage, to get my attention that he was craving and didn't receive yet that night."

What a great example of setting up the right language that gives a child a way to get a parent's attention in a healthy way!

This was a positive account of gaining attention, but how many times are we in a situation where we refuse to listen or pay attention to our children? I know these types of situations come up for me often. Sometimes it comes when they are competing for my attention. That happens when I am focused on just one of their siblings, working, talking to my wife, or on the phone. How about when they are yelling and screaming for attention and we put them in their rooms because we decide, "They need time to settle down on their own."

Our kids want our attention, and if they don't get it in positive ways, they will find negative ways to get that attention. And if they don't feel seen or heard when they are acting in a positive way, but they DO feel seen and heard when they are acting in a negative way, that is the behavior they will repeat.

In those situations, a child feels neither seen nor heard. Now, do me a favor and relate that to a time when you didn't feel seen or heard. Maybe that happens in your marriage or partnership. Maybe it happens with your parents. Maybe that has happened to you with friends, or at work, or any other place where relationships matter. Now imagine that relationship was with the first person you ever knew, the one you relied on, trusted, loved. You are that singular person to your children, you are that relationship and because of that they are going to try even harder to get your attention!

I am not advocating for giving in to every single desire of a child, far from it! There are ways however to make sure your kids feel seen and heard without becoming a pushover. What I want to know now is, what can you do to make sure they feel like they are being seen? What can you do to make sure they are being heard?

Dale Carnegie put it like this, "Wanting a feeling of importance is a human frailty. When arguing with someone, they get their feeling of importance by loudly asserting their authority. But as soon as you recognize their importance and stop the argument, their ego expands and they become sympathetic and kindly human beings."

Once you understand that concept, how are you able to recognize their importance? What are things they do where you can see and hear them be brave? When do you see and hear them being smart? When do you see and hear them being kind? On the flip side of that, when do you miss seeing and hearing them being brave? When do you miss seeing and hearing them being smart? When do you miss seeing and hearing them being kind? And a more important question—what happens to them when you miss those opportunities to see them?

Positive attention to BSK reinforces those actions. It makes them more interested in showing you more of what they are capable of. It's a subliminal message that makes a connection in their brain between positive acts and attention. It's habit-forming, and even greater than this, it's character-forming. Likewise, when they don't receive the positive attention they seek for their BSK acts, they will do the opposite to get the negative attention. They'll put their chin down when they are supposed to try, they will turn their brain off when they need to think, and they will close their hearts when they interact with others. Negative actions are habit-forming too and, more dangerously, character-forming. The only way out of this is to either pay attention and recognize the positive behaviors OR hope that the people they find to fill those holes in their life are people of high character.

CHAPTER 5 TAKE HOME

- Find your kids' favorite stories. Identify the brave, smart and kind moments and call them out.

- Ask your children to tell you their favorite story of courage, their favorite story of someone using their brain, their favorite story of kindness.

- Ask yourself what happens when you don't feel seen or heard.

- Think about where your kids get their feeling of importance.

- Notice and recognize when they are brave; standing up for something they believe, doing something hard or scary.

- Notice and recognize when they are being smart; using their creativity, problem solving, knowing a specific piece of information.

- Notice and recognize when they are kind; using their manners, giving attention to a friend, helping others or caring for themselves.

CHAPTER 6

FUNDAMENTAL VALUES

I have worked in educational leadership organizations since 1998. What has always intrigued me is how leaders shape their decision-making process, how they succeed, how they fail, and how they relate. What I have found is that the answer to all of these questions boils down to individual values. The inherent traits we have been defining and developing over years of living.

Definitions are tricky, which is a strange concept because we quite literally have books that give us definitions for words. What dictionaries however have not been able to sort through is context, culture, language, upbringing, etc. Words mean different things to different people. Here are some textbook definitions of our central theme:

Brave: having or showing mental or moral strength to face danger, fear, or difficulty; having or showing courage

Smart: having or showing a high degree of mental ability

Kind: of a sympathetic or helpful nature

I am not going to knock Merriam-Webster, but there is so much more to these words than simply their definitions. At the same time, those are great places to start because we all have strength to overcome, we all have ways to show mental ability, and we have ways to be helpful to others or ourselves. Some ways bring us together and other ways take us further apart. Our goal here is not to agree on all values, actually that goes very much against what we should do. We all need to come up with our own definitions of our personal values. Your brave is different than my brave, your smart is different than my smart, your kind is different from my kind. In the case of parenting, it's a difficult and yet necessary realization when we find that our values aren't always shared by our children. So, let's do a gut check here.

> **Is your purpose to have your kids have all of your values, or is your purpose to raise kids who have their own?**

Take your time with this one because it is pretty important. I get it, the answers are nuanced.

This book is going to do a little of both. We are going to help you understand your values so you can use them in raising your children AND we are going to help you identify your children's values because—whether you like it or not—their values will not mirror your own. The best we can hope for is that we pass down the best of us, know that they'll absorb some of the bad, and help them understand the rest that they'll pick up from an infinite number of people and experiences.

DEFINING VALUES

I suppose the first definition that matters is actually defining what a "value" is. It might seem trivial, but if I look at the word count right now, the word "value" is repeated in this book more than 600 times. I guess that makes sense since I am a values-based leadership coach and my purpose is to raise kids who are brave, smart and kind. But if we can't agree on what values are, then there isn't a lot of use in continuing. For this I am going to lean on one of the all-time greats when it comes to values, Mahatma Gandhi. Here is what he said about values:

"Your beliefs become your thoughts,
Your thoughts become your words,
Your words become your actions,
Your actions become you habits,
Your habits become your values,
Your values become your destiny."

While I think we can get an earlier jump on values, it still shows the importance of defining "values" as the beliefs, thoughts, words, actions and habits from which we live. Destiny isn't predetermined, it is something we work towards, and that is what we will be doing in this book. We are working towards our purpose—understanding our beliefs, thoughts, words, actions and habits through the values of brave, smart and kind.

Brené Brown talks about the same concept, but as a sense of worthiness saying that, "A strong belief in worthiness doesn't just happen, it is cultivated when we understand the guideposts as choices and daily practices."

If we are able to understand values, our guideposts, we can create habits for ourselves and our children and do so from a place of authenticity.

If we are able to do that regularly, then what happens is we are quicker to act from our positive values. What it also means is that it's easier for our children to act from their values as well. If we start with basic values when they are young, then we can create positive habits in them and add to those habits and their values as they get older.

In the last section I told you how I defined the brave, smart, kind values for my girls. In this section we are going to look at how we can define brave, smart and kind for anyone. Like we said, my definition of brave might be completely different from yours. Our differences matter and are at the heart of these values.

All values tell you how to overcome challenges, how to critically think and how to treat people. This isn't to tell everyone that we are putting a box around their uniqueness, this is to say that values are only original in their definitions. Yes, you still get to be a big, bright, beautiful butterfly—unique and brilliant.

I started training people in values-based leadership in 2017, not only helping people find their values, but also how to speak and act from those values. After I began digging into values with the girls, I started to notice the same patterns in adults. What I have found after working with thousands of leaders is that ALL values in their purest form boil down into essentially three questions:

1. How do you overcome?
2. How do you critically think?
3. How do you treat people?

Too simple? Try to find a value that doesn't fit into at least one of those buckets. I've been trying for years, and have yet to find one.

Some of the most common values are authenticity, determination, creativity, wisdom, empathy, loyalty. And some are more unique values people have shared like grit (resilience), be a seeker (learn), give a shit (care).

Understand this, everyone is raised with values. Every person has values inside of them! They could be the saintliest person in the world or the most evil. Each person has values guiding their thoughts, their decision-making processes, their actions. You may not agree with who they are or what they do, but values are present, always.

Values are the driver AND they start to develop at a very young age and become more concrete as we get older. Consider this excerpt from the Center on the Developing Child, "The brain is most flexible, or 'plastic,' early in life to accommodate a wide range of environments and interactions, but as the maturing brain becomes more specialized to assume more complex functions, it is less capable of reorganizing and adapting to new or unexpected challenges. For example, by the first year, the parts of the brain that differentiate sound are becoming specialized to the language the baby has been exposed to; at the same time, the brain is already starting to lose the ability to recognize different sounds found in other languages. Although the 'windows' for language learning and other skills remain open, these brain circuits become increasingly difficult to alter over time. Early plasticity means it's easier and more effective to influence a baby's developing brain architecture than to rewire parts of its circuitry in the adult years."[5]

The part I want you to focus on is the early plasticity of a child's brain versus an adults. (When working with adults, we are simply helping

5   "InBrief: The Science of Early Childhood Development," Center on the Developing Child (2007), Accessed June 14, 2022, https://developingchild.harvard.edu/resources/inbrief-science-of-ecd/#:~:text=Sensory%20pathways%20like%20those%20for,built%20upon%20earlier%2C%20simpler%20circuits.

them find their values that have been shaped over the course of their lifetime.) The opportunity we have with children is to actually shape their values with greater purpose.

As I looked to my own children I had two choices: I could be a good father, raise them and see what values they developed OR I could be intentional, and help them develop their values now so that they learn to understand, reason, act and speak from their values. So,

1. How do you overcome? Through being brave.
2. How do you critically think? By being smart.
3. How do you treat people? With kindness.

As they get older, brave may become authenticity or determination or grit. Smart may become creativity or wisdom or be a seeker. Kindness may become honesty or loyalty or give a shit. I don't know how they will end up, and that's ok. Our values come from many more sources than just our parents, this is just where we are first exposed to them.

What happens when parents and teachers start working off of the same framework? The influential adults who surround our kids begin to use the same language, to reinforce the same actions, to create habits that form courage, critical thought and kindness at the most critical stages of character development for children. The result is, we begin to grow a nurturing community based on fundamental values.

I have seen so many children struggle with their identities stemming from what is expected of them and what is noticed. What happens when we start to notice who our kids truly are? We meet them in a place of pride and confidence, and we get to build them up based on character, not necessarily their math or reading scores. I know I am preaching to the choir right now because you are already reading this book. What we need now is for the choir to sing it out so loud that the rest of the world hears it. Yes we are looking to inspire others, but only if that inspiration creates action.

6.1 DEFINING BRAVE

The Merriam-Webster definition is, "having or showing mental or moral strength to face danger, fear, or difficulty : having or showing courage." For argument's sake, let's just say that courage and bravery are synonyms. That gives us, "mental or moral strength to face fear, danger, or difficulty."

One of the reasons that I like this definition is because it doesn't fall into the narrative that fear is a necessity of bravery. Yes, the abuse of fear was the main reason that I chose "brave" as one of the definitions of beautiful, but it doesn't mean that we all have to live with fear to be brave.

I think it's important to acknowledge we can be courageous even in the absence of fear. I remember when my parents were going through their divorce, people would come up to me and say, "You're being so brave going through this." Even at that young age, it didn't feel like bravery to me because I wasn't scared to begin with. I felt confused and sad, but not unsafe.

Looking back, I can say I was courageous because of the way I was showing up. There were a lot of tough emotions during that time and I had the ability to move on and overcome them. All of this to say, when you discuss bravery with your kids, don't forget that fear isn't the only place their courage shows up. It can emerge in a difficult conversation that's had with compassion. It can be overcoming doubt and trying something new. It can be finding peace in a sad situation. It can be a belief that better days are ahead. It can also be the way they stand up against you, rebel, and ignore what you are saying. It's harder to see it in those moments, but it doesn't make it less true.

When we look at defining bravery, the key aspect is how we overcome. In those times of danger, fear or difficulty, what is our character? Of all of the values, bravery is one where people believe you either have it or you don't. You can work on your "smart" and you can decide to be "kind," but bravery is considered a bit of an enigma for those who don't believe that they have it.

I disagree.

I think we are raised believing that bravery is rare because of the stories and myths that we give to courage. Naturally, we all enjoy hearing stories of intense bravery. We are told stories of heroes, warriors, those who have overcome seemingly insurmountable odds. I read an anonymous quote that said, "Sometimes courage isn't a lion roaring. Sometimes courage is a quiet voice saying, that is enough for today, I am going to try my best again tomorrow."

This is how I view bravery. It's how we show up on a regular basis. It's how we overcome our challenges. One can show courage by jumping two feet in the fire to the cheers of many, and one can show courage through restraint and not buying into what others say. Brave can be getting out of a difficult situation OR sticking with a difficult situation. It can be fortitude OR it can be a willingness to show weakness.

If you are thinking, "But PJ, that means ANYONE can be brave, and that no one is special!" That is not what I am saying. Yes anyone can be brave, as a matter of fact, everyone is. And, people are different, and that difference is what makes them special. In addition, what a better world it is to live in when we can get people to see the courage that they have inside of themselves instead of creating a myth that only the strongest or the fearless have the courage to overcome challenges.

The most important step in our own journeys is to find out how we are brave. Do you find bravery from being your true self? Is your bravery the ability to step out of your comfort zone? Maybe your bravery is resilience, to embrace the suck. Your brave may not be the same as my brave, and that is exactly the way it's supposed to be. Do yourself a favor and reflect on how you show up in times of fear, danger, or difficulty. Then learn to maximize those strengths. These are your superpowers.

Here are some words you can use to help you define your brave:

Accomplishment	Conservation	Frankness
Accountability	Conviction	Freedom
Activeness	Decisiveness	Gallantry
Adaptable	Dependability	Grace
Adventure	Determination	Honesty
Aggressiveness	Discipline	Honor
Agility	Discovery	Hopefulness
Artistry	Diversity	Humility
Assertiveness	Dreamer	Impact
Audacity	Drive	Independence
Balance	Elegance	Individuality
Bold	Endurance	Integrity
Calmness	Energy	Intensity
Candor	Exploration	Justice
Capability	Expressiveness	Optimism
Carefulness	Faith	Originality
Challenge	Fierceness	Passion
Competition	Firmness	Perseverance
Confidence	Fortitude	Proactivity

Prudence	Sophistication	Transcendence
Resolve	Spirit	Uniqueness
Restraint	Stability	Virtue
Sacrifice	Strength	Vivacity
Security	Success	Wonder
Sexuality	Traditionalism	Zeal

Defining Brave In Parenting

"It is ok to be afraid. Even if you are scared, make the right choice." This was the very first definition that I gave my daughters. It has held up pretty well over the first seven years, but it naturally needs to expand as my kids start to overcome more complex, mature challenges.

If we look at the Merriam-Webster definition again, "mental or moral strength to face fear, danger or difficulty," we have a pretty good starting point in how to define brave for kids.

Fear was worked into our original definition for the kids. It is the most popular definition of brave because of the common perception that fear is a prerequisite of courage. The topic of fear is pretty extensively looked at throughout the book, but the important part of your family's definition isn't fear itself, it's how you want to deal with it. Is it with honesty, grace, boldness, security? All of those definitions give your kids different angles of how they can deal with fear. Honesty says, "Come to me, talk it out." Grace says, "It's ok, everyone gets afraid sometimes." Boldness says, "I'm going to laugh in the face of fear!" Security says, "Let's see if what we are afraid of is actually dangerous." There are no wrong answers here people, but there is choice.

Danger is a worthwhile addition because kids so rarely accurately feel danger. While kids can have innate fear from dangerous objects, danger is usually learned from past experience. What is dangerous and how do we want to act when danger is present? I would highly suggest you talk to your kids about what IS and what ISN'T dangerous and how to act when those situations arise. Which "brave" characteristics do you reinforce?

Lastly is difficulty. While fear is the most popular idea presented with courage, I find difficulty is the most common. In my life, I am presented with difficulty much more frequently than fear. This feeds our fundamental description of needing to overcome. Difficulty happens most days. How do you want your kids to work through difficult situations—with grit, curiosity, energy, stability?

All of those definitions say something to a child, and you are the person who will be saying it.

6.2 DEFINING SMART

I have been truly fortunate to travel and experience new people and new places. Living in four U.S. states and moving eight times by the age of eleven, change was a constant in my life. I continued that trend, after failing in my first attempt at university and pursuing various careers, ending up as confused as ever living in Southern California. My decision from there? Join a touring musical organization and travel further from home of course!

At that time, our tour went to a new city every three to four days. I had already seen much of the U.S., but for my international experience, I had only been to Niagara Falls and Tijuana. (For any Canadians and Mexicans reading this book, I know those locations don't count as international.)

My first real trip abroad was to spend six months exploring the Netherlands, Germany, Denmark and Sweden. People were infinitely kind and it was fun to learn of the various customs and cultures. As we opened ourselves up to new experiences, one concept kept coming up into conversations—culture shock.

People love to talk about culture shock when experiencing something surprising or different to what they are used to. Trying herring on the streets in Amsterdam, entering a Finnish spa where everyone is naked, or simply missing the comforts of home over an extended period. My story is slightly different.

When we arrived in the eastern part of Germany in late 1998, you could still very much see and feel the remnants of the Soviet Union. From the architecture to the city infrastructure, you could picture what life might have looked like. The people were very welcoming, but aesthetically you were transported in time.

East Germany and West Germany had only officially been reunified since 1990. East Germany was part of the former communist Soviet Bloc. There is so much history we can unpack here, but for the relevance in this story we just need to look at how communism was discussed in the U.S. as the root of all evil.

During the Cold War, the stories we heard in the West were about families being separated, or people being shot as they tried to escape over or under the Berlin Wall. Along with mainstream media, there were countless movies depicting the Soviets as the bad guys and the Americans as the good guys. (I may be speaking to a specific type of 1980s movie-goer, but think *Red Dawn*, *War Games*, *Rocky IV*, etc.) These are just a few that speak to the environment I grew up in where the term "commie-bastards" was frequently used. I was raised to believe that the opposite of freedom and democracy was communism. And communism was so horrible that even the people living under its rule were dying trying to escape.

When the Berlin Wall started to come down in 1989, I remember my dad calling me over to the news and telling me how important this moment was in history. That memory will always be in my head, and he was right, the significance was world changing. The fall of communism was a moment, in my mind, when good triumphed over evil, and humanity was headed down the right path.

In November of 1998, we were visiting a village called Prenzlau which is 100km north of Berlin, and 40km west of the Polish border. A panel of German speakers were going to speak about German Reunification. I didn't know a lot of history, but to hear from people who lived through the fall of the Iron Curtain, uniting families and a nation, what a fun and insightful talk this was going to be. I wasn't wrong about the insightful part.

It started out quite friendly with the panel discussing what life was like when they were growing up. It wasn't "us against them" talk, just their memories from childhood. The panel started to take a drastic turn when one of the West Germans said they still wanted to be called "West German" instead of "German," and one of the East Germans said they didn't want the reunification at all.

My mind started spinning. "Excuse me, what'd you just say?" This isn't computing. The dialogue was something along these lines:

East Germans: "We didn't want the Wall to come down."

West Germans: "Of course you did, we freed you!"

East: "We didn't want to be freed and the West just wanted the wall down to take advantage of the cheap labor to make more money for themselves."

West: "Maybe if you were not so lazy and worked harder, you'd be able to afford more."

East: "You are capitalist pigs."

West: "You are lazy and worthless."

This argument played out over the entirety of the panel discussion, but the conclusion was that German reunification was not this amazing success story where democracy triumphed over communism. It was a messy, political and economical shit storm that had been manipulated in the media, on both sides, and was not AT ALL what I had been told.

When the talk was over, everyone got up and went their separate ways and here was a twenty-one-year-old PJ Brady, stunned and huddled up in a corner, shaking and crying because his mind and body could not handle the apparent break in reality between what he just experienced and everything he thought he knew. THIS was culture shock. It wasn't discomfort, it was a feeling of collapsed beliefs and a feeling of being failed by a world that I trusted. It felt like betrayal.

I had a couple of life-altering realizations that day.

Firstly, I learned something that I suppose I probably should have learned in high school. The opposite of communism isn't democracy, it is capitalism. Communism and capitalism are economic structures. The opposite of democracy is dictatorship, those are political structures. You can have democratic communism and autocratic capitalism. Maybe it was because of what my mind was ready (or not ready) to learn, or maybe the thought of democracy being better than communism had been reinforced so many times that I didn't even think to question it. The lesson was that I needed to question everything more often.

Secondly, I learned the lesson that we all live with bias. Rarely is bias presented as "bias." Bias is sneaky because it latches on to us at such a young age, and comes from so many sources. Most of the time we don't even have the power to stop bias because we have no idea it's there. Bias is like carbon monoxide of the mind. You can't see it or smell it until it destroys you. Understanding bias is understanding that we all have knowledge and experience that has come to us through various lenses.

We've been given "facts" that were really just opinions. We were given "knowledge" that was really just perspective. Being smart is our ability to look at something through another lens. It's taking the steps to actively seek new facts, new knowledge AND new opinions and perspectives.

The last realization I had was one of those sliding-door moments. Right after that session, I knew I needed to seek out new facts, knowledge, opinions, and perspectives. I wanted to go abroad to study international affairs and politics. I needed to be surrounded by people from different backgrounds and cultures, who had lived under different economic and political means, so I could learn from them. And that is what I did. For any extreme patriots, don't get so huffy. I love my country, and I also acknowledge that significant growth comes from stepping outside of our comfort zones to experience new things.

While my experience listening to this panel discussion was the most significant example of how I shaped what the "smart" value means to me, it is by no means the only one. I have countless lessons where I was under one assumption, and it happened to be wrong.

"Smart" is the value I find people disagree on the most. For instance, it's easy for two people to come to severe disagreements if one is very logical and the other is very contextual. For the logical, many issues are black and white. They understand what the "right" and "wrong" decisions are very plainly. For the contextual person, they play in grey areas much more often. This doesn't exist as much within the brave and kind values. In bravery, people look at overcoming challenges and they recognize there are many ways people do that. In kindness, the world accepts many different versions. Because "smart" is at the heart of how people critically think, and they are able to debate thought. Debating bravery or kindness is much more difficult.

Here are some of the values that describe how people critically think:

Accuracy	Creativity	Influence
Adaptability	Credibility	Ingenuity
Alertness	Cunning	Inquisitiveness
Artistic	Curiosity	Insightful
Awareness	Depth	Intellect
Certainty	Diligence	Intelligence
Clarity	Direction	Introspection
Clear-mindedness	Effectiveness	Introversion
Cleverness	Efficiency	Intuition
Competence	Expectancy	Inventiveness
Confidence	Expertise	Investing
Connection	Flexibility	Knowledge
Consciousness	Focus	Learning
Conservations	Growth	Mastery
Correctness	Healthy	Maturity
Craftiness	Imagination	Meaning

Mindfulness	Reason	Spontaneity
Nature	Reasonableness	Structure
Order	Reflection	Teaching
Organization	Resourcefulness	Truth
Perception	Sagacity	Vision
Persuasive	Saintliness	Wisdom
Practical	Scientific	Wittiness
Pragmatic	Self-control	
Rational	Shrewdness	
Realism	Speed	

Defining Smart In Parenting

A school principal in Singapore sent this letter to the parents before their exam:[6]

Dear Parents,

The exams of your children are to start soon. I know you are all really anxious for your child to do well.

But please do remember, amongst the students who will be sitting for the exams there is an artist, who doesn't need to understand math... There is an entrepreneur, who doesn't care about history or English literature... There is a musician, whose chemistry marks won't matter... There is an athlete, whose physical fitness is more important than physics... If your child does get top marks, that's great! But if he or she doesn't, please don't take away their self-confidence and dignity from them. Tell them it's OK,

---

6 Jackson, Abby, "The internet is freaking out over this note a principal sent to parents during exam week," Insider, November 22, 2017, https://www.businessinsider.com/principal-note-to-parents-testing-2017-11.

it's just an exam! They are cut out for much bigger things in life. Tell, no matter what they score, that you love them and will not judge them.

Please do this and when you do, watch your children conquer the world. One exam or low mark won't take away their dreams and talent. And please do not think that doctors and engineers are the only happy people in the world.

I love this representation of how people can take multiple definitions from the value of smart. In this example you can see that smart takes on multiple faces depending on the audience. The principal tries to reconcile these to relieve the pressure on students from their home.

Smart can mean:

- Good exam grades to academics
- Creativity and logic to the artist and musicians
- Problem-solving for the entrepreneur
- Intuition to the athlete

There are so many definitions for you as parents to take pride in, and when you take pride in something that your child has done, THEY take pride in what they have done. It reminds me of the saying that is often misattributed to Albert Einstein, "If you judge a fish on its ability to climb a tree, it will live its whole life thinking it is stupid." Finding a definition of smart that works for you and your family is going to be tough, especially because there are so many types of "smarts" that individuals take pride in.

From my girls first definition of, "think before you act," they are given a broad spectrum of where their smart value lies. The type of critical thought that I like to give my girls is more around problem-solving, creativity and intention. Let's unpack those three for a second.

Problem-solving is one of the unique skills that is hopefully a future proof skill. Yes, we can use technology in an infinite number of ways to come up with the variables required to make decisions, and yet at the same time, a person's ability to be creative, think under pressure, not make a big deal out of small issues, etc. are skills that we can start teaching our children. These are skills that breed confidence and success—however you define it.

I have a long list of events that I have attended and organized. Before my teams have ever hit the floor of those events, there are a couple of ground rules, and none more important than, "If stuff starts to go wrong, don't look for who is to blame, just look for the solutions." Lots of people say they are solution-oriented, but wait until the pressure is on and the shit start to hit the fan. I want a team of people around me who can outsmart that problem, come with solutions, and essentially tell me what we should do. If, as parents, we can start to include our children in solution-finding, this is a skill that grows. If, however, every time something goes wrong, we as parents start to point fingers at who or what may have caused the problem (a teacher, the school system, a coach, a teammate, our partner) then you can be sure that your kids will follow suit and hopefully have some other influences in their lives that will show them the right way to find solutions.

For my girls, they have problems daily, and I do my best to not necessarily give them answers, but to help them figure out the issues and come up with potential solutions. For now, there is a lot of hand-holding, but I have faith that it won't be for long. Soon I'll be the old guy showing up at their door giving them solutions, and they'll be like, "Dad, we got this, don't sweat it." Later they will be at my door giving me solutions.

6.3 DEFINING KIND

In defining kind, the essential questions we need to ask are, "How do we treat people and how do we treat ourselves?" Defining what kind means sounds easy right? Well, let's see. Funny enough, "kind" started out as the easiest value to define for children, but I have found that it's the most complex to adapt into adulthood.

The Merriam-Webster definition of kind is to be, "of a sympathetic or helpful nature." This definition doesn't quite fit for a fundamental value. Why? It doesn't fit because there are some kind people who are not very sympathetic or helpful. Maybe they are respectful, and that is how they treat people. To be respectful is kind, but it's not necessarily sympathetic or helpful. I have searched many definitions and none of them work for me.

Perhaps it's so hard to define because of the range of ways that we teach children to interact with others—be polite, help others, say nice words, share—AND we also need to teach them to have boundaries, how to say no, how to love themselves. The balancing act that we expect out of children is tough! I'll rephrase that. The balancing act that we expect out of all humans (especially the expectations we put on ourselves) is impossible! No wonder this is a struggle for parents.

Instead of using some universal definition of kind, I want you to think back to when you were a kid and think about the examples of kindness OR lack of kindness that you witnessed. Remember that these can come as lessons of who we wanted to become or who we knew that we didn't want to become.

My first thought goes to my mother. When I was younger, my mom was a stay-at-home mom, but we didn't stay home often. She was the leader of my sister's Girl Scout troop, which I then usually attended because my Dad was traveling. There I saw her impact young ladies with the activities they would do, and the volunteerism. She was the youth leader at our church where I saw her dive deeper into faith to overcome some very difficult times. She was part of a group called Chorus of Hands who would go and perform songs for deaf audiences, many times children. My mom was a giver of her time, attention, and love to others and I couldn't be more proud of her.

I also saw kindness from my father who sincerely did care for others. I saw it from my sister who I remember stood up for me when there were some bullies on a playground. I saw it from my step-dad who isn't much of a talker, but showed up to every single soccer game to root me on. I have seen it from countless host families, close friends and complete strangers. There is no lack of kindness when you look around.

And now the examples of what you saw that you didn't like. Kids picking on other kids or adults picking on kids. The adult who promised something and didn't show up. The lack of respect coming from a person of authority. Choose the ones that impacted you the most, because if you remember them, it means it shaped you, and you need to work those into your definition of kind.

It is a wonderful exercise to define what "kind" means to you and your children because as parents, we need that definition as much, if not more, than our children do.

Here are some values of kindness that you may identify with:

Abundance	Encouragement	
Acceptance	Entertainment	Patience
Accessibility	Enthusiasm	Peace
Acknowledgement	Ethical	Philanthropy
Affection	Fairness	Presence
Appreciation	Friendliness	Recognition
Approachability	Fun	Reliable
Attentiveness	Generosity	Respect
Belonging	Giving	Responsibility
Calmness	Gratitude	Selflessness
Charity	Guidance	Self-respect
Charm	Harmony	Sensitivity
Commitment	Heart	Sensuality
Community	Helpfulness	Sincerity
Compassion	Hospitality	Supportive
Connection	Humor	Sympathy
Consistency	Inspiration	Synergy
Coolness	Intimacy	Teaching
Cooperation	Involvement	Teamwork
Courtesy	Joy	Thankful
Credibility	Lively	Thoughtfulness
Devotion	Love	Trust
Directness	Loyalty	Volunteering
Discretion	Modesty	Warmth
Duty	Motivation	
Empathy	Openness	

This list isn't even exhaustive. There are so many values to describe what you and I may see as the same things. Well guess what, when it comes to other peoples' values, what you and I think doesn't matter. All that matters is what they think about them. And if we disagree, then we are completely free to change our own values.

Defining Kind in Parenting

I get a range of interesting answers when I ask parents how they want their kids to be kind. Many say they want their kids to be polite, some want their kids to show compassion, some will settle for their kids to stop yelling and hitting (I've been there too by the way). The most common answer is that, generally speaking, parents know what they think "kind" is for a child, but when you ask the question, "How do you define kindness for your family?" people haven't given it that much thought at all, and they definitely haven't written it down or even had a specific conversation about it.

I find this interesting because "kindness" is something that we all hope for as our kids are getting older, and yet it is the one value that we struggle with when we don't feel like our children are achieving that goal. I have spoken to many parents who struggle with the concept of kindness altogether. They don't like the word kind as much as they like respectful, polite, authentic.

Kind to me as a parent means that I want to know that my kids are helping others. I know I am succeeding in this when my girls want to give money to anyone living on the street, they are the ones who stop to help when other kids fall, they are the ones who have genuine concern if anyone in our family is having a bad day. They pay attention to helping others. Why? Because we defined that for them and we back it up with action. When our neighbors asked for eggs to make their dinner, we said yes. When we saw a cyclist on the side of the road who had fallen, we stopped the car to check on him. When one of their friends needed a place to throw a birthday party, we offered our home—AND we proactively ask people if they need help when they are struggling.

We define kindness, we create language around what that means to us and as parents we use that language. Now, getting my daughters to help others is easy, getting them to help each other is a struggle, and one that we are still working on. I'll let you know how that progresses!

The second part of kindness in parenting is helping our kids look at how they treat themselves. This concept is actually significantly more difficult than how they treat others. At some stages, children can be completely self-obsessed. It comes with possessions, so we teach them, "samen spelen, samen delen" (a Flemish rhyme that translates, "play together, share together" equal to our "sharing is caring"). At other stages, we hear negative self-talk like, "I'm stupid, I'm fat, I'm not good enough." For our kids, this started around eight years old. In many stages, and often daily, our kids go between deeply caring about members of the family and then disregarding everyone's feelings except their own.

And from what I have seen and read, this is all very normal behavior. If it's normal behavior, should we just leave it alone and let them be? My answer is yes and no. Yes we can acknowledge that kids are going to be both kind and unkind AND no because acknowledgement doesn't mean acceptance.

Whether it's how they are treating others or how they are treating themselves I can accept "normal" behavior, but my job as a father is to be able to reinforce the positive attributes and guide them through the negative ones. One simple thought that helps me do that is to understand that what gets noticed gets repeated. If I see that my kids are being kind to themselves, I notice it and I build it up. Sometimes they take the time to consider their own feelings or they tell me that they need to take some time alone to cool down when they are in the middle of an argument. That one is harder for me to let them do if I am also heated. I notice it, and that behavior gets repeated.

Then there are times I notice my kids treating themselves unkindly. If what gets noticed gets repeated then won't bad self-talk get repeated if I call attention to it? The answer is yes it will IF that is the only thing you notice. If we only pay attention to our kids in their most unkind moments, their craving for attention will drive them to be unkind more often. If however we give them positive attention for their kind moments and can identify and meet their needs in unkind moments, they are better able to discern the type of attention they require. This is a skill that many adults could use as well.

There is also a balance to be had which can be confusing to kids. Where do we draw the line at helping others vs. helping ourselves? As a matter of fact, that isn't only confusing to kids. Many adults, including myself, struggle with this. If you are looking for a singular "right" answer to this, I don't have one and quite frankly if anyone else is selling you the absolute truth to this question, please don't buy it. We all have our own answers, and most of us will fail many times before we find that balance. For me it came by defining what "kind" meant to me personally.

Take Care of Others

1. Kindness is Badass.
2. Smiles and Laughter are Contagious. Share yours as often as you can.

3. Appreciate others. Their time and care for you is precious, treat it as such.

4. You can't take care of others if you aren't taking care of yourself once in a while.

5. Be humble. We are all warmed by fires we didn't light, we drink from wells we didn't dig. No one is self-made.

Yes it is only five points, but believe it or not I spent a lot of time thinking about these and have gone through multiple versions over the years. I know when I am at my best, I am living in this space. I can use these to find my balance between taking care of others and taking care of myself, and because of that clarity, I can use these in parenting and help my daughters to find their values as well.

What You Value vs What Are Your Values

As a values-based leadership coach, I will challenge every time someone tells me that their value is "family." Naturally, I will never question their love, devotion, or loyalty to their family. It's just that family is more of an intense extension of your values. Typically, someone's courage, critical thought and kindness are not limited to their relatives. People put family down as one of their values because that is where they prioritize their time and energy. They understandably value their family above others, and they place such a high importance there that it can feel like a value. But values aren't objects. "What do you value?" and, "What are your values?" are two separate questions. People value many things: family, friends, homes, money, jobs, etc. If you can touch it, it's something you value, not one of your values.

The value could be dedication, love, loyalty, togetherness—there are many ways we show our values towards those that we care about. If dedication is the value, and they apply that to their family with great sincerity, usually I find those people are also very dedicated to close friends, and many to their teammates, work colleagues, etc. They extend their dedication to other areas of their lives. So their own personal definition of that value and where they extend it, is more appropriate than saying that one of their values is "family." Family can, and should in this instance, be included in their own personal definition of the value but rarely as a value on its own. This just goes to show how important it is to define your values for yourself.

CHAPTER 6 TAKE HOME

- Go back and highlight five words you would use to define brave.
- Highlight five words you would use to define smart.
- Highlight five words you would use to define kind.
- Find the words in each list that would describe your children. Ask yourself, "What is their superpower?"
- Which of your kids' values are different from yours?

LET'S GET GEEKY

Firstly, allow me to qualify the word "geeky" for a second. Geeky is awesome. Geeky to me is when someone gets so far into the details of anything that they stand out from the rest. Sure, geeky can be math and science, numbers and context—AND geeky can also be Dungeons & Dragons. It can be the baseball buff who sits in the stands detailing the pitch count. It can be the dinosaur enthusiast, the stamp collector, or the person who can recite all 154 Shakespearean Sonnets. Every single one of those people would have been made fun of in high school for something they love, AND these are people who make the world a better place to live in. We need more geeks in our lives!

In my area of expertise, I like to geek out about leadership and values. How can values be geeky? Well just you wait and see!

Allow me to introduce you to m'peeps! And by "my peeps," I mean most of them have no idea who I am. I have only met a quarter of them. What I do mean is that I rely on their perspective, knowledge, for calling out BS and for setting things straight. Note, I don't always think they are right. I can disagree with them, but IF I go against something they say, it is because they have given me a perspective to work off of and it comes from a place of immense respect.

I refer to them throughout this book, so it is better that we get to know them now.

- Brené Brown - Researcher/Storyteller on shame, vulnerability, and leadership
- Dale Carnegie - Author of *How to Win Friends and Influence People*
- Stephen Covey - Author of *The 7 Habits of Highly Effective People*
- James MacGregor Burns - Author of *Leadership*, and founder of leadership studies
- Bernard Bass - Co-author of *Transformational Leadership*
- Richard Mulholland - Author of *Here Be Dragons* and all around badass dude
- Warren Rustand - Author of *The Leader Within Us*
- Muniba Mazari - The Iron Lady of Pakistan, motivational speaker, artist, advocate
- Sheryl Sandberg - Co-author of *Lean In: Women, Work, and the Will to Lead*
- Theodor Geisel, better known as Dr. Seuss - Say what you want, dude was enlightened

Part of my "kind" value definition from the last chapter was inspired by one man on this list, Warren Rustand. He frequently says, "We are all warmed by fires we did not light, we all drink from wells that we did not dig." These are the people who contributed to the fires that warm me and the wells from which I drink. I have pulled courage and perspective from all of these individuals whether they know it or not. In this chapter we are going to focus on James MacGregor Burns, Bernard Bass and Stephen Covey.

I suppose the bigger question is why does leadership matter to parents? Parenting is EXTREME leadership.

If we understand certain types of leadership are power-based AND yield the least results, then how do we recognize, respond and recover in those situations? How can we apply these examples in parenting?

If we know other non-power-based styles of leadership are about motivating a team, helping people find their identity, following a larger vision and being a role model within that vision then we can find ways to lead and parent with intention.

The long-term goal of leadership is to turn followers into leaders! Unless you want your child following you around for the rest of their lives, I am all for helping my young ones lead! This section is about how leaders lead with greater purpose. That sounds a lot more like the parenting I want to do than simply laying down the rules and trying to get my kids to follow them.

This is relevant because we can take all of these leadership components and treat them as components of parenthood. When we take a values-based approach to leadership and parenting, what happens is that we are able to intrinsically motivate our children, help them find their own identity, give them a larger vision to aspire to, and then hold ourselves accountable for walking the walk.

All of these authors, speakers, and thought leaders have taken stances on leadership that move the needle. These m'peeps!

TRANSFORMATIONAL VS. TRANSACTIONAL

Have you ever heard of transformational leadership? If your answer is, "Hmmm, rings a bell," or "nope," then you'll be in the majority. Technically speaking it's exactly what it says it is, leadership that transforms others. Now that we have that covered, we can skip to the next chapter, right? Wrong. Geeks don't move on, they dive deeper!

Transformational Leadership is a theory that was introduced by leadership pioneer, and Pulitzer-Prize winner James MacGregor Burns in 1978. Bernard Bass then extended that research in 1985 to understand the psychological underpinnings of leadership theory; which is still widely used in organizational psychology. If you are starting to fade out, stay with me for a little bit, I promise it will be worth it.

The end goal of transformational leadership is to create positive and meaningful change. It transforms followers into leaders. Transactional leadership is a managerial approach where outcomes are determined by behavior.

Here is the quick summary. Essentially there are eight components of leadership, four that are transformational and four that are transactional. (For our scholars out there, I know I have shortened the names and the descriptions. I want to make them easier to read and remember.)

Transformational

- Inspirational
- Intellectual
- Individualized
- Influential

Transactional

- Reward-Based
- Active Exception
- Passive Exception
- Laissez Faire or Hands-Off

Transformational Leaders

Inspirational: See the long-term vision and motivate others to follow.

Intellectual: Look at things from various angles, have good perspective and/or creativity.

Individualized: Understand that everyone is unique, and they need to be taught and interacted with as such.

Influential: Are the ones that walk the walk, consistently do the "ethical or moral" thing.

Transactional Leaders

Reward-Based: Lay out the rules, and actively reward positive behavior.

Active Exception: Lay out the rules, and actively punish negative behavior.

Passive Exception: Don't lay out the rules, but actively punish negative behavior.

Hands-Off: Take the approach that people need to learn on their own.

Now that we have given the description of these components, we really get to geek out! Bass wanted to see not only which leadership styles people responded to best, but also to see which ones were more effective than the others in getting results. Bass' research showed the difference between whether a leader is "liked" OR "is getting the job done."

You can see how incredibly relevant this research is in finding effective leaders. There are some leaders that say, "I don't care if they like me, I care if the job is getting done." Similarly, you have parents who say, "I don't need them to like me, I need them to do what they are told." Most parents would not SAY those exact words; however, their actions show that they would rather have obedience and control with results over love and connection without results.

Let's see if any of those theories hold water in practice. Here is what the research shows:

We can start with active exception (lay out the rules, punish negative behavior). Leaders who primarily engage in active exception are not necessarily liked or disliked. They are quite neutral. Perhaps not coincidentally, leaders who engage in active exception are equally ineffective. They don't necessarily fail, but they also don't necessarily succeed. See this as the mediocre zone of leadership.

In specific order of leadership styles that most liked by followers:

Individualized

1. Inspirational

2. Reward

3. Intellectual

4. Influential

Here are the leaders who are disliked:

1. Hands-Off
2. Passive Exception

This says IF a leader wants to be liked, they engage in actions that treat people as individuals, are able to motivate others, reward positive behavior, add perspective, and walk the walk.

Leaders who are unliked do not see the need to engage or when they engage, they punish behavior that without laying out the expectations.

Honestly, this all makes sense, right? There is no real insight here... yet. Let's see what happens with the leaders who get results.

In specific order, these leadership styles get the job done:

1. Influential
2. Intellectual
3. Individualized
4. Inspirational
5. Reward

Here are the leaders who don't get the job done:

1. Hands-Off
2. Passive Exception

Now there are a couple of quick observations to be made before we bring in our values.

From the leaders who are liked AND the leaders who get the job done, all the same traits exist. If you engage in that behavior, people enjoy working with you AND are effective. For the leaders who are unliked, they also don't get the job done

This means that leaders who say, "I don't care if they like me," … you should care! For parents who prefer obedience and control with results over love and connection without results, it is proven that if you can create love and connection, you DO get results. It just might take longer to get the results you are looking for.

I hear some parents say, "Sure PJ, we want kids to like us, but they also don't know what is good for them. They'd like me more if I gave them a piece of candy instead of a piece of broccoli." And you're probably right, they would, but now let's bring in some BSK.

We need to understand if we are being transformational parents or transactional parents. Honestly, I can look back and see that I have been all of those at certain moments.

TRANSFORMATIONAL PARENTING

- Inspirational: We inspire our children by helping see the long-term vision of who they can become.

- Intellectual: We help them find new angles, perspectives, information.

- Individualized: We treat them all as they need to be treated, we cater our parenting approach.

- Influential: We "walk the walk" as parents, and show them a good example.

TRANSACTIONAL PARENTING

- Reward-Based: We tell them what is expected, they do it and are rewarded.

- Active Exception: We tell them what is expected, they don't do it and are punished.

- Passive Exception: We don't tell them what is expected, they are punished if they don't meet our expectation.

- Hands-Off: We don't tell them what is expected, and we don't engage to teach them new things.

I think that our biggest hurdle isn't to know that transformational parenting is more effective than transactional parenting; it is that many parents don't know how to engage in transformational ways. Many have only been exposed to the transactional side of parenting; this means that they rely on rewards and punishment to influence behavior. They set up a rewards system for kids doing things well because we know positive reinforcement works. Active exception is looking at the rules and knowing what the consequences are when those rules aren't followed. An easy example to show is concerning how parents dole out allowances for children.

Let's say a kid gets five dollars per week if they do their chores. Reward-based would say, there are five chores you need to get done this week. For every chore you do, you will get one dollar. Active Exception would say, you are entitled to five dollars, but for every chore you don't do, you get one dollar taken away. Active Exception deals with punishment if someone doesn't do what they are supposed to. Reward-Based is telling them what is expected, and then rewarding them for doing that. Please don't negate this scenario because you believe that kids should simply help out around the house because they are part of the family, this is just an example between the difference of reward and exception. If you want kids to help out because they are part of the family, then keep reading because that comes with transformational parenting.

The bigger problems I have been guilty of as a parent are when I engage in passive exception. I see my daughters doing something that I consider wrong and I ASSUME that they know it is wrong also, which then leads to a negative reaction and possible punishment with zero preparation or communication from my side.

A common topic of conversation is how parents engage with their children. Some feel it is their duty as parents to make sure their kids are always entertained. Do not confuse "hands-off" parenting with letting your children be bored. Boredom actually has a great effect on creativity and problem solving. Hands-off means you just leave your kids to learn how to live life on their own. I fully agree that sometimes kids need to find the answers on their own; however, hands-off means not paying attention at all, assuming it is going to work out, and not really caring if it does. If you are reading this part thinking, "Oh no, I am a hands-off parent," you aren't. Want to know why? Because you are still reading this book! Hands-off parenting is absenteeism with a lack of desire and/or ability to try. Unless you are locked up and forced to read this book, that's not you.

Transformational parenting is being inspirational, motivating your children through overcoming challenges. For me, this is the brave value. I go back to the quote I was given, "Act as though when your children think of the word integrity, they picture you." FYI, I fail at that A LOT, but it's just as important for them to see me working towards integrity and failing than not thinking about it at all.

Transformational parenting is being intellectual with your children. For me, this is the smart value. How are we gaining perspective, how are we critically thinking? How do we work with our children to problem-solve, gain information, and create a mindset?

Transformational parenting is treating our kids as individuals. This is our kind value. Our children are unique and need to be treated as such. They will learn at a different pace, have different skills, passions, ways to deal with conflict, etc. If you think one-style of parenting is always going to work for all kids, then I don't know if you have interacted with enough kids.

Transformational parenting is being influential. It's making ethical and moral choices and doing your best to live up to what you tell others to do. It is the moral of the "What the Bubbles" story. It isn't just leading by example; it's leading by a great example. As far as BSK is concerned, this doesn't fall into one singular value, it falls into all of them.

For the sake of research, it's easy to separate these types of leadership, but even in that capacity there are many leaders who use a multitude of these components to lead. Rarely, if ever, do you find someone who just relies on one. The same goes for parenting. Parents can be inspirational, intellectual, individualized, influential, and use rewards and punishments; AND that could all be before breakfast!

THE SPEED TO ACT

One of the benefits of viewing your values through brave, smart and kind is that these three words are easy to remember.

I am a big fan of Stephen Covey. His most notable book is *The Seven Habits of Highly Effective People*. I was talking to a friend the other day who owns a successful consulting company and Covey's name came up. He said that he loves the seven habits; and for a bit of fun I asked, "Yeah same here, remind me what they are," and he said, "Listen first and... begin with the end in mind... and... sharpen the saw... hmmm, I don't remember the others..." He got two-and-a-half right.

BINGO!

I am not taking anything away from Stephen Covey. His effect on the world has been tremendous and he has guided world leaders to make some incredibly difficult choices. I just don't go through all seven habits when making split-second parenting decisions.

As parents, we make decisions in real time. We take action. We live our lives according to our own code. If you are able to remember and live the seven habits, then sincerely I take my hat off to you. I do not remember things like that. If I ever read an article like, "The Top Ten Tips to Becoming a Better Parent," or "Fifteen Steps to Get Your Kids to Stop Yelling"—I don't remember fifteen things!!! I don't even remember why I walked into a certain room in the morning.

Brave, Smart and Kind give us short and digestible ways to make our decisions. They guide us in knowing the right questions to ask, and in making the right choices towards our destinations. For me, that is about taking care of people, acting with intention, and continuing to prepare and show up. I defined my values, I work to understand them better, and I act upon them in a positive way. I understand how I fail, and I am able to recognize that, respond to it, and recover from it.

Quick reminder for those who are still trying to come up with all seven of Covey's habits but didn't want to pause and look them up online:

- Be Proactive
- Begin with the End in Mind

- Put First Things First
- Think Win-Win
- Seek First to Understand
- Synergize
- Sharpen the Saw

For those who want to see Covey's habits through another lens:

Brave: Be Proactive

Smart: Begin with the End in Mind, Put First Things First, Sharpen the Saw

Kind: Think Win-Win, Seek First to Understand, Synergize

You might think, "PJ why does it matter, you just reordered them under new headings." And you are right, that is exactly what I did. And by reordering them, they sit differently in our minds. This is what brain doctors call "clumping" and it is a way for you to remember things easier. That is why it is easier to remember the numbers twenty-four, thirty-two and ninety-one instead of remembering two, four, three, two, nine and one. If you are able to put information into groups it becomes easier to remember. That little nugget comes from neuroscientist Dean Burnett in his book, *The Idiot Brain*.

What Covey is actually saying is to be brave, be proactive and get ahead of your challenge. To be smart, start at the beginning but keep the end in mind, and don't stop learning. To be kind to yourself and others, create win-win situations, listen before you speak, and work well with others. Is it rocket science? Nope. Could his seven habits possibly be the most influential leadership advice of all time? There is a solid argument to say yes! Why is it so powerful? Because he put tremendous effort into defining and living those values. Those who follow his habits sincerely do become incredible leaders.

The next question you might be asking is, "If Covey figured it all out, why is this BSK book necessary?" Well, truthfully, if you find Covey's definitions work for you, then by all means use them. I use them often AND I have another angle. I think the success of Covey's habits are that they cover each of the fundamental values of brave, smart and kind, and that he dedicated his life to teaching them to others. Do you think if habit number seven was, "Face each fear as it is presented," then he wouldn't have appealed to the masses? Covey's magic was in making it applicable, and there are many other applicable values in leadership and in parenting. Covey knew this, he even added an eighth habit fifteen years after his original seven were published, "Find your voice and inspire others to find theirs," which could fall into the brave and kind buckets.

I have seen leaders and parents who are highly successful who do not live by Covey's habits, they live by their own. The Brave Smart Kind Framework is built on you finding out what you stand for and how to act from those values.

CHAPTER 7 TAKE HOME

- How do you walk the walk? Do you lead and parent by great example?
- How do you add to your child intellectually? Is it with perspective, sharing knowledge, ideas, etc?
- How do you treat your children differently based on who they are as individuals?
- How do you inspire your children? Do try to get them to see beyond themselves?
- What behaviors do you reward with your time, attention, words?
- What behaviors do you punish, and what punishments are used?
- Do you have any unsaid expectations of your children?
- Are there times when you run away?

SECTION THREE

FRAMEWORK

CHAPTER 8

IT'S A JOURNEY

When I started studying leadership, I would always hear people say, "You either have values or you don't," "You either lead with your values or you don't," and, "Live a values-driven life," and, "Good leaders, lead with values," which then implies that bad leaders don't lead with values. People think there is something special about people who have values, people who live their values. I am afraid I am going to burst a few bubbles here...

Values aren't unique to people who are successful. They aren't unique to incredible leaders who have shaped the world. They aren't reserved for the impactful teacher, the supermom, or the Nobel Peace Prize winner. It isn't that you have values or don't have values, it's either that you know what your values are so you get to live them with intention, or you don't know what your values are and you live them by accident. The goal is to get from accidental living to purposeful living.

Some might ask, "Why does that even matter? If I am living my values without knowing them, then at least I am living as my true self with authenticity." It is a valid question to ask and yet it actually matters a lot. Live by accident or live with purpose. As we'll discuss in this chapter, if you know your values you can use them to your benefit. If you don't know your values, you can become a prisoner of them. The difference is that people who know their destination are much more likely to actually get there.

If you discover what your values are, you will discover that you have been living your life according to those values all along. You will also find that the times when you have had issues with someone else, or the times when you have had issues with yourself were never due to a lack of values.

We deal in two worlds as it relates to our personal values causing issues. We either deal with the abundance of values and we deal with the clashing of values. I simply haven't yet seen a situation where values don't exist.

With an abundance of values, a singular value can be taken too far and work against you. With a clashing of values it simply means that you either have two of your values clashing against each other OR you have a value that is clashing with someone else's value. Once our values become actions and are out there for the world to see, they are no longer our values but are the reflection of us through the eyes of someone else who may or may not share our values. There is never an absence of values but a conflict of value in comparison to another party.

As you begin to think about your own values and those you want to share with your kids, it's only natural that from time to time, you will find yourself in some discomfort. Defining your values and using them as your guiding force can become complicated as you interact with the world and with the people in it. Not only that, but defining your own values often requires you to unlearn beliefs that were imprinted in childhood and to undo some bad habits or harmful thinking. It's no easy task!

In this section, I want to highlight some of the issues that are inherent in values construction, so that you may be more aware of the reasons behind those moments of discomfort. And, in those moments, remind yourself that living a life on purpose is hard. Knowing your destination makes all the difference because the truth is that your accidental "true self" gets your butt in trouble more often than your purposeful "true self" does.

HAVES OR HAVE NOTS

We live in a world right now that is SO divided. One reason is because we think that good people have values, and bad people don't. If we attack values, and make it into a "have" or "have not" situation, then it's very easy for us to draw a line in the sand and say, "I'm right."

If however we approach this as, "We all have values and sometimes they help us succeed, and sometimes they help us fail," then we get to operate in the middle ground. We get to a place where curiosity reigns over judgment. We get to a place where we listen before we talk, and—more importantly—before we act. If we can look at people as differently motivated, and we can see what they truly stand for, then maybe it isn't so different from what we stand for.

The easiest place to see this is how politics has been misconstrued to make everyone believe that they are on the side of good, and the other side is evil and/or ignorant. One beautiful example to dispel this idea comes from former U.S. Supreme Court Justices Ruth Bader Ginsburg and Antonin Scalia. Ginsburg was a badass, glass ceiling-busting liberal. Scalia was a family-loving, Italian-American conservative, constitutional-originalist. AND they were best friends because while they disagreed on the law, they saw courage, intelligence, and kindness within the other. They cared for AND influenced each other through their years of bonding.

I'd like to be very specific with this following point. Operating in the middle ground does not mean that we don't have non-negotiables. We SHOULD have non-negotiables in our world, but our non-negotiable can't be that we will be afraid of everything the other side says or does.

If your courage to be wrong shuts down, you become irresponsible with your life and the lives that you influence. Our non-negotiable can't be that we avoid the hard conversations.

If your critical thought shuts down, then you become susceptible to the influence of others. Our non-negotiable can't be intolerance of those who disagree with us.

If your respect for others is dependent on their respect for you, then we find ourselves in a never-ending loop of discord and eventual violence.

> *"Out beyond ideas of wrongdoing and rightdoing,*
> *there is a field. I'll meet you there.*
> *When the soul lies down in that grass,*
> *the world is too full to talk about.*
> *Ideas, language, even the phrase 'each other'*
> *doesn't make any sense."*
>
> **RUMI**

Now, I am not saying you need to walk into a KKK or Neo-Nazi meeting and say, "Hey, can't we just all get along?" But you can't go anywhere screaming, "Listen to me!" and not be willing to listen. You can't go into a situation saying, "See me!" and not be willing to acknowledge others. The very first place that this rule applies is in your homes with your children and your partner.

The answer to the question, "Are you living a values-driven life?" is simple and finite. The answer is yes you are—and so is EVERYONE else. We all are driven in life by our values. Sometimes our values drive us towards success and sometimes our values drive us right off a cliff… into a pool full of sharks… covered in chum.

8.1 NEGATIVE VALUES

We all understand that we use our values as filters for our decision-making processes. What we are trying to do here is make your values explicit so you can make the right choices for the right reasons. It's important to note that nobody else can "invent" your values. There aren't any exercises you can do that CREATE your personal values. Your values are already inside of you, we are simply pulling them into the light.

It's funny because whenever I do exercises for audiences to identify values, they come up with a barrage of answers. Honesty, determination, intention, loyalty, caring—the list is long. After some sharing of values, my "go to" question is, has anyone written down a negative word? Has anyone written down rude, stubborn, manipulative? Not surprisingly, no one writes down a negative value. But something doesn't fit here. If we agree that values drive decision-making, but everyone has positive values, then shouldn't it mean that we all make positive decisions? Can we agree that many times, we make poor decisions? So, how does that work?

Well, let me ask you this. Which direction does a tree fall? No this isn't a trick question, it's a scientific question and I want you to give it a little thought before reading… I'll wait right here for you to think…

The most common answer that I get to this question is "down," which isn't inaccurate however not what we are looking for. The next most common answer I get is that a tree falls whichever way it is cut. That's what we've been taught right? You make a v-shaped cut in a tree and it falls in that direction. The truth however is a lesson I learned from *The Lorax* by Dr. Seuss. Which way does a tree fall? A tree falls whichever way it leans. Let that sink in for a second.

A tree falls whichever way it leans. Sure, you can TRY to get it to fall in the direction you want it to, but you can't take the physics out of that equation. Well guess what, you fall in whichever direction you lean too. So do I. So does everyone else.

8.1.1 VALUES DRIVE YOU... RIGHT OFF A CLIFF

Values are the direction that we lean. Our values are our operating systems. When we make decisions, when we treat people a certain way, when we evaluate situations, when we think and act—all of these operations fall into our values system. These are the ways that we lean AND these are the ways that we fall.

After we do the values exercise, I ask who in the room has honesty as a value to raise their hands. It's a fairly popular value, especially in Germanic, low-context cultures that appreciate directness. Then I ask those people to keep their hands raised if they have ever been accused of being rude. Predictably nearly all the hands stay in the air. I call these our **negative values**. Negative values are when your core values get taken to an extreme.

- Honesty can easily become rude.

- Determination can lead to stubbornness.

- Intentional can lead to manipulation.

- Loyalty can lead to favoritism.
- Caring can lead to being weak.

This list is infinite. For every positive value, we can find a negative value that pops up when we are stressed, tired, hungry, overwhelmed, etc. When we have little or no time to think, our gut takes over. Our values dictate what we say and what we do. If honesty is your value, then when you are under stress you feel the need to be absolutely honest. Many times, this honesty comes without concern for other people's feelings and you come across as rude. Naturally, there are times when honesty can be taken too far, just like other values.

You might be able to relate with this fable of a job interview gone wrong:

Interviewer: Tell us about your weaknesses?

Interviewee: I have been told that I can be too honest.

Interviewer: I don't think that honesty is a weakness.

Interviewee: Yeah well, I don't give a f*ck what you think.

In parenting, it is very easy for our negative values to take over. There are a couple of reasons for this. Firstly, we love the crap out of our kids and any time we have intense emotions, we can easily get swept up in the moments. I am here to protect my girls, and sometimes I can imagine danger that doesn't really exist. That can result in me taking my values too far. Secondly, kids are emotional little humans too and can raise the stress level in your relationship in an instant. When we get stressed, we feel we need to stand on our values even stronger, so we do. (In the past, when you have felt your most defensive, see where your values took you.) Thirdly, we take this job as a parent seriously and sometimes that makes us live in fear of who our kids are, or who they are going to become. *What do they need from me? Am I good enough?* I am all for taking your job as a parent seriously, AND for breathing and relaxing. We need to be able to recognize the conditions under which our values can go too far.

Also realize that negative values can be subjective. People subconsciously think more about our own viewpoints than we do about others. We focus on life through our own lenses. This applies to our values because we rarely consider that people might not value the same things that we value. If you value brutal honesty and you meet someone who prioritizes compassion, odds are you are not going to be very popular with them. And if you are like the brutally honest people that I have met, odds are also that you aren't very bothered by that fact.

Let me be very clear, I am not advocating for you to shape your values to the needs of others. I am a firm believer that people need to be more authentic in the ways that we act and the ways that we communicate. What I am saying is if you are wondering why someone isn't responding to you in the way that you would like, maybe you should look at your values compared to their values. It may give you an explanation at the very least, and from that point you can adapt (or not adapt) your behavior as you see fit.

8.1.2 WHAT PUSHES OUR VALUES NEGATIVE?

If we look at values as more of an operating system rather than a golden beacon of light, then we are better able to recognize and accept our failures and shortcomings. If we give our values a place in our failure, then we can better learn how to recognize, respond and recover from them. Negative values give us a place to start. When we are able to identify one of our values in its extreme, creating our failure, we then get to ask a much more important question: *why?*

The truth is, there are plenty of reasons why, and it might take more than reading this book and years in therapy to get you there.

Often, when we go down the negative values route, it's because we feel a negative emotion as we make the decision. We take our values to the extreme when we are stressed, when we are angry, when we feel fear, insecurity, anxiety, or pain. I'd like to say it's different for everyone, but the root causes are pretty clear.

In typically less severe (yet extremely important and controllable cases), we can look at what affects our mental state—lack of sleep, hunger, bad weather, restlessness, being surrounded by negativity, etc. I know some people who get "hangry." Their emotions are tied to their stomachs. Others need nine hours of sleep. These can be easy ones to control. Anything that keeps us in an irritable state can lead to our negative values. What are some of the reasons that your values get pushed to the negative side of the spectrum?

One day Alex and Em were maneuvering to see who could annoy the other more, Josephine was on a warpath from the second that she woke up, Violaine was rushing to get out the door, and I had a late night writing. The pinnacle was Violaine driving away as Joey was screaming because her shoes were on the wrong feet and Emmeline had locked herself in the bathroom while Alex pounded the door to get in and ran out of patience. I picked Joey up, grabbed her bag and started walking towards school telling the eldest two that they had the choice of beating each other up and being grounded for a month or walking to school together in the next five minutes. I may have also thrown in a, "What the bubbles is going on today!" somewhere in there. Parenting fail.

I am not an expert on stress, anger or fear. I am not a life coach that monitors and corrects your sleep, your diet or who you surround yourself with. I am simply a father who falls on his ass sometimes and wants to know why and do better. And because I have been able to identify how I fail, I am usually able to recognize the root cause much quicker than I could before because I have put time in working on my values. Then I get to see if any of those causes are things that I can recover from. Most of the time, I can. Most of the time there are easy fixes. Then there are times I fall flat on my face. Then I look back again and ask why, how, what happened?

I know why I failed with the girls that day. The bigger reason is because "intention" is one of my three values, it is how I critically think. My intention is to be a kind and loving family and that morning we missed that intention by a LONG shot. The smaller reasons are because I was tired, my patience waned, and I didn't have the energy to take care of others in all the ways that I know I am capable of. There are some things that we deserve "do-overs" for, but for me, the quicker I am able to come to terms with why I got upset, the quicker I am able to talk to them about it. I got Joey outside, put her down, gave her a hug and asked what was wrong. Without the chaos around her, she better explained to me that she just wanted help with her shoes. I waited around the corner for Em and Alex to get there so I could apologize for leaving them, and they apologized for causing trouble with one another. We didn't have to go through the day disappointed or angry with anyone, we got it out there and got past it. An earlier version of myself wouldn't have been able to do that.

The current version of me recognizes that if I talk about being brave, then I need the courage to admit where I messed up. If I talk about being smart, I need to give a little more thought as to why something is happening. If I talk about being kind, then I need to be the first one to apologize as opposed to expecting a level of maturity from my kids that even many adults don't have. One of the benefits of intentionally raising my daughters to be brave, smart and kind is that I need to strive to be that myself. If I don't, it will never work.

The "why" matters here, because understanding the reasons for our own shortcomings directly relates to us understanding, and even more importantly, accepting our children's shortcomings.

Trauma

I know from my side that my past emotional baggage can be a trigger. There are certain words or phrases that can set me off and there are times I have full control. For instance, my Dad traveled weeks and months at a time for work. I can handle it if my girls tell me that I work too much because quite frankly speaking, my girls have absolutely zero idea of what constitutes "too much." I know what they are really saying is, "Dad, I want to spend time with you so I'll say anything I have to, even if it hurts, to get that attention." We work on better ways for my girls to express themselves.

Then there are times when I do not have full control like when my girls yell at Violaine saying, "You don't do anything for us, it is all about YOU!" (Enter childhood PJ who saw his mother nearly break while devoting everything she had to her kids. Then see me now, as a husband who wants his wife to prioritize herself more because she consistently puts our needs above her own.) I lose it every time. And that is just one trauma-based response.

We all have some sort of baggage we carry. Some are adults who were abused as children, ones who grew up without parental figures, ones that were surrounded by drugs or other chemical abuse. Some are people who have come from war and deal with the PTSD that follows. Some are fathers who have no idea how to be a father because their dad died when they were four. Some are mothers who saw her mother drink herself to bed every night. And the trauma doesn't even need to be that extreme. The sister who was bullied, the brother who was told he was fat, the siblings who saw the family next door playing in their pool in the late night summers while their own parents were arguing about bills. Some people go through these situations and come out unscathed while others build up scar tissue and only need one reminder for it all to come flooding back.

From my side, I don't know anyone who is unscathed. Everyone has something that sets them off, some have more than others. Some people have healthy techniques to work through their pain and it goes away without much effort. Others struggle on every front. Most of us fall somewhere in between.

It isn't my place (nor anyone's place) to judge what you are going through and where you have come from. I hate it when people say things like, "I've gone through terrible things before too, and you don't see ME <insert behavior>."

This reminds me of a powerful poem called "Lost Voices," written and performed by Scout Bostley and Darius Simpson in 2015 at a poetry slam. It's about what it means to be a black man and what it means to be a woman. "To tell me you know my pain is to stab yourself in the leg because you saw me get shot. We have two different wounds, and looking at yours does nothing to heal mine." Judgemental comparisons aren't helpful.

Our experiences are infinitely different, as are our psyches. I find that diving in to understand my past helps me live with more purpose in the present and work towards the future. If my trauma (however severe or mild) takes me to a place where I am a worse father, I feel an obligation to work through that for my children. And as I work through it, I still fail. I just fail less, or maybe fail with less severity.

I've come up with tactics to relax. Sometimes that is tagging in my wife—WWE-style—to take over. Sometimes it's taking some time to breathe. Sometimes it is preemptive, like making sure I get out on the soccer field at least once a week, and spending some extra time outside of the house. I call old friends, I write, I lose at chess online. Other times, I spend one-on-one time with each daughter because they need that individual attention from me, and I need that individual attention from them.

The point is, I do what I need to do so that I don't let my negative values define me. It doesn't mean they aren't there, and that I don't struggle with them. It simply means that once I recognized my negative values and identified them as my positive values taken to an extreme, I gained more control over them. I get to think about what triggers them, and because I put in that work, I am able to come up with actions to help me overcome.

NEGATIVE VALUES OF BRAVE, SMART AND KIND

As I have implemented BSK into the lives of my children, I have seen firsthand that even the best intentions can take a negative turn. Here are some of the foundational negative values that come with living an unbalanced value-driven life.

A negative value of "brave" is recklessness.

The way that I started to define bravery to my girls was to tell them "It is ok to be afraid," but it has evolved to discuss overcoming danger or difficulty as well. In times of stress, people who value bravery can become short-sighted and miss dangers that present themselves. They can be hasty in their decisions because of their perceived need to be decisive. You can put risk-takers into this same basket. Sometimes people miscalculate risk and they need another perspective because their "brave" value makes them leap before they look.

When you trend towards your courageous side, it is also easy to underestimate the effect you have on others. Think about the times when you need to be brave. Many times it's because you have a challenge in front of you, and regardless of who else is involved, you show up in "go mode" and get the problem solved. (Think "bull in a china shop" here.) Many leaders and parents are problem solvers, but taking bravery too far has also been known to alienate those you are trying to care for.

A negative value of "smart" is becoming an egotistical know-it-all.

I have tried to define smart as "making good choices" but that is too easy of a definition. As the girls get older a more necessary definition is "to be able to think critically." Looking at options and acting with intention is a more accurate and deserving definition of "smart" in their lives.

What happens when people become too smart—or at least too smart for their own good? Some of the smartest people in the world have become irritable know-it-alls, and I don't mean people who know everything, I mean people who THINK they know everything. You notice them because they don't let the little things slide. They are at the center of every debate and they very seldomly admit that they are wrong. Many times, they end the conversation with "agree to disagree."

Those of us who lean into our smart value often find ourselves stuck in analysis paralysis. People who take their brain value too far keep thinking, debating and analyzing over and over. We can get so worried about making the right choice that we end up making no choice at all. We keep telling ourselves we need more data, more information.

It often keeps us up at night. Many of us who overuse our smart value have trouble getting out of our heads, and our decision-making skills suffer.

One negative value of "kind" is to be weak or a pushover.

Like the other values, I started my daughters with a very limited definition of kindness. We said kindness was "to be nice to people." And for under-nine years old, this definition works pretty well. With my eldest, we have started to discuss empathy in kindness. How can we try to consider others and treat them with kindness? And like all of our other values, there is a negative.

People's inability to say "no" can become a problem when it leads to burn out, chronic stress or resentment. People who take kindness to an extreme can easily be taken advantage of. They can become people-pleasers and ignore their own needs and desires. These are also the people who avoid confrontational situations or unpleasant conversations.

Many times running away is a natural reaction for kind people when they aren't feeling valued. Outsiders can see this as an unkind, cowardly or selfish act when that isn't necessarily the case. "Kind" people, or those who think about the well-being of others, can feel like they are doing everyone a favor by not being around, especially when they are in a bad mood.

As with many things, knowing your negative values is only half of the battle. The next step is what to do about them.

8.2 PRIORITIZATION OF VALUES

I'd like to start this section with a disclaimer about prioritizing values. We are going to follow the 90% rule in this chapter. (I actually like to follow the 90% rule in most aspects of my life. Real or not, it gives me the perception of wiggle room for exceptional cases.) We are going to discuss what happens 90% of the time, not the "what if" scenarios about exceptions to the rule. We are going to use our values of being Brave, Smart and Kind and figure out which one means the most to us and why that self-awareness matters.

Why am I prioritizing values you ask? Because this is my book and I can do whatever I want, write your own book if you want to start a Spanish Inquisition! I'm kidding, it's a valid question. We are prioritizing our values for two reasons. The first is because typically, we have one value that is pulling in a negative direction more often than the others. Identifying which value pulls to the negative is a key step in solving that issue. The other reason is because the most difficult decisions that present themselves are often because of a conflict of value rather than an absence of values. This happens either when one value is contradicting itself OR when two values are working against each other. Knowing which value to prioritize allows us to work through those decisions with greater clarity and comfort, even when they are hard.

8.2.1 TWO VALUES ARE WORKING AGAINST EACH OTHER

If we go back to our *Alice in Wonderland* scenario, imagine you are at a fork in your road. You now know your values, except one value is taking you on one path and the other value is taking you on another. Many people call these types of decisions moral dilemmas and they are right to say these are some of the most difficult decisions to face. My hope is that once you have defined your values and prioritized them, the "correct" choice becomes much clearer.

Let's imagine two of your values are trust and kindness. You define trust as being honest with others and allowing them to be honest with you. You protect that honesty with the strength of your word. You define kindness as helping others achieve their goals. You give unwavering support to your friends in their pursuits. (Yes, I know there are many definitions to these words, let me roll with this hypothetical situation.)

You have a friend at work who is working their butt off for a big promotion. Your manager told you in confidence that the promotion is going to go to someone else, but that they are obliged to see all the internal candidates who applied. Your friend asks what you think about their chances, and to help them prepare for the interview. How do you proceed?

1. Keep your mouth shut, it would be unprofessional to say something.

2. Tell your friend the truth but ensure they don't say anything to the boss.

3. Don't tell your friend the whole truth and still help them prepare the best you can.

4. Avoid your friend at all costs until after they have interviewed.

As you can imagine, there is no "right" answer. Even in this example there may be variables like:

- How strong is your friendship?

- Do you have a vested interest in your friend getting this position?

- Do you have two weeks of vacation saved up to avoid them for that period of time?

The issue here is that you need to choose one value over the other. You don't get to be kind with your friend because it would break the trust with your manager. Or you don't get to maintain your trustworthiness with your manager because you want to be kind to your friend and help them in their pursuits.

Some people will look at this basic hypothetical and say, "Of course the answer is <insert letter>." This situation may or may not be an easy one to evaluate at face value, but this is just for the sake of explanation.

What about when this applies to parenting with purpose? What happens when your career gets in the way of your ability to be there for your children? Let's take a very common issue that parents have. You are a dedicated hard worker. Your career is advancing and you take pride in your accomplishments. Your hard work pays off in terms of a promotion with greater responsibilities, expectations, and time commitment. You also value the presence that you have with your children. This new job will definitely take time and attention away from your family. What do you do?

1. Take the job and give more financial security to your family.

2. Take the job but negotiate terms so you can still be present in your kids' lives.

3. Have a family discussion to see how you can work through the upcoming challenges.

4. Turn down the job outright, your presence with your kids is everything.

Still no right answer. Much like our example above, there are variables to all of these situations that might change your answer. Some people can easily state what they should've, could've, or would've done. For some of us, it isn't so easy.

8.2.2 ONE VALUE IS WORKING AGAINST ITSELF

Let's use my personal value of "taking care of others." Caring for people is a measure of kindness that many people use, but have you ever been caught in the middle of an argument between your children? Better yet, have you ever gotten caught in the middle of an argument between your child and your partner? What happens when there's an argument, but your child is the one who is right? Here are some of your choices.

1. You could declare yourself Switzerland and stay out of it all together. If this is your choice, remember that silence and neutrality have consequences just as standing up for what you believe is right does. You'd probably alienate your partner who is looking for support. That would also mean that your child sees you back down from the "right" choice due to fear and/ or a lack of caring. That might also mean that your child feels disregarded. Fear trumps integrity.

2. Back up your partner. After all, "one united voice" is a pretty common parenting tactic. The lesson for your child is that sticking up for your partner is more important than doing what is right. Loyalty trumps integrity—or loyalty to your partner trumps loyalty to your child.

3. Back up your child. You decided to either publicly or privately support your child, which means that even if you THINK you are doing the "right" thing, you have just discredited your partner, thrown them under the bus, given them no legs to stand on, etc. Integrity trumps partner loyalty—or loyalty to your child trumps loyalty to your partner.

4. Take both sides. Search for the middle ground. There is plenty of room for this option, except that if you clearly agree with

one side, you are still going against what you believe in. Harmony trumps integrity.

Yes, the choice is harder when we don't know what the situation is. What if your partner and child are arguing over chores? What if they are arguing over the person your child is dating? What if they are arguing because your partner just won't listen to your child? What if your child is about to run away? Yes, it is all nuanced. Yes, your answers are going to change.

The point is that if your value is to take care of others, the waters can get muddy pretty fast and your values can start to work against you.

The issues above are caused by your conflict of caring for others. You are going to have to make decisions that both live up to your value AND go against it. Sometimes those choices cause minimal stress and damage, but as your children grow and decisions become less black and white, the choices get harder.

What happens when you have been working your butt off to provide a better life for your kids, and then you wake up and realize that you don't have a relationship with them. Do you keep working hard to provide safety and security, or do you provide safety and security by nurturing a relationship that has been neglected?

What happens when you have a choice to make between telling someone you have known for years that they are abusing your friendship, or letting them continue to do it because you know how hard of a situation they are facing at home?

What happens when you have a marriage that is broken. Do you stick with it because anything less would go against your value of loyalty? Do you end the marriage because true loyalty is allowing your loved ones to find happiness?

What happens when you notice your friend's wife shows signs of being psychologically abused? When your elderly father is endangering others when he drives? When your partner strikes your child?

These can be times of immense stress because a singular value is working against itself. I have some discouraging news; living to be brave, smart and kind is not going to make the difficult situations go away. At the very least it is going to help you notice it, see where you stand, and help you to both cope with it and talk about it.

8.3 FILTER QUESTIONS

The two most important steps to take with your values are to determine what they are and how they are defined. After that, life should be pretty simple right? If you know what your values are, you know your negative values, you have prioritized them, and you reach Alice's fork in the road, you will obviously know what path to choose, correct? Yes, this is a set up question. Of course you won't! The sign is not going to say, "Brave choice to the right, smart choice to the left." You need to be able to visualize what is down each path and fit it to the definition of your values. Knowing what your values are does not give you answers unless you know HOW to use them.

This is where filter questions come into play. This notion of filter questions is not new. Many of us are adept at considering the consequences of our actions. We make pro and con lists even if they are just in our heads. Weighing options and making a decision is routine even if occasionally difficult. The only thing that I have done differently is to give that decision-making process parameters so that after you have made the decision, you have done it with the best intention possible and therefore have fewer regrets or second thoughts.

If your decisions as a parent are going to help you take your children down an intentional path, then these questions are here to help you do that.

Questions to ask to understand your "kind" value:

- Who does this decision affect?
- How are my decisions going to affect them?
- What are they going to feel?
- How are my decisions going to affect me?
- Am I treating myself with kindness?
- How do I want to be treated in these situations?
- Who do I need to prioritize?
- Will this cost me any of my energy or happiness?

Questions to ask to understand your "smart" value:

- Do I have the information I need?
- If not, how can I get what I need?
- Do I trust the information, and/or the people involved?
- What is the goal?
- How can I prepare myself?
- What are the other angles to consider?

Questions to understand your "brave" value:

- What is there to be afraid of?
- What are the risks?
- What are the possible consequences?
- What is the right thing to do?

- What is worth doing even if I might fail?
- What is worth doing knowing that I'll surely fail?

Now, just because you have answered these questions isn't to say you won't make poor choices. Remember, failure is not a consequence of making the wrong decisions. Failure is an inevitability of action. The more actions you take, the greater the number of failures you have.

8.4 CHECKS AND BALANCES

Well now we have screwed everything up haven't we? I've spent the majority of this book telling you how helpful it is to instill values in your family, how to be brave, smart and kind; and then I went and jacked it all up telling you that these values can actually ruin you. I get it! When I figured out that it isn't just our greatest moments of success that are determined by values, but that our biggest failures come from our values too, it was a real kick to the groin.

I am a big proponent of being solution-oriented and that identifying an issue is the biggest step in fixing it. So, now that we know how damaging our negative values can be, is there anything that we can do about it to fix it? The answer is absolutely!

How do you keep yourself in check when it comes to your negative values?

As an American who has spent a significant amount of time outside of America studying politics and history, I feel that I am qualified to love my country for all of its greatness and be critical of it for all of its shortcomings. One of the things I love about the U.S. is that it implements a system of checks and balances. For newcomers to American history and politics, this means each of the three branches of government, executive (President), legislative (Congress), and the judiciary (Supreme Court), all exist to perform their own functions; and at the same time, have the power and responsibility to keep the others in check. Note this is not a uniquely American system. It was created by the Romans and included into the U.S. Constitution by Montesquieu, a French political philosopher. As a matter of fact, there are many governments that have this separation of powers: Australia, France, India, Iran, Malaysia, and Pakistan, to name a few. The point is that no one branch of government can function without the others. It also means that no one branch can grow too powerful. This is the system that helps explain the BSK framework.

We have discussed negative values and how essentially, we are playing a winless game where our values will raise us up and trip us up at the same time. (Sounds a lot like a political system to me.) Each value has an essential function to govern lives and at the same time, can become dangerous if power is concentrated.

Our values are essential pieces to our lives that govern our beliefs, our thoughts, our words, our actions, our habits. AND can turn negative when they act alone. Recap:

Brave left unchecked leads to recklessness.

Smart left unchecked becomes egotistical.

Kind left unchecked gets you walked all over.

How do we even these negative values out? We apply a values-based system of checks and balances that I call the Reciprocity of Values.

CHAPTER 8 TAKE HOME

- What are your negative values?
- List the reasons that your values get pushed to the negative side of the spectrum. What sets you off?
- Ask yourself what you can do to stay in the positive; get more sleep, have more time to relax, get help with… whatever you need help with but have a hard time asking for.
- What are your non-negotiables outside of your house?
- What are your non-negotiables when it comes to your children?

CHAPTER 9

RECIPROCITY AND EXTENSION

My daughters know by now that every day after school I ask them if they were brave, smart or kind. Now they are getting to the point where they discuss these topics with me whether I ask or not. When Emmeline was six years old, she got in the car after school with a frown and didn't want to make eye contact, which for her (and similarly my Bernese Mountain Dog) means that they have done something they are ashamed of. I was just hoping for Emmeline that her look didn't mean she pooped on the lawn. I asked her what was wrong, and she looked up with her sad green eyes and pouty lips and told me that she wasn't very brave today. She said that the boys in her class dared her to climb up to the top of the slide and to jump off but that she was too afraid, so she didn't do it.

Emmeline felt ashamed because in her mind, she gave in to fear. It took me all of two seconds to lift her chin up, make eye contact, smile and sincerely tell her how proud I was of her. She was immediately confused. I told her that one of the bravest decisions we can make is to tell our friends no when we know what the right choice is. Standing up to people is hard enough when we don't know them but standing up to our friends is even more courageous. Then I helped her break down her decision.

Me: "Why didn't you jump off the slide?"

Em: "Because I was scared."

Me: "Scared of what?"

Em with a DUH look: "Because it would hurt."

Me with an AHA look back: "So... you took the time to think about it, and you made a smart choice to not jump off of the slide because you didn't need to do it, and you might get hurt?"

Em with a smile: "Yep."

Me: "I am proud of you because you made a smart choice."

I cannot emphasize enough that stopping to explain what these values mean in everyday situations is one of the most important gifts I can give my kids. Taking the time, discussing the important stuff is a habit I want to continue because at some point the important stuff will be more than just decisions about jumping off slides.

I helped Emmeline see that you can't just act out of bravery. Bravery without critical thought and without kindness is recklessness. We can move way beyond the slide example for this. There are many ways to define bravery that unilaterally end in recklessness. At the core of bravery is the understanding that fear is a normal part of life, and being afraid of something shouldn't allow your fear to dictate your actions. However, if this is the simple definition we work with, fear can be ignored quite efficiently—and dangerously.

Here are some examples of when I had to overcome fear:

1. Deciding to invest money into a startup business.

2. Going against someone I cared about who wanted to change me into someone I wasn't.

3. Choosing to step out of my comfort zone to do our own home renovations.

In principle, all of these situations required courage in the face of fear.

The startup was my own company, 42Walls, that was going to have an inaugural two-and-a-half day training event in Budapest, six months after launching. I spoke with many friends and family who said that, "they would LOVE to come to my first event," and that was good enough for me. I figured I'd only need thirty people to sign up to break even. So, with that extensive research (sarcasm) I rented a venue in Budapest, did some half-assed marketing and got exactly THREE people to register, three. I ended up losing several thousand Euros on my very first monetary investment into my company.

The relationship was a serious girlfriend who wanted me to dress to impress, wear fewer t-shirts and more collared shirts and sweaters. As someone in his early twenties, this was a moment to stand my ground and live up to every single signature in my high school yearbook that said, "don't ever change." P.S. "don't ever change" is probably the worst advice anyone has ever given anyone in the history of... ever. She insisted so much and I resisted so much it came to be a real source of friction. The difference is that from her side, she didn't care what I wore at all, she loved my style. The problem was that she came from a more "high-society" family and was getting all sorts of pressure at home to not date the "commoner," and by simply wearing a different shirt that wasn't promoting a Grateful Dead tour, I would have spared her a lot of grief from her family. I am exaggerating a little, I had SOME shirts that weren't from the Grateful Dead, I was also really into Phish.

The home renovations in question are when we decided to order 175 lbs (80 kg) cement blocks to build a retaining wall in our backyard. My wife was away for the weekend, and I was alone with the girls. The bricks were delivered on Friday, so I decided that me and my Superman-complex were going to do this alone. I was going to shimmy these huge-ass blocks into the hole I had dug for the foundation of the wall. It took me all of thirty seconds to push the first block halfway into the hole when it slid on the uneven dirt and tipped over—smashing my pinky between two blocks like a little piece of uncooked sausage. I'll leave out the gore, but it ended with a trip to the ER, crushed nerves, two broken bones, surgery, pins, a cast and a little finger that will never look or bend the same again.

Each of these situations took some amount of bravery. The problems, as you have already imagined, were that bravery alone wasn't enough.

1. The investment in 42Walls needed more thought, it needed more research, it needed to be smarter.

2. The relationship needed more compassion, it needed more understanding and empathy, it needed to be kinder.

3. The retaining wall needed patience, needed humility, needed… a professional wall builder… which we ended up getting after all.

Each of these situations needed the other values to keep my "bravery" in check.

Why "Reciprocity"

When I was looking for terms to name the effect that keeps our values in check, I kept thinking about the system of checks and balances. In essence, that is what these values do. They don't allow any of the other values to get too strong to the point of failure (when used properly). But this idea is more than simply a practice of limiting each value; that doesn't give the concept enough credit. The idea here is that each value is able to enhance the others. Yes, it does keep them from becoming negative values, but more so it creates more depth of understanding and application.

Brave becomes purposeful and compassionate.

Smart becomes courageous and thoughtful.

Kind becomes confident and meaningful.

Brave, Smart and Kind all exist with their own merit, but together they create a trifecta of lasting strength and beauty. Reciprocity technically means, "the practice of exchanging things with others for mutual benefit." I can't find a better term for what these values mean for each other. One without the other two fails; one depending on the other two succeeds. If you need a mental reinforcement of this idea, it is why the BSK logo was designed in a triangle. Each one leaning on the others to make itself stronger.

When working on personal or corporate values, I encourage my customers to see how their values can be taken to the extreme, when they become negative values. Then we evaluate the reciprocity of the other values to see if they can work together; not only holding each other in check, but making each one stronger.

From a parenting perspective, this is an opportunity we have to grow with our children.

- Brave taken too far: talk about how recklessness can be overcome by thinking about who we affect, and what perspectives we should consider.

- Smart taken too far: talk about how overthinking can be overcome by the courage to take a chance, and the support if they fail.

- Kind taken too far: talk about how always saying "yes" can be overcome by the courage to say "no" to people, and the thought and kindness in prioritizing yourself sometimes.

In doing so, we can discuss what actions we take with our kids and what actions they take with others. We can ask them if they have thought about all three values in making their choices. When something is going wrong, we can ask them which of the three there is an issue with, and because we have defined our values, we have better language to use with them. Thinking on our feet all the time is exhausting. This gives us some go-to phrases that work. If there is nothing else that BSK gives us, it is context to have these conversations. It is important to have the definitions that everyone agrees on to frame a discussion.

9.1 NEGATIVE VALUES AND RECIPROCITY IN ACTION

Over a twenty-four-hour span in 2021, three of my top clients called me up or sent me a message saying they had to cancel their events. All the business suddenly dried up. I called my accountant in a panic saying, "Don't do any work for me. I can't pay you. Do nothing!" I called anyone that I owed money to and explained what was happening.

The morning after, I woke up feeling exhausted, frustrated and scared. Normally in the mornings, I like to turn on music and let my girls wake up to some cool jams. I smile and I tell them I love them. I do all these things to set the right tone for the day. Once in a while, one of them will give me lip or won't get out of bed and typically I'm cool. I give them a hug. I give them some love. I give them some attention, whatever they need.

At seven in the morning, I walked into the hallway between the girls' rooms. I put on a playlist of either their favorite songs, a "girl power" set, some Bob Marley, etc. to wake them up in a good mood. I make sure they are tightly covered, rub their backs and give them a kiss on their heads and say good morning. Then I open up the curtains to let the light shine in. Alex's room is closest to ours so I wake her first. She is our sleepyhead, it takes her a good amount of time to come out of her zombie phase (I was the same way as a kid). Emmeline usually greets me back with an, "I love you," or, "good morning." Joey sleeps on the bottom bunk, so I get to lay down next to her and cuddle up for a bit as she rolls out of bed. We usually play some sort of game and she wakes up giggling. Well... on this morning, NONE of that happened.

I walked into Alex's room and she just says, "UGGGGHHHHH Dad, you are so annoying, go away." And on any normal day, I could have put that statement aside and talked to her in a normal tone, like "adults" are supposed to do. Not this day! I engaged. Engaging in an argument in the minutes after waking up is never a good idea. I let her know that she had just lost her screen time for the weekend and of course she started flipping out. I walked over to Joey and Emmeline's room. I rubbed Em's back and then went to bend down to wake up Joey. As I bent down Emmeline's voice came from the top bunk and said, "HEY! Why didn't you give ME a kiss!?!?" I peeked back over the top bunk where I saw my genetically-passed-down furrowed brow and angry green eyes staring at me. I kissed her head, said sorry and let her know there are nicer ways to ask for a kiss. With a loud, "hmmpppffff," she slammed her head back into her pillow.

By the time I bent back down to wake up Joey, I saw that she was already peering up over the covers at me. I smiled and said, "Good morning sweetheart," when she threw the covers off and said, "Why did you kiss Emmeline before me!?!" As I went to give her an explanation, she pulled the cover back over herself, turned to the side. Defeated and deflated, I took a deep breath and went to walk out of the room. Angry is no way to start a morning, and I had already engaged in an argument that was still waiting for me to resolve one door down. As I turned to walk away, I heard, "Stommerik," from under sheets of the bottom bunk. "Stommerik" is the Dutch word for dummy, but not as cute.

There are times when you have your "adult hat" firmly on your head. You know that arguing with children is a losing battle both in the short and long term. Then there were days like this one...

I didn't talk at first, I simply proceeded to take the covers off of each of their beds as they were crying at me that they were cold. Then I grabbed their stuffed animals and opened up the attic door and tossed them in. I let them know that this "crap" was not going to fly and that if they wanted to have a terrible day making others feel bad, then that is exactly what they'd get. I got Joey dressed as she was still flailing away and let the other two know that I would be taking Joey to school at eight-thirty and that I'd be leaving without them if they weren't ready. I fireman-carried Joey downstairs where my wife was looking at me as though to say, "WTF just happened?" I plopped her down in her seat and then went back upstairs to take a deep breath.

The morning didn't offer anything else of substance. The girls felt terrible, my wife unsuccessfully tried to mediate before leaving for work, I was riddled with guilt and shame, and I ended up leaving early with Joey to get to school because I just didn't want to be around anyone else.

As the eldest two arrived at school, they both gave me hugs and apologized. I said that I was sorry too for how I reacted. When I got home, I slumped down in my chair. I had been awake for less than two hours and felt like a complete loser and an inept father. My one big task for that morning was to write a chapter on "Raising Kids to be Brave, Smart and Kind"—well... bubbles. That wasn't going to happen. How can I write about a topic I'm currently failing at? Side note, writing about what we are failing at is actually an incredible exercise to help bring us clarity.

In this particular story, can you see which of my values was taken too far? If this is your first time doing this, you might look at my values and say, "None of them, kids are occasionally monsters and it is normal that you flip out from time to time, welcome to parenting buddy!" Hey, you aren't going to get an argument from me, AND I tell my girls all the time, "It is ok to feel whatever you are going to feel. That is natural. The only choice we have is how we react to those feelings. And you don't get to control other people's reactions, you only control yours." At the same time, if I don't look at the parts where I contributed to the fallout, then how am I going to learn anything?

Back to the original question, "What value was taken too far?" The answer is all of them.

In "taking care of others" I can give too much credence to the belief that my girls need me to wake up to a "good vibe" in the mornings. If I want to take care of them, I need to make sure they know I am there for them. The problem is that because this is my value, when they don't return that value, I feel it is broken, and when someone else breaks one of our values it can be difficult, sometimes impossible, to move forward.

With "intention," I know what my goal is for the morning and I take active steps to get there. I want to create a positive environment with smiles and laughter and my girls out the door on the right foot. And when my intention is met with grumpiness, then I try HARDER to make it happen. Ever get your finger stuck in one of those chinese finger traps? The more you pull the tighter it gets.

In "creating my luck," I cheat and put two parts to this. One is the preparation and being ready to meet various situations, and two is to continue to show up even when I am scared or unsure. When I take this to an extreme and continue to show up, it gives me a distinct disadvantage in my ability to walk away. I don't like to give up!

So how do I pull myself back? The answer is that I try to have a bit more balance. Think about the reciprocity my values offer. My solutions are always found in the same place as my problems, relating them back to my brave, smart and kind values.

How can I take care of my girls and not be so reliant on their happiness? I change my intention to be how I treat them, not how they treat me. I know they will mirror me. I take care of my stress level so I am mentally prepared to be a good father.

How can I change my intent so I am less dependent on the reaction of the girls? I keep taking the brave steps to show up, even when I mess up. I get support from my wife when I need it.

How can I prepare myself to show up and know that walking away is still a perfectly acceptable response? I keep my perspective from

"Father Forgets." They are just kids. I breathe and take care of my health, because I need to make sure my mask is on before I can help them with theirs.

It doesn't take me long to figure out how I failed, it can, however, take me longer to learn the lessons and then apply them next time. I feel that I have a distinct advantage BECAUSE I have put in the work to determine what my values are and to define them. Because I have done that in advance, when I have those mornings, I am able to recognize much faster than I have in the past, I can recover and I can respond.

9.2 EXTENSION OF VALUES

As we have previously noted, people live and die by their values. It isn't just people with strong convictions that succeed and people with weak convictions that fail. We all triumph and fail based on our belief systems and the thoughts, words and actions that come from those beliefs.

The distinction between people who succeed based on their values and those who fail based on their values is twofold. The first is to be able to stay balanced as our system of reciprocity shows us. If you can keep your values in check using your other values, you can do better to stay out of that negative zone.

The second is just as important to realize, and yet much more difficult to enact and/or correct when it goes wrong. This is because the second issue is relational. I call this the extension of our values. It is the idea that we all have values and yet we don't necessarily extend our values to everyone in the same way. Who do we extend our courage to? Who do we think about? Who are we kind to?

I have grappled with this concept for a while. For all the examples I find of people failing because of their values, it can also appear that they are going *against* their values and I wanted to know why. It's too easy to say someone doesn't have values, an idea I have struck down as many times as I have thought it.

The reason we say someone isn't living up to their values or that they are hypocritical in their words and actions is because we are viewing their decision-making process in terms of how it affects us, or a certain group, or the environment, or <insert any object here>. We make judgement on someone's decisions through our own lens with a distinct destination in mind.

Why is it that brave people can act without courage? Why do thoughtful people go against their own instincts? Why have we all seen (or been guilty of being) kind people who occasionally do unkind things?

I had a girlfriend in college who was one of the kindest people I had ever known. She constantly went out of her way to help others. She gave people the benefit of the doubt. She was passionate about global injustice and the environment. She was incredibly empathetic and sympathetic. And at the same time, whenever she felt like she was betrayed by a friend, her mother, or me; she flipped a switch and could actively do things that she knew would hurt them. Does that mean that she didn't have values? No, of course not. She was one of the most ethical people I knew. She did it because she was hurt and instead of directing her values outward, she directed her values inward. She began to self-protect, used her courage as a defense mechanism, and turned her thoughts and her kindness towards herself. This part is important to note—it wasn't because she lost her values or didn't act out of her values, she just decided not to extend them to the people who she thought wronged her.

When other people go against a value that we hold dear, it's very easy for us to redirect that value in a different direction. That can happen when someone hurts us, it can also happen when someone hurts someone or something that we care about. It's easy to stop extending that particular value outward, but instead turn inward. We focus on the hurt party (ourselves or who we feel connected to) and consider the offending party undeserving of our values.

Imagine that one of your kind values is empathy and you have a friend whose partner is mistreating them. Obviously, you aren't directly hurt by the offense, but someone you care about was. Rarely does someone with that empathy value treat a friend's abusive partner with any sort of kindness or understanding. Even more so, if your friend and their partner patch things up, that doesn't mean that you would let your distrust go and be able to treat that partner with genuine empathy. (This is understandably so as you weren't part of the original equation nor were you part of the healing process that they went through. And quite frankly, sometimes that is what a good friend is for, to look out for our friends when we don't feel they are looking out for themselves.)

But here is the thing, you are still living your value. You are extending it to your friend as opposed to extending that empathy to the partner that messed up.

I remember we had a surprise party for my mom's fiftieth birthday. Her friends came from all over to celebrate. My stepdad had put together a slideshow of my mom's life. Obviously, as she and my father were married for fifteen years and had two children together, he was a huge part of her life. What happened when his picture came up? All of my mom's friends booed. I was twenty-three at the time, so I could handle it, but I also thought it was terribly unfair and shot some deserved dirty looks around the room.

Extension of values is an individual choice. It seems to be personally and situationally specific. Sometimes, we are able to hold disappointment and empathy in the same hand simultaneously. For example, when my parents got divorced, my Aunt Judy (a close cousin of my mom's) was the only one who still spoke nicely of my father and treated him with respect. It had nothing to do with whether his actions deserved respect or not, but it had everything to do with what she thought that all people deserved. That made a pretty significant impression on me. Her kindness wasn't limited to just her friends or herself.

Some people have that rare ability to extend their values to everyone around them, regardless of circumstance. We see this ability amongst the greatest leaders in our history.

Nelson Mandela extended his values to everyone he met. He would host world leaders at his house for lunch and invite their drivers to dine with them because they were also guests in his home. He once invited another man to eat with him who he spotted at a restaurant. The man uncomfortably sat and dined with him. Afterwards when asked who that man was, he said it was a guard at his prison who once pissed on him when he told him he was thirsty.

Some of the most heralded leaders of all time like Mandela and Gandhi did not have a limitation on where their values applied. This also came at a price—alienating their families who did not share the opinion that values should be extended to all. That is a choice.

I am not telling you or anyone else that we should hold ourselves to Mandela's standard of kindness. I would not have been able to treat someone with such forgiveness in his case. I am simply using him as an example of what it looks like when your values are extended to everyone.

Extending Our Values Inwards

On the opposite side of the spectrum, we have people who only extend their values to themselves, and those who only extend their values towards their inner circles. This can happen for so many reasons, some as a result of how they were parented or educated. Some experience trauma early on in their lives. Most people who have been taught to operate in their own sole interest find the message is reinforced on a regular basis. They turn their values inwards without conscious thought and have built it into their daily decision-making process including into their parenting.

There is middle ground, however, between Mandela and self-centeredness.

What would you do if you saw your child being bullied? You are a kind person; would you treat the bully with kindness or would you direct your kindness only to your child? Most people would take care of their own. I have seen it and I have done it. I have also known some of the bullies, and I know that their parents were going through a rough divorce. I have known some of the bullies and seen their fathers punish them with an iron fist. I know some were hungry, I know some were sad or hurt or scared. I know all of them had been taught to bully from either their parents, siblings, grandparents, neighbors, or others. Is that an excuse? Absolutely not, but it *is* a reason, and perhaps a bit more empathy would help even when we don't accept their actions.

I had a summer job taking care of kids aged four to sixteen who had to be pulled from their homes due to abuse, drugs, mental issues, etc. and were placed in a children's shelter. Before working there, I had to go through training on how to restrain kids in case they lost control and hurt themselves or others. One four-year-old boy was unhappy with something I had asked him to do, and he looked me dead in the eye and said, "Fuck you, Mr. Patrick." With only four words he told me that he had learned to swear when he was unhappy AND that he was supposed to be polite by saying Mr. and Mrs. in front of adult's names. Do you think he deserved my kindness? Of course he did!

I think back to the quote on my wall, "Kids who need the most love ask for it in the most unloving ways." Should child bullies be any different just because we don't know them? What about adult bullies?

My friend Warren was in a not-so-great part of Los Angeles. He was walking to his car late at night after an event and could feel somebody behind him. Warren took out his money clip, turned around and saw a huge dude with a knife in his hand. Warren looked him in the eye with kindness and said, "Here. You might need this more than I do. I'd like to buy you breakfast."

The two of them went to an all-night breakfast place and Warren listened as the guy told him about his life and about his dreams. Warren is still in contact with him today.

The situation could have turned out differently if Warren had responded with anger, aggression or fear, but he chose to see the attacker as a human being and responded with kindness. Not only did he de-escalate a potentially dangerous situation, he greatly impacted a young man's life.

Abraham Lincoln, for all of his greatness and his shortcomings, had this brilliant bit to say about why we shouldn't criticize others, "They are just what we would be under similar circumstances." I am not saying that we should tolerate bullies at any age, AND maybe if we understood their circumstances, they might stop being bullies. If however, we refuse to extend our values to them, it will just reaffirm that they aren't worthy enough to receive them. Where do you think that leads?

When it comes to us as parents, there are two sides that we need to consider in raising our kids to be brave, smart and kind. Firstly, we need to examine the example that we show our kids outside of our home. How far do our values extend, where do they have limits? Secondly, we need to look at the interactions inside of our home. How do we extend our values to our children? How far do our partners extend theirs? And perhaps most importantly, how do we extend our values to ourselves?

9.2.1 EXTENDING BRAVERY

How our bravery extends beyond ourselves doesn't really matter unless we have previously defined what it means to be brave. For my girls, the very first definition I gave them was, "It is ok to be afraid but you still need to make the right choice." So what specifically does it mean to extend our brave value? Well, we look at where we show courage and where we give in to fear. How do I want my daughters to extend their courage outside of themselves? Who are they brave for?

I would say the majority of my girls' courage is shown within the walls of our home; between them and their sisters and with my wife and I. They stand up for themselves often—even when they are dead wrong. They also have plenty of courage in standing up for each other when one of them is being punished. Maybe the sympathy they feel is a result of memories of their own past punishments. All three of them—even Joey at age six—ask us to be more lenient with the others when they are getting in trouble. I put on a tough face, but I will occasionally give them a win on those occasions because it is important for them to feel like their courage is recognized and rewarded.

School also offers the girls a place to extend their bravery. Teachers have shared stories from school when the girls have stood up for others. At my children's school, the older kids do a pretty good job of taking the younger ones under their wings—protecting, correcting, advocating and consoling, when necessary.

My children and I often talk about who else we should stick up for. We talk about current events a lot. Things like the #MeToo Movement, Black Lives Matter and anything LGBTQ+ related. We talk about what it means to stand up for yourself in those moments and how we can stand up for others. One of Alex's best friends is half-Dutch, half-Congolese, which created a personal connection for a conversation about the Black Lives Matter movement. This gave us an added opportunity to talk about the role that courage played in this social uprising. We talked about having the courage to speak up when there is injustice. The courage to admit our own wrongdoings and those of the generations before us. The courage it takes to call out friends who make racist comments or jokes. What does courage mean to our LGBTQ+ friends and how do we extend our courage to that circle when they need it?

We talk about all of these things because it's important to teach our kids that courage needs to be extended past the events that affect our lives. Awareness means looking for the parts of life that make us uncomfortable, and doing something about it. Will that have consequences? Absolutely! But guess what? Silence has consequences too. If we act with the purpose of bravery, then the consequences tend to be worth it.

Knowing that kids will follow both our good and bad examples, we must also consider how they see us showing courage for people we don't know. Where and when do we choose to extend our values? I try to talk to my girls about this as often as I have fear, which is regularly. Most importantly, I talk about how I get courage from others, and how maybe I can inspire courage in others. I tell them how they make me a braver person and how I would defend them from anything.

I genuinely believe that those with the ability to overcome challenges have the responsibility to help those who are not able to. I can think back to times when I have neglected to help others out of my own fear, and those are moments I am ashamed of. I can chalk it up to being young, but when right and wrong don't have any shades of grey to them, and we still act in our own self-interest, those are moments when the extension of our values need to be questioned.

9.2.2 EXTENDING CRITICAL THOUGHT

Those who have the ability to extend their "smart" value into moments and circumstances that are bigger than themselves have such an incredible impact on the world. And yet, critical thought is completely irrelevant without action. We need to consider how we extend our critical thinking into the world and into our childrens' worlds. Critical thought without courageous or kind actions is a wasted gift.

From the moment parents scold, "think before you act," children witness a broad spectrum of how people value "smart." Some believe "smart" is being intelligent or wise. Pure high IQs can be applied to the rare few and wisdom in children is rare and often stems from some childhood trauma that made them grow up faster than their years. I don't focus on those two definitions. The type of critical thought I like to give my girls is more around problem-solving, creativity and intention. Let's unpack those three, in terms of how we either keep those to ourselves or extend them into the world.

"Smart" can be a difficult one for me to manage as a parent. There is a spectrum of extending your brain into the world versus keeping all of your thoughts to yourself. When it comes to problem solving, I think a good place to start is to look at what problems we personally face and what problems the rest of the world face. I want to be very careful not to mix this with our kind values and how we extend them. This has to do with how our brains work, and I think they work better in groups. Don't get me wrong, some of my best thinking has come from sitting alone in my thoughts, but how much better are those thoughts when I am able to build on them in a group of people?

Are you able to share your thoughts and create synergies with others? Imagine the possibilities to have an impact on the world if we share our thoughts with others. Contrary to that, how limited is our impact on the world if we only keep our thoughts to ourselves?

It's equally important to ask who we welcome into our thoughts and who we allow to influence them. Listening to others is such a critical tool to teach kids, not simply out of respect to others, but the perspective that it can bring to people. Much like my story about the German panel of speakers blowing my mind into culture shock and shaping the rest of my life, I would have never reached that conclusion if I was sitting there in my own world, like I had been doing for the previous twenty-one years.

Extending the reach of our "smart" values is to know the value of pushing our minds to the limits and coming back with new perspectives to consider. Our failures of critical thought come when we become too set in our ways to consider new information and new opinions. It also comes when we hold on to our thoughts, reluctant to share.

How do we navigate these waters with kids? I have a couple of strategies. Sometimes they work. Sometimes I simply hope my girls are storing the information somewhere so they can whip it out at exactly the right moment. Creating a safe space for learning is the first step. Kids have to have the space to share their ideas. We give them time at the table to clarify their thoughts in front of everyone. I try to ask them hypothetical questions to see where their mind is at. Also when their friends are over, we engage in some thought dialogue, like what they want to do when they grow up, or we play problem-solving games with them.

I am sure there will be a time when friends come over and the girls will want to have their private time and space with them, but that hasn't happened yet. So, we try to capture the thoughts of other people around us and give the girls the chance to share too. My hope for the future is that they are going to be able to share thoughts in a meeting or relationship, even if they are the dissenting voice. I don't want them to keep their thoughts to themselves because rarely has that done anyone any good.

Exposure to perspectives is key. If we want children to be able to extend their thoughtfulness past their own minds and outside of the family, then we need to be able to give them that practice.

Likewise, what do our kids hear us talk about? As in Eleanor Roosevelt's famous quote, "Great minds discuss ideas; average minds discuss events; small minds discuss people." What are the ideas we are discussing? Are we discussing things that only affect us? Do we take on ideas that are out of our realm of influence yet still matter? How do our kids hear us talk about certain circumstances and scenarios that are out of our control? How do they hear us talk about people? Let that question sit there for a second. What do our kids hear us say about others? Do we say positive things? Are we respectful? Are we uplifting? Or are we complaining, degrading, and shining a negative light on others and on ourselves?

Our minds absolutely must be able to extend outward to others and not only inward to ourselves. Inward thought speaks to our own egos.

Inward thought tells us we are right—about both positive thoughts and negative ideas. Outwardly, we are able to work with others on what needs to get done. Outward, we become more interested in the solution than who came up with the solution. Outwardly, we reward other's creativity and take pride in contributing our brains towards something bigger, and that only happens if we apply our knowledge. Brené Brown refers to this as the difference between being right versus getting it right. If we push out our brains, I am confident we will have a new generation of kids who approach problem-solving in a more collaborative way.

9.2.3 EXTENDING KINDNESS

> *"Tell your spouse, child or employee that he or she is stupid or dumb at a certain thing, has no gift for it, and is doing it all wrong and you have destroyed almost every incentive to try to improve. But use the opposite technique, be liberal with your encouragement, make the thing seem easy to do, let the other person know that you have faith in his ability to do it, that he has a undeveloped flair for it, and he will practice until the dawn comes in the window in order to excel."*
>
> **DALE CARNEGIE**
> *HOW TO WIN FRIENDS AND INFLUENCE PEOPLE*

I suppose out of all of the values, kindness, or how we treat others and how we treat ourselves, is one of the easier ones to technically define but comes with much more complexity because it is relational. We have two personas to whom we extend our values; others and ourselves. I find there is often a disconnect between those two personas. How we treat others can be in direct opposition to how we treat ourselves. I don't like to live in the world of "shoulds," but I don't believe we should treat others any better than we treat ourselves, and I don't believe we should treat ourselves better than we treat others. One side is self-deprecating and the other side is conceited. That doesn't mean that in certain moments we don't need to prioritize others over ourselves or that there aren't times when it's necessary to put ourselves over others; it's just that the way in which we make those choices both fall under our kindness value.

Outward Kindness

Let's cover how we treat others first. It will be the easiest to discuss because when most people think of "kind" they understand that to mean how they treat other people. It is also easier because we very naturally put an order to the people that we know. We have best friends, close friends, friends from a certain place or group, and our 3000 closest Facebook friends (sarcasm). We have our immediate family, our extended family, our distant relatives. We have our next-door neighbor, our community, our state, and our country. We have our communities of religion, professions, sports, etc. At work we have our team, our department, our company. There are those we know and those we don't. Those we share common interest with and those whose interest goes against ours. And we naturally prioritize who we will support and who we won't. We all do it, but it's the extent and circumstances that matters.

I'd like to think that my kindness extends to everyone on the planet, but that simply isn't true. There are some for whom I would gladly lay down my life, and there are those who I avoid answering phone calls from. (Because, quite frankly, I just don't want to listen to a family member complain for thirty minutes that everything in their life is against them and they are pretty sure Covid is a government conspiracy to curtail population growth.) My job isn't to tell you who to extend your kindness to. It's to question it with this specific prompt: Who do you want your kids to be kind to?

The quick answer to this question is, "I want my kids to be kind to everyone... but not toxic relationships."

"Ok... everyone who deserves it."

"Ok... everyone who deserves it, and people who are going through a hard time, but definitely your family."

"But not if you don't have a healthy family environment, then take care of yourself."

"And don't just limit it to your family, you can't be in the house ALL the time."

"So your friends too AND people who might become your friends... but you don't have to be kind to people who aren't kind to you!"

"Unless of course those people are actually hurting, then you should show them some kindness...but don't risk your own mental or physical health being kind to those who aren't kind in return...and remember the Golden Rule... always."

Maybe this "kindness" stuff isn't as easy as previously thought. If kindness is hard for us to figure out as parents, think of how hard it must be for kids who have much less context and watch us struggle with kindness regularly. In many ways, kindness is simple to young kids. They don't think about who to extend their values to like we do. When Alexandra was at preschool, she used to walk up to any grandparent who would come to get their grandkids. She would hold their hand and walk around with them and ask if she could go to their house—seriously, how did she not get kidnapped?!

More importantly, kids learn who they will be kind to and who they won't be. They will learn at different ages and in different ways. Your kids probably won't be kind in the same ways. When the eldest two girls were five and seven, we were on a vacation in Barcelona. Their aunt had given them a couple of euros to buy a souvenir and as we were walking down by the water we saw a homeless man sitting on a blanket in the shade. Alex asked me why he was there and I told her that he didn't have a home. We walked further for a couple seconds when she stopped and asked me if she was allowed to give her euros to the man. "Of course my dear, they are yours and you can do what you want with them." She went and put them in his hat and came running back. She said, "Emmeline, you can give your euros to the man too!" Em looked back and said, "Nah," and kept walking forward.

I am not concerned with Emmeline not wanting to give her money away. I don't give money to every person I walk past who is homeless. At the same time, I am proud that Alexandra wanted to. It was the first time that I saw her extend her kind value outside of her immediate circle of friends and family. My job is to help her recognize it so we can discuss it. Kids get their sense of worth from attention, and it can be negative or positive attention (not unlike adults), so when they extend their values outside of themselves, the positive attention they receive from that goes a long way in shaping the person they become.

I remember that my father was extremely insistent on manners during my childhood. He helped teach me those manners, but what I noticed and appreciated was the acknowledgement I received from so many people I didn't know. "Wow, what a polite young man," or,

"You use your manners so well." It made me want to use them more often to gain compliments. And while at first it gave me an inward sense of pride, it later translated into using my manners because it's a way to show respect and kindness. Don't discount the situations where selfish reward can lead to positive habits.

Just as important as who we extend our values to, is the understanding of where we limit our values. Even while writing this, my first thought is, "That's terrible, who would exclude others from kindness?" Unless you are at the level of Mother Teresa, Gandhi, or Mandela, the answer is that we all do it. Yes, we all limit our kindness to either the people we know, or the people we think deserve it. If you don't think that is true, then let's change that statement to the idea that we can always think of someone who doesn't deserve our kindness. We can start big like serial killers and pedophiles. We can go to abusive parents or rapists. You might be thinking, "Ok PJ, you just used the worst of humanity as examples!" And you're right, I did to show one end of the spectrum. How about lawmakers you disagree with? What about someone who says that all lives matter when you say that black lives matter? Politics is too sensitive? What about perfect strangers? Have you ever *not* moved over for a car that is tailgating you? Yeah... me too. What about family members you have a strained relationship with? Friends who unintentionally wronged you? Is forgiveness followed by kindness or irrelevance?

Just because my gut feels uncomfortable here, I want to repeat that I am not advocating for you to show kindness to everyone at all times. It's neither simple nor realistic in my own mind and even if it was, it would be unfair to have that expectation of others. Yes, there are some who are all-inclusive with their kindness, and either they have reached some zen-like pinnacle of existence that I can only dream of, or they are literal saints. My goals aren't so lofty.

It's worth examining who your values extend to and who they don't, and not in some aspirational way but in an accurate, truthful context. Who are the people that you don't show kindness to and why? Why is that an important question? Because you set an example for your kids. And before you say "everyone," remember that person who cut you off in traffic and what you called them. "Everyone" might be a stretch.

We use language that reinforces where we direct our values all the time:

Family above all else

Take care of your own

Blood is thicker than water[7]

America first

I have heard this sentiment in quasi-political debates, "Why should we help the poor kids in Africa when we have children starving right here?" I say quasi-political because most people who say that don't understand international politics or economics. And the real answer is that we have the power to take care of all of them if we decide to, but that conversation is for another time.

The point is, we tell our kids where to prioritize their kindness and oftentimes want to teach our kids what *ought to be done* as opposed to what we do. I will never tell anyone to NOT put their family before others. I do it, I believe in it. The question I want you to ask is, what is the limit? Who do you help? In raising my girls, the answer is, "The people who need it." There is, however, a balance.

---

7 Here's a fun fact! This phrase is used in the exact opposite way than it was intended. We say blood is thicker than water to mean that we should stand with our "blood" or family over non-family relationships. In actuality it was used to talk about comradery of military troops and that the blood spilt on the battlefield was thicker than the water of the womb or "your family." Neat huh?!?

My role as a father exists because of my kids. While most of that role is to take care of my own children, some of that role is to take care of their friends much like the fathers of my friends took care of me. I can also extend it to my neighbors, community, or as far as I have reach.

The limit of where I extend that kindness is usually a balance. Am I able to extend kindness AND still take care of those I care about? If so, then do it. When I start to sacrifice that kindness in my inner circles, then I need to reevaluate how far I extend myself.

Becoming a parent, in my opinion, is the greatest lesson in humility. Even if we are just able to follow the lessons that we teach our kids we become infinitely better humans. And if we learn to extend our kindness out to more people, then it serves as a greater example for our children to follow.

Inward Kindness

Now let's cover what it means when the person we extend our values to is one's self. This concept gets a bad rap too often. Thinking and acting in our own self-interest can be a form of egoism and can also be a form of self-therapy. Like all of our values, we can take it too far and view ourselves as the center of the universe or we can neglect ourselves completely which can take us to a dark, oftentimes lonely, place.

From my work, I find inward kindness is the one that people say they neglect most often, and it's easy for us to do as parents. Firstly, we have the responsibility to take care of our kids. (If you want to call it a pleasure, a passion, a gift; sure by all means go ahead and do that, you're right. You won't get an argument from me. If you want to say it's hard, overwhelming, energy draining; I am right there with you. I feel the phrase "personal responsibility" is the bare minimum to describe what we feel in raising our kids.) Secondly, we have a personal responsibility to take care of ourselves too. "Put on your own oxygen mask first" isn't a selfish instruction. It means that if you can't breathe, you can't help others breathe either. There is nothing to feel guilty or ashamed about with self-love.

Here is where we get into issues of extending our kindness inward. Guilt is a great hindrance of self-love and self-appreciation. Guilt for spending money on yourself instead of your loved ones, guilt for taking a weekend away from your family, guilt for working a full-time job, guilt for not being as good of a cook as your mother. Most mothers I know remind me of Cersei walking from the Red Keep— naked and being pelted with tomatoes, a bell ringing behind the angry crowd and a strong female voice pronouncing over and over, "shame… shame… shame…" In many cases, the person walking naked, the person throwing the tomatoes, the person ringing the bell, and the person shouting shame, are all the same. It is you. (For all of our non-Game of Thrones readers, this means we all play a starring role in our own guilt and shame.)

It is an easy trap to fall into because there are so many expectations put on us as parents, and with a huge sense of responsibility, comes just as much worry that we don't want to be the ones to mess up our kids! So we prioritize ourselves last in that equation right up until we feel so under-appreciated, so powerless, so hopeless that we have a parental burnout and the kids are eating pasta and eggs for the fifth night in a row because, "Meh."

Sometimes you HAVE to make yourself the object of your own kindness because an unhealthy you will have a much harder time raising healthy kids. Should we repeat that for the people in the back? Parents, PLEASE take care of yourselves because your health is important to both you and your kids. You will be their example, their voice in their head, and they hear you when you say you aren't doing enough or aren't being enough.

Once you define your "kind" value, make sure it has two distinct personas to extend to—others and yourself. If you aren't able to treat yourself with the same value you use with others, then you need to keep searching for the right definition because after defining it you need to back it up with actions. Respect, love, time, laughter, humility, grace; if you are able to give it away, you are able to show it to yourself. It might take more work, but it's worth it. Your kids will notice it, you can talk to them about it, and you can help them discover what their kind value is and how to apply it to themselves. And when they are parents, get ready to remind them because they are going to forget.

Here is a question I want you to answer for yourself. How often do you choose yourself over others? It is a fair question. Do you choose others right up until you feel uneasy, and then you choose yourself? Do you choose yourself right up until other people are watching and then choose others? I don't think anyone reading this book is going to qualify for sainthood. It's ok to admit to ourselves that at some point we choose ourselves over others, even in ways that we teach our kids not to. We teach kids to share. How much do you share? When you share, is it because of an expectation of your community or because you want to? Do you give money to causes bigger than yourself? Do you give time to causes bigger than yourself? What does service mean to you? What are your limitations of giving? Many people only give when they feel like they have enough for themselves. Would you define that as greed?

These questions aren't there to make you feel uncomfortable. Growth doesn't often happen in areas of comfort. They are important questions to ask so you can feel comfortable in your choices AND you can guide your kids to see where their kind value extends to.

I am not one to judge where and to whom you extend your values. Many people prioritize their families over others. Many people prioritize their schools, their communities, their regions, their states, their countries over others, and it is encouraged. Some extend it to certain genders, races, people of certain socioeconomic standing. Which do you condone, which do you condemn? My job is just to make sure that you are realizing it and then are able to see what the consequences are of those actions.

The smaller the circle you extend values to, the more times that your values are going to be self-serving. For those who we see have the greatest good are the ones who extend to the largest circles. They are the ones whose values, thoughts, words, actions and habits are applied to everyone regardless of who they are, what position they hold, what their nationality is, what their skin color is, how big their bank accounts, house, car, or influence is. Living a life and parenting with purpose means that you need to be fully aware of how your actions affect others, and this is a big one. Your values most likely have limitations. It is up to you to dictate which values, and under which circumstances, you draw the line.

BSK is universal but subjective

The beauty of brave, smart and kind is that everyone has their own way to define these values. We aren't raising all kids to think and act the same (just like no adult thinks and acts the same as any other adult). It isn't enough to simply accept brave, smart and kind as your values and then all of your thoughts, words, actions and habits fall into place. Each value needs context so that when you act, you do so within your own personal definition of that value.

If your smart value is to use logic for decision-making, then it's very simple when I tell you to draw a tree. It's green, leafy, and has a brown trunk.

If your "smart" value is creativity, then it is very simple when I tell you to draw a tree. It might be Autumn, with orange, yellow and red foliage. The wind is blowing so the tree sways in one direction. There is a man sitting at the base of the tree, learning up against it with his hat over his head taking a nap. The trunk has a hole in the middle where an owl lives.

You both show me the pictures and logic says, "You just told us to draw a tree, not an entire picture or story that goes along with it." Creative says, "That is what I picture when I think of a tree." There is obviously not a right or wrong in this situation. There are two different people who see things from a different perspective. And that is the point.

Your values still make you unique. When there are three of them, they are easier to remember but that doesn't mean they are easy to interpret. Keeping things to be brave, smart and kind are simple for kids to remember AND they are foundational values which gain complexity as we gain experience.

CHAPTER 9 TAKE HOME

- Think about how you pull yourself back from the ledge, from your negative values.
- Do you extend your kindness value to yourself? How?
- When do you choose yourself over others?
- Consider how you want your kids to show kindness to those who are unkind.
- Write down times you have let fear stop you from helping someone.
- What does it mean to show bravery to a stranger?
- Think of a bad decision and which of your values caused that failure. What did it need more of?

SECTION FOUR

JUMPING HURDLES

SECTION FOUR

INTRODUCTION

"What is one thing people get wrong about you?" I was once asked this question on a podcast. I answered, "Everyone assumes that because I talk about being brave, smart and kind; that I am indeed brave, smart and kind."

My experiments with values do NOT mean my life is constantly enriched with courage, critical thought and kindness. My values become negative like everyone else. Sometimes I don't extend them at the right times or to the right people. Being values-driven is not a path to an easier life. As a matter of fact, knowing your values arguably leads to more challenging decisions. Here is why.

Have you ever watched competitive hurdling? You have these insanely fast humans who work hard to time their steps, focus on their footwork, and hurdle over barriers at breathtaking speeds. The more you work at something the better you get at the basics, the faster you run, the harder you push yourself. Have you ever seen one of them get tripped up? Imagine an Olympic hurdler whose foot just barely hits the hurdle as they are barreling forward. They trip over one of the hurdles and fall with incredible force to the ground. They don't only fall, they fall hard; face-planting with their limbs twisted in bars. And at their speed, the damage of mistakes is greatly magnified. The same goes with living a values-driven life. The same goes for parenting with values.

Imagine yourself on that starter block. Imagine you are looking down a track of hurdles. If I am there and I start running towards those hurdles, I promise you, I am not going to fall very hard. I am not particularly fast nor a great jumper. Bottom line, I don't know how to hurdle and I don't really care to be great at it! So, I am going to be slowly stepping over those barriers, I may even go around a couple of them. If I fall, it might be hilarious, but I won't be breaking any bones in the process. To make those jumps dangerous means that I'd need to put myself out there far enough to feel pain—that is called bravery, vulnerability.

Now I don't mind being considered an amateur at hurdling. I won't go through the gruelling regiment that it takes to run 110 meters in under thirteen seconds. However, in life we are all looking down a track of hurdles, aren't we? While I have no interest in winning the 110m hurdles, I do want to live my life to my fullest potential. I want to live my life with purpose. I want to be able to succeed while feeling proud about HOW I overcame obstacles. I want to be grateful and happy in my relationships. I want to understand why I fail, so I can grow. I want to set good examples for my kids, and be able to talk with them about what matters in life. This is how I define success, and I will absolutely go through the gruelling regiment to live my life with purpose.

The more I know about my values, the more conscious decisions I make from them. The more intentional a life I lead, the more magnified my mistakes are. Failure is a consequence of action, not of mistakes. The more intentionally you live, the more mistakes you make. If how you define success is to lead an error-free life, well then don't take action. Your likelihood of "success" is much higher. If the two choices are to be a person who spends their time on a couch watching E! Network OR to be an Olympic hurdler, I'll choose to be the hurdler. Ok, well a metaphorical hurdler.

If you are looking for this type of success too, challenge is a prerequisite. You need to live with purpose and intention. No success has been unchallenged and like all other mental expansions, identifying your values, defining them, understanding what you stand for at your core leaves you without the excuse of ignorance. Once you know your values, once you are able to identify the right choices for the right reasons, you are not magically transformed into a mistake-free, all-knowing three-eyed unicorn wizard. You are as human as you have ever been, and you are also a more aware, intentional version of yourself.

After realizing how you succeed from a place of authenticity, you will be confronted with a renewed sense of morality and responsibility to make the tough choices. You see, your former self has plausible deniability of your poor decisions, truth notwithstanding. Your future self will no longer have that deniability to stand behind; you will have new challenges that you need to overcome, that most likely will be even more difficult than your former challenges because you will have broken through to a new level of self-realization. You will have new challenges with more complex answers not questioning WHAT to do, but the ways in which you CAN or SHOULD. This is the life equivalent of moving from checkers to chess, and the complexity that comes with it. Living with values, living on purpose is not meant to make your life easier, it is meant to make your life more meaningful. Those are two very different results.

CHAPTER 10

THE STRUGGLE IS REAL

10.1 ENERGY IN AUTHENTICITY

"This isn't me…"

"I would never do that… I would never be like this."

"How did I get this way?"

"This isn't what I wanted."

"I am going to do better tomorrow."

"Shit, I said I would do BETTER tomorrow, this is worse."

"I don't know where to start."

"I don't know what to do next."

"I keep trying, and I keep failing."

"What is wrong with me?"

Inner voices can be real a-holes! Have you found yourself saying the above phrases to yourself? I have, and I do. I would love to chalk this up to human nature, and maybe that's all it is. Are we all hardwired to criticize? My intention is to instill strong values into my children. I want them to be confident. How am I able to do that if I can't stop my inner voice from tearing me apart all the time? How can I instill confidence in my kid when I struggle with it myself?

In the 2021 Pixar film *Luca*, the two main characters have a great way of addressing their insecurities. Whenever they feel fear getting in the way of their goal, they say, "Silenzio Bruno!" They have named their negative fear, and once they give it a name, they speak directly to it. I like this example because it separates our positive self from our negative self. Then if we can get the negative part to keep its trap shut, our positive gets to shine even more.

Here is the thing, we all have insecurities. In leadership I like to use a John Maxwell quote that says, "Good leaders are always good learners." The most dangerous leader is the one who thinks they have arrived. I could say the same thing for parenting. We need to keep growing and pushing ourselves for growth. In the absence of growth, we begin to hear our Bruno. Our fear is loudest when we stop feeding our courage and critical thought.

One of my goals is to help leaders and parents succeed by taking actions towards their authentic selves. I know, "being your authentic self," sounds so vague, it sounds like a hippie, incense-burning, alternative-science approach. Everyone is already their own "authentic self" so what kind of phoney baloney is this? Well, have you ever heard anyone say, "It's so exhausting trying to be the person that everyone else wants me to be"?

Go ahead and substitute "everyone else" in that sentence to:

- It is exhausting trying to be the person that my kids want me to be.
- It is exhausting trying to be the person that my partner wants me to be.
- It is exhausting trying to be the person that my employer wants me to be.

If you want to put yourself in the shoes of your kids, go ahead and add:

- It is exhausting trying to be the person that my mom wants me to be.
- It is exhausting trying to be the person that my dad wants me to be.
- It is exhausting trying to be the person that my teacher wants me to be.

Shouldn't simply "being" not be so exhausting? How we interact with our values can often determine the abundance or depletion of our energy.

We are all at different places when it comes to understanding ourselves and our values. Here are some places you may be at:

1. I know my values and I act from them with intention.
2. I know my values but don't actively use them.
3. I don't know my values, but I feel comfortable in my own skin.
4. I don't know my values, and I am struggling to be myself.

If you are saying, I feel like all of those are me at different times of my life with various people, well you are not alone. The difference is that when we know our values and act from them, we are doing so from a place of authenticity. We don't need to use up energy being the person that people expect us to be, but we get to use our energy being the person we simply are. We might get to the end of the day exhausted, but it will be satisfied exhaustion where we have a smile on our face looking forward to whatever is next. If we end the day, mentally exhausted, saying things like, "I don't know how much longer I can keep this up," well then getting to a place of authenticity might not be such phoney baloney after all, although getting there might not be as easy as you think.

As you clearly define your values and try to live according to what's important, you'll become more comfortable in your own shoes. You'll be leading by example and be in an energized mindset which will allow you to teach and guide others—including your children. Once we are able to name our values, then we are able to live by them intentionally, to parent by them, and most importantly, help our children to live by theirs.

Please, please, please pay attention to that last obvious and yet difficult point. Once we know our values, we can help our children to live by THEIR values, NOT by ours.

10.2 YOUR KIDS WILL HAVE THEIR OWN VERSION OF BSK

In the movie *Gladiator*, Commodus, the son of Marcus Aurelius says, "You wrote to me once, listing the four chief virtues. Wisdom, Justice, Fortitude and Temperance. As I read the list I knew I had none of them. But I have other virtues, father. Ambition, that can be a virtue when it drives us to excel. Resourcefulness. Courage. Perhaps not on the battlefield but there are many forms of courage. Devotion, to my family, to you. But none of my virtues were on your list. Even then, it was as if you didn't want me for your son." Commodus then went on to suffocate his father to death, so we obviously know the lesson to learn here. Make space for your children to define their values OR get those breathable pillows and learn to sleep with one eye open.

On a historical note, Marcus Aurelius died of unknown causes in his military chambers at the age of fifty-eight, he was only fictionally murdered because he tried to force his values on his son.

Many times the struggles I have with my kids occur when I don't feel like they are living up to what I believe they should be. I teach, I coach, I yell, I discipline, I set boundaries, I set expectations, I let them set their own expectations. Then I need to hold them accountable when they forget their own expectations! The struggle is real, and it is in an infinite loop. No, my advice is not, "Oh well, looks like there is nothing we can do. Might as well go get some wine." My advice is to say, you might need to change your lens. You might be looking at these situations through your own values, and not your kids.

Over the years, I've worked to find my own personal definitions of BSK, and how I want to embody those values.

- Brave: Create your own luck

- Smart: Be intentional

- Kind: Take care of others

I have defined all of those thoroughly, and do my best to create great examples for my girls. When I see them NOT taking care of others, not thinking something through, and not preparing and/or showing up, I tend to go a little crazy. That is where the foundational levels of BSK start to show up and help me deal, or at least accept my own crazy.

> As my girls get older, their brave doesn't have to be my brave. Their smart doesn't have to be my smart. Their kind doesn't have to be my kind.

Oddly enough, teaching them that they are unique little beings is coming quite naturally. However, dealing with their individualism is difficult because oftentimes it doesn't align with what I think, say or do. HOW DARE THEY! <sarcasm>

My kids are still forming their values. They are still absorbing influence. I don't get to dictate what their values are, but I do need to be patient while they define them. And the more that I understand what "being authentic" means, the more I understand that all values deal with how we overcome, how we critically think and how we treat others and ourselves, then the more energy I have in "being me," and the more I can help my little ones in "being them."

There have been numerous times when Alexandra has struggled with her studies and broken down in the middle of her homework crying saying, "I'm not smart." Emmeline struggles with feeling angry and when she was six years old she came up to me with those eyes looking up for acceptance and said, "But Daddy, what if I don't feel kind in my heart." Man, does this kid just speak my truth sometimes or what?!

One thing I didn't anticipate when teaching my girls BSK is how unintentionally confrontational it can be. How do you respond to a child who doesn't feel kindness in her heart? I don't get caught off-guard too often but Emmeline's comment got me. I responded in the most honest, empathetic way that I could. I knelt down to her level so we could be face-to-face (it's amazing how often this tactic works when so many other attempts have failed) and I told her, "I don't always feel kindness in my heart either sweetheart. Sometimes I feel anger or sadness. And when I feel those things, you know what I try to do? Nothing." She gave me the same confused face that you might be giving right now. "I try to not talk, because I might say something unkind. I try not to act, because actions from anger or sadness usually don't turn out very well. I try not to get upset at myself or the situation, because most of the time it will pass. For a couple of seconds, I don't do anything. Then I take a couple of deep breaths before I do anything else. Should we try to do that together?"

When I get stuck for words, I try to go back to my own values. When I know which value to focus on, I find it isn't hard to put myself in the mind of a child. We were all kids once. Getting in touch with that side can be very difficult when we lose it. But when we find it again, it gives us a window to peer through, remembering love or heartbreak and how we lived in those extremes for so long. It gives us less grey to consider and more simplicity and clarity of thought and action.

So after my monologue to my little angry angel, you know what happened? She looked me straight in the eye, took a couple of deep breaths and then said, "Yeah Dad, it's not working," and she stomped up the stairs. Well... bubbles. But guess what, habits take time. We still go through the same stuff, and she is learning to breathe. She recognizes that she needs to take some time. And she still acts like a maniac too.

Being intentional with my words helps me be more intentional with my actions. I can easily say, "make the brave choice, make the smart choice, make the kind choice," and I do. It helps a little, but what I have found to be even more impactful is helping them find their own values.

When they are scared, or when they need to overcome, I can say, "Chin up, find your brave."

When they are having a hard time figuring something out, or looking for an angle to approach an issue, "Brain on, find your smart."

When they aren't feeling the kind in their heart, when they need to consider others or themselves, "Heart open, find your kind."

This helps in a couple of ways. Firstly, it identifies that they don't have the same values as each other or as their parents or as their friends. It encourages individualism and uniqueness that I believe will help them find their confidence and feel comfortable in their own skin. I find the majority of adults don't get this for themselves, so I am giving my girls a head start. Secondly, instead of me saying, "be smart," it can imply that they aren't smart and they need to "be" something they aren't. "Find your smart" means that it is there inside of them all the time, and while it might be hard to find when we need it, it doesn't mean anyone is undeserving or not enough.

It also puts an emphasis on me as a parent to help them find what their individual values are instead of superimposing my own. Because everyone has a value that is brave, a value that is smart, a value that is kind; there isn't a lack of values at all, just a different way that we approach those fundamental pillars in our lives.

I say this in coaching, workshops, keynotes and I'll say it over and over as a parent. Living with purpose is hard. Living by accident is easy. And please remember, our goal as parents isn't to HAVE brave, smart and kind kids—our job is to help get them there eventually. They'll show us flashes of that brilliance and they will fail miserably.

10.3 SCARED, STUPID, SELFISH

I once got advice from a good friend of mine who I greatly admire. He said, "Look, if you want to sell the idea of brave, smart and kind, then you need to be able to sell people on the other extremes. You can get people to listen if you define the opposite of brave, the opposite of smart, and the opposite of kind." He suggested the idea of, "Scared, Stupid and Selfish." I immediately felt uncomfortable with the idea.

For one, the reason I chose bravery in the first place was because I was tired of people using fear to control others. If I was trying to convince people that bravery was something we needed MORE of in the world, I definitely cannot go around making people scared of the lack of bravery.

Secondly, scared, stupid and selfish aren't necessarily the opposites of those words. Bravery isn't about not being scared. It is about understanding fear, confronting it and overcoming it. Stupid isn't the opposite of smart. Mindless might be a more appropriate notion, as defined as, "not aware of or not concerned about what is happening around one." Stupid implies that you don't have choice or opportunity to change. Selfish is a loaded word. In part, some people need a little more selfishness in their lives. The disconnect between how we treat others and how we treat ourselves is vast.

My friend wasn't being underhanded, he wasn't trying to get me to trick people. He was being helpful. He was trying to help me get in the minds of my audiences, and to see things from their viewpoint— which is a fantastic and empathetic way to approach people. What I learned from that exercise is that the words, "scared, stupid and selfish" are used so often to describe people that we naturally come to those conclusions when people aren't being brave, smart and kind. My friend was right in the sense that people are attracted to negative values just like they are attracted to negative news headlines. People so often define what they are, by what they aren't. Brené Brown talks about how in her research, when she asked people about love, belonging and connection, they gave her stories of heartache, exclusion, and disconnection. When you are able to speak to what they aren't, they are more apt to listen.

My friend also wasn't wrong in that when I talk to my girls about brave, smart and kind, and they are having a difficult day, they say things like, "I am so scared, I am so stupid, I am so selfish." Those are issues that we need to deal with. When I have found myself in those situations, I have quickly jumped to blame myself saying, "of course they feel scared, stupid and selfish. I have been so focused on talking to them about being brave, smart and kind, their negative emotions take them directly to the opposite, and guilt and shame set in when they do something against what I have programmed into their brains!"

There are times in life where I give myself too much credit...

One of the reasons I know that my kids feeling scared, stupid and selfish aren't a result of teaching them brave, smart and kind is because in talking to other parents, their children also say that they too are scared, stupid, or that they are a bad person. One of the reasons I know that BSK is foundational, is because everyone measures themselves by those same values. And when they go awry, as they often do, parents are so quick to jump to self-judgement and the judgement of others. Kids see that, hear that, feel that, and they respond in-kind.

How do we know that they know? Because scared, stupid and selfish aren't the only words kids use, they could say, "chicken, moron, jerk." Kids have ideas on what the opposites are of brave, smart and kind, and they use them to attack others AND attack themselves. Want to take those words to the next level? When was the last time you heard someone call a person a "pussy, retard, or bitch." If you find those words abrasive and completely inappropriate, you're right, those are some of the worst words out there. I cringed even writing them (sorry Mom). If you think your children won't or haven't heard those words, you're wrong. If you think your children haven't or won't USE those words, you may be in for some eye-popping moments, and that bad language isn't necessarily reflective of you as a parent. My parents didn't use any of those words and yet as a teen, I used all of them. Not frequently, but enough. So did the guys on my soccer, baseball and football teams, so did older kids, so did coaches, so did other parents. And guess what, this book won't change any of that.

My goal isn't to get everyone in the world to stop weaponizing values and calling each other names. My goal is to make sure that MY kids understand how we look at the world in the best light and in the worst light. And in the worst light, we attack people by telling them that they lack courage, lack thought, lack kindness in extremely hurtful ways.

The beautiful part is that if we can teach our budding adults to understand fear and that it's ok to be afraid and make mistakes, then we are taking steps in the right direction. If we can get them used to using their own critical thought through creativity, logic, curiosity, then we are taking steps in the right direction. If we can get them to treat others with understanding, openness and respect, and connect that with how they should treat themselves, then we are taking steps in the right direction. As they get older, my kids will see people attack them because of the aggressor's own fear, thoughtlessness, and insecurity, not the recipient.

10.4 WEAPONIZING VALUES

When I talk to people about speaking in public, we have to review the topic of fear. Public speaking can be scary because it offers a level of vulnerability. Speaking is scary because what you say has consequences, and by speaking up you become an active participant in those consequences. But here is the part that people forget. There are consequences to staying silent as well.

The same goes for your values. The concrete steps of values are to define, display, and discuss. This is how you start to live your values intentionally. They are no longer in your head; they are active in the world. You have voiced them. AND similar to being read your rights, "anything you say or do, can and WILL be used against you," your values can and WILL be used against you at some point too.

There are so many ways your values can be weaponized and it's important that you are aware. As with many things in life, what is good and well-intentioned can be turned around and used to destroy. One person uses fire to warm their home, another uses it to burn down a village. Harnessing electricity has led to exponential human advances, it can also bring a 300-pound man to a screeching halt. Nuclear power has the ability to bring power to millions, and it has the ability to level cities. All forms of energy have the ability to give us power and the ability to unleash power upon others. They can bring us both light AND darkness.

The first reason to discuss weaponizing values is to make sure we aren't guilty of this offense. When we understand values CAN be weaponized, hopefully we look inside of us and stop whatever we might be doing to others. The second reason is so both parents and kids can recognize when other people are doing it. That way, you (or your child) can instantly say, "That person is using values against me. I'm not going to take that bait. I'm not going to take that crap." Then you can have the strength to truly live by your values instead. It's powerful when you see the punch coming because you have a moment to decide how you are going to react instead of getting smashed in the face by it.

Glasshouse Fallacy

I'm the guy who's always talking about being brave, smart and kind and one of my biggest fears is that someone will use this against my girls. I'm worried some dope is going to say, "Your dad's always talking about kindness, so you'd better be kind. Your dad talks about courage but aren't you being a little coward right now?"

Those people can just as easily throw my values back into my own face as well. I'm not perfect. I'm still human and there are moments when I don't show up as I'd like to. It's so easy for people to look at me when I'm not my best self and criticize my actions, "Well, that wasn't very smart!"

"Those who live in glass houses should not throw stones." Well guess what, if all parents and leaders were not allowed to help people on topics that they themselves have failed at, we would all be sitting in silence.

The glasshouse fallacy has been misappropriated and used as an argument for why one individual should not talk about anything that they are guilty of themselves. "Let he who is without sin be the first to cast a stone," and all that. The valid glasshouse perspective should be that people should not judge others because we all have made errors. It should not be the reason for silence, it should be the reason for empathy.

Here is what it sounds like at a basic level:

"How can you say that when one of your values is kind?"

"For having smart as one of your values, you do some really stupid stuff."

"If you were really brave, you wouldn't be so scared."

The trick is having the ability to observe what is going on while reserving judgement. Instead of being judgmental, we can try to be curious. Instead of creating a story and saying, "This person is acting this way because..." we can ask questions. We all make mistakes and there's usually a reason behind them. I want my girls to understand this too, so they can show compassion to those who throw stones from time to time.

Typically this comes to the surface if someone in their world has bullied them. I reassure my girls that I'll help them find safety—whether that be talking to the appropriate adult like the principal at their school, their coach, another parent. But then, I sit my girls down and explain that kids who bully have usually been bullied themselves. It might be an older brother or sister. It might be a cousin or uncle, or could be parents. It could be something that they learned on TV. I don't know. I remind them how important it is to try to not judge others for who they are right now. They definitely don't have to accept the other kid's actions, but let's at least try to understand where they might be coming from.

These conversations are paying off. I swear! There was recently a bully in my eldest's class. As my daughter was telling me about this boy she said, "Daddy, he's going through some really hard stuff at home." The fact that she could see past his behaviors and extend some empathy was a win. By being compassionate, she felt less afraid of that boy and took away his power. That's what brave, smart and kind looks like, folks!

Negative Self-talk

Many people think they can't lead with the values of brave, smart and kind because they're guilty of being the opposite. They think they aren't living the values and this disqualifies them from teaching brave, smart, kind to their children.

They think, "Well how am I supposed to talk to these kids about being brave when I've stayed in the same job even though I hate it? I haven't taken the risks that I wanted to in life because I've been scared yet I'm telling my children to go take these risks." And quite frankly, people can weaponize that against you too. "Who are you to tell me to go take risks? You haven't a single risk in your life."

But that's not the point of it. It's not to say you can't teach from your own life experience. In fact, you can share, "I've done some things based on fear. So I am actually probably the more qualified person to talk to you about fear stuff. Yes, I've done some terribly unkind things to people and it's hurt people. And so I can talk to you about what has happened when I've hurt people."

We discredit ourselves out of shame and self-judgment. We overthink our decisions and find ourselves paralyzed. We beat ourselves up when we make mistakes.

These are only a few ways we take our values and use them against ourselves.

How to Weaponize BSK

If you look at weaponizing values, go no further than politics and political-leaning media. They are both fantastic at triggering people to see a non-existent danger and create fear around it. When you are triggered, you open yourself up to negative values. You feel the need to be "brave" but you have now aimed that bravery at a perceived threat. How does outside influence feed that bravery? They give you "information" to feed your "smart" value. They do this by misusing statistics or straight up lies that have recently been named, "alternative facts." For the full trifecta, they will feed your "kind" value to tell you who in your life will be affected, your kids or your community. When people want to weaponize values, they can mobilize people in great numbers. As Mumford and Sons so brilliantly wrote, all they need is to give you an "enemy bigger than your apathy, and then they have won," or at least then you are engaged.

The textbook definition of brave is "having or showing mental or moral strength to face danger, fear, or difficulty : having or showing courage." This means that people can misuse a call to courage for non-existent danger, fear or difficulty. There is a distinct formula that people use to trigger your negative values, here it is:

1. Tell you what you need to be afraid of (satisfying your brave value)

2. Manufacture specific knowledge or data (satisfying your smart value)

3. Tell you who in your life is at risk (satisfying your kind value)

I could pick plenty of historical or current events to demonstrate this point, but let's just jump to one that most people finally agree on, a woman's right to vote.

In my circles, I don't think I know anyone who disagrees with women voting, but in the late nineteenth century there were massive anti-suffrage movements. Let's look at how those messages were spread.

1. "Women voting leads to the erosion of society where a man's role in politics is balanced by a woman's role in the home." (create fear)

2. "The majority of women don't want to vote." (manufacture knowledge)

3. "Think of the children, if women are involved in politics they have less time raising kids." (use who you care about are at risk)

You can go ahead and lump any group of people together that you want to create a campaign against and use this formula to do it. Democrats, Republicans, Socialists, rich, poor, men, women, black, brown, white. If you want to sway public opinion, go ahead and use this formula. When people want to weaponize values, they can mobilize gangs in great numbers.

If you think, "PJ, you are giving away the formula to get people to hate others!" Trust me, hate-mongers already know this formula. People have been doing it since the beginning of humankind. What I am doing is giving people the ability to recognize it, respond to it, and recover from it.

As parents, not only can we not fall into the trap of non-existent fear, we have to be able to show our kids the difference. Learned fears are so incredibly powerful and dangerous. We can help our kids with them but only if we see them in ourselves first.

CHAPTER 10 TAKE HOME

- Ask if who you want your kids to be aligns with who they want to be.
- Think if there is anything you are guilty of and don't feel qualified to talk to your kids about.
- What are you scared of for your children, do you pass that on?
- Consider which non-existent fears you have. Question them.
- When has someone used values against you?
- When have you weaponized values against someone else?
- Try putting yourself in the mind of your child... regularly.

PARENTAL GATEKEEPING

In Sheryl Sandberg's book, *Lean In*, she shares stories about how you need to have a partner who is willing to shoulder the personal load of life if you want to be able to also take on a professional load. In her specific case, she was talking about a husband's willingness to take on routine responsibilities at home in order for women to focus more of their attention, if desired, on their career. She says one of the obstacles to achieve this balance isn't simply for a man to want to share the load, but for the woman's ability to let him. She outlines a concept she calls "maternal gatekeeping" where a husband is doing his part in the home only for the wife to come in and do it "her way" thereby dictating the terms of how the man takes on certain roles. This type of gatekeeping is a "you can't have your cake and eat it too" scenario. If a couple desires to find this balance, they need to give up a certain level of control.

This is a hugely relatable concept not only for all the partners of the world who have been told exactly how to load the dishwasher, dress the kids, or make the meals; but also for the ones who have been told exactly how to track their finances, handle a car salesman, or parallel park. The principles of maternal gatekeeping are universal. Hold on with too much control and you will limit yourself and those who are wanting and willing to help.

In applying this gatekeeping concept to parenting, there are two discussions to focus on—one, ensuring we don't block our partners from parenting with values, and two, ensuring we don't block our children from learning how to live with values.

11.1 GATEKEEPING A CO-PARENT

Are we able to share the load in raising our kids WITHOUT telling our partner how to do it? Do we allow our significant other to live their values, and are we on the same page when it comes to raising kids with values? Is it even necessary to have both parents in agreement on the values?

If I am being completely honest here, this is the area I have struggled with most and it has also created the largest rift between my wife and I. You see, we are polar opposites when it comes to most things. Just so you know, this story is being published with her permission with the sole objective of hoping we can help other people with our experiences.

My wife is introverted and private. I am extroverted and put myself out there more. She would much prefer quiet time at home, while I enjoy being out and about with people. She likes walks in the woods, I'd prefer going to a pool. She loves city trips, I'd rather go to the beach. She thrives in organization, I thrive in chaos. In getting angry, she has a shorter fuse but a smaller explosion. I have a longer fuse, but when it goes off there is a boom. She is more of a realist, I am more of an optimist. When people come over to the house, she takes pride in creating an incredible culinary experience and I open the bag of nacho chips, or whatever is in the cupboard. This could go on, but no need.

Here is part of the beauty. When it comes to being brave, smart and kind, we both are those things AND we both struggle with those things. My wife is amazingly courageous. She did a year abroad in high school though she barely knew how to speak English. She broke off an engagement close to the wedding date because she realized they weren't meant to be together. She works harder than anyone I have ever known—at everything. She was one of the most decorated students in university, winning an award for best honors thesis. She was a Fulbright scholar. She is also one of the most loyal people you'll meet. She takes care of people in ways they might not even realize they need, and she does it without expectation of anything in return. She is incredibly brave, smart and kind.

Her "brave" is hard work, her "smart" is knowledge, her "kind" is loyalty.

My "brave" is to be present and create luck; my "smart" is to live with intention, and my "kind" is to take care of others.

And here is the deal… our values still clash.

Sometimes her "hard work" clashes with my "take care of others." That causes tension when the time it takes to complete a project at home means that we don't get to enjoy our time on weekends with each other, kids, or friends.

Sometimes my "create luck" clashes with her "loyal" when it means that I take risks in my career so she feels she needs to make more responsible decisions for the sake of the family stability.

Sometimes her "knowledge" clashes with my "intention" when I have a specific timeline in mind and she is still processing all the available information. She sees my actions as hasty, I see the time she is taking as wasteful.

There are numerous examples where values clash in relationships and our marriage is no different.

Here is what gatekeeping a co-parent looks like:

- One parent punishes a child, one parent pardons.
- One parent challenges their children, one parent protects.
- One parent is optimistic with the kids, one parent brings them down to earth.
- One parent rewards results, one parent rewards effort.

None of these examples are as black and white as they come across here. My wife and I are parents who both punish and pardon, challenge and protect, are optimistic and realistic, and reward both results and effort.

The first question in gatekeeping is, do we allow our partners the freedom to parent as they see fit, or do we step in? If your answer is yes and no, then you are catching on to this book. That isn't for me to tell you, that is the conversation you need to have with your significant other.

The second question is, where is the line? We have to be able to talk about the places we disagree as parents and see that the popular, "Stand together, one united voice," doesn't always work and can send even more mixed messages to your little ones.

Co-parenting is a values-ridden battlefield. Talking about difficulty and failure, I had an interviewer ask me a question I hadn't anticipated. She asked, "Seeing as you are so in touch with your values, how you succeed and how you fail… what is it like when you argue with your wife?" For someone who spends a lot of time visualizing potential situations, this one never crossed my mind. I naturally had to answer the question, but I struggled. Knowing that understanding the complexities of a values system does not void you from failure. If anything, the more you know about values, the more opportunities you have to fail in your values completely.

So to answer the question, how do I argue with my wife? Intensely, with difficulty, painfully, apologetically, but with the intent to heal. Arguing is an extreme form of communication and issues should be worked through with better communication styles. However, the other extreme form of communication is silence. In silence, relationships die.

Knowing that our children will develop their values from all over the place, I feel fortunate that their mother and I don't share all of the same values. Do we struggle at times? Hell yes! Do the kids see that? Not all of it, but yes they do. And because they see it, they also see that brave, smart and kind have different meanings and interpretations. They will see us as individuals who love them very much and approach our relationships with them from different angles. Knowing this, my wife and I don't have to subscribe to one parenting style, and that gives our kids permission to find their own brave, smart and kind too.

11.2 GATEKEEPING BSK FROM OUR KIDS

Do we act as parental gatekeepers by not allowing our kids to live, learn and fail at the values because we want to protect them? Are we taking away the opportunities for our kids to show courage, to be smart, to show kindness? How can we have them learn to be brave, smart and kind in a safe environment? Is there such a thing as a safe environment?

I find my own difficulty with allowing my children to fail at their values goes in the specific order of brave, smart and kind. It is harder for me to let my children be brave than to be smart or kind. One of the occasional ingredients to bravery is fear. Except the problem is that many kids DON'T HAVE FEAR! We condition our children to be afraid. We tell them what to be scared of. We tell them who to be scared of. I probably tell my girls to "be careful" every single day. Other popular hits include:

"Watch out!"

"Don't jump off there!"

"Why would you do that?"

"Take that out of your mouth!"

"That'll hurt if you have to poop it out."

The irony is, my own fear is robbing my girls of opportunities to practice their own versions of BSK. I need to get a handle on my anxiety and get out of their way. The worst thing I could do is imprint my fears onto my children and create a worry for them where there wasn't one before. Fear, like anything else, can be taught.

11.2.1 GATEKEEPING THEIR BRAVE

There are two types of fear, innate and learned. There is something to be said for teaching children about innate fear because heaven knows jumping BEFORE they say, "Dad, catch me!" might be funny, but carries a great amount of risk. At the very least we want our kids to know the risks of the decisions (smart) before making the decision to jump (brave). So allowing my girls to be brave is a struggle for me because I know the potential consequences. We have an innate need to keep our kids safe because, quite frankly, they suck at keeping themselves safe.

Innate vs. Learned Fears

While there are plenty of things that people fear, essentially they can all be broken down into two types: innate fears and learned fears. If the titles didn't give them away, innate fear is the classification for the fears that we are born with, while learned fears are those that have been taught.

There was a study done between the Max Plank Institute in Germany and Uppsala University in Sweden. They took a sample of six-month old babies and showed them pictures of snakes and spiders to see what their responses were. The consistent reaction was that the children had dilated pupils pointing to a stress result in their brain.[8] One journal cited this report and identified evolution in developing an innate fear of animals that could harm us, as humans who did not have a healthy innate fear of these animals died more often, thereby removing their genes from the world. Other critics say that the report simply points to a heightened focus as opposed to an actual fear. But the focus didn't occur when the infants were shown pictures of flowers and fish. Why does this matter? Because realizing what fears your children are born with versus what fears they develop is significant. Would you like to know the relation between your children's learned fears and parenting? Much like the anti-drug ad in the 1980s, your kids might say, "I

---

8 Hoehl, Stefanie, "Itsy Bitsy Spider…: Infants React with Increased Arousal to Spiders and Snakes" Frontiers in Psychology, October 18, 2017, https://www.frontiersin.org/articles/10.3389/fpsyg.2017.01710/full.

learned it from watching you!" Ok, your kids aren't just watching YOU to see what you are afraid of, they are watching others as well.

Your kids are also testing the limits of their courage to see where you will stop them. (We all know the talents of a child who is pushing their limits.) Most of the time, however, we as parents see that as us needing to put our foot down to draw the line in the sand of what we will or will not tolerate.

> Have you ever considered that the first place children test their bravery is with you? At that time, what do you want your response to be? Is it anger and/or punishment?

Are you going to ignore them? There isn't a right answer to these questions without knowing the circumstances surrounding them. It is, however, worth the thought when considering how to raise your kids and the type of parent you want them to have.

Innate Fears

When it comes to innate fears, think of it in terms of evolution. Some organisms have been so incredibly brave they've reached the point of being reckless. The more reckless a species was, the more they were removed from the gene pool. So, innate fears are very healthy to have. They have kept us scared and alive for two-and-a-half million years.

While we aren't able to do much about our innate fears, fear itself is a feeling. I use a very simple and common adage when speaking to my girls about feelings. "We can't control our feelings, but we can control our actions." I try my best to let my girls know that they are entitled to any emotion they are feeling. I want them to feel present and aware of their emotions, because when they understand them, then they are able to make better decisions. Not understanding an emotion, or being overwhelmed by one, makes it much more difficult to act with purpose. Whether it's their DNA or their upbringing, I am not concerned with my daughters feeling or showing their emotions, including fear. They got that covered.

When we sense innate fear, there are two types of actions we take: active or passive. You've heard of these many times if not in other words. An active response is fight or flight response. The passive response is to freeze or faint.

If innate fears are hardwired into our DNA, then first of all we need to be able to recognize them. Why is that important? If we can't recognize them, we can't talk about strategies to address them. If freezing is an option, then it can be done with intent. If fighting is an option it can also be an intent. The problem with fighting is that most people aren't taught how to fight, and more importantly they aren't taught what to fight for.

I am not necessarily talking about fighting in a physical sense, though I do feel that is important. When you live a life of courage, you need to also be able to discuss how you stand up for people and stand up for yourself. One of both Gandhi and MLK Jr.'s principle values was that of nonviolence. Please don't mistake that for not fighting. Nonviolence is a very defined and effective way to fight. It is an active nonviolent resistance to evil that chooses love over hate. These iconic leaders knew what they stood for and they had a strategy to get there. If we were all so clear of what that meant to each of us, then we would find our world in a much better place.

Take some time to make a list of what your kids should fight for and what they shouldn't. I do not want my daughters to punch people AND I want them to be able to defend themselves. So I have taught them how to block punches and restrain people. I want them to be able to deal with insults from bullies, so we talk about what to say and when to walk away. As they get older we will be talking about what to look for regarding their relationships and their bodies. Right now we break those down into principles like "no means no," so if I am tickling them and they say "stop," I stop.

Write down the techniques in which you want to teach them how to fight—like when to stand up for themselves. I cannot stress enough the importance of taking the time to teach them how to overcome certain situations. If they don't learn that from you, I promise you they will learn it somewhere else. And just like our values, realize that even if you do teach them how to deal with these situations, they are still going to witness others who use their courage differently. You were never going to be the only person they learn from.

Learned Fears

Learned fears are the ones we have a much greater power over, and with that power comes a great deal of responsibility (RIP Stan Lee). We have both an intentional and unintentional impact on our kids in relation to the fears we teach them to have. Of course there are positive effects. We want them to have a little fear in situations where they could be hit by a car, burnt by the stove or injured by the scissors they were running around the house with. I try to reserve striking the fear of God in my children for just such occasions.

Each of the girls had at least one instance of walking into the middle of the road at age two or three and because I was attentive, I was able to purposefully prevent anything bad from happening. Each time I saw those chubby legs on the sidewalk about to step into the street without me, I watched from a safe distance. We live on a street in the suburbs where there is a decent amount of traffic but it is a long street and I can see where cars are coming from. So I would let the scene play out, knowing what would happen next. It was always innocent enough, they would be looking at something on the other side of the street and start to make their way across. No cars were around, but they couldn't see that over the parked cars on the side. They'd get to the middle of the road and I would shout in a voice-of-God fashion, "Joey! Get out of the street!!!" I'd run over and pick her up with haste, tilt my head down with my eyes up, and very forcefully tell her that she can't walk in the street and that she could get hurt by the cars. Each word and tone is intentional and breaks my heart with every second that passes knowing that she had never seen me like this before.

After instilling that fear, I would then give her a big hug and explain everything to them. Remember, heightened emotions create memories. I used that to my advantage in those situations. Same as when they all reached for a hot pan on the stove. Sometimes I caught that in time, sometimes they learned with a burnt finger and a blister to remind them.

Then there are the fears that we put inside our children without thought or intention. Think about how many times a day you tell your kids to "be careful." When we do this, we imply there is an element of danger and they should be scared. We've projected our fear of them getting hurt.

The other day, Joey was walking on a ledge and I told her to be careful. It wasn't even a tall ledge! If she fell, she would have been fine. After I said it, she looked at me with fear and I knew it was a result of my overprotection.

We also need to see the fear we are digesting from the media who use these tactics to get our attention. We hear a story about a baby dying of SIDS and we're in our child's bedroom watching them breathe while they sleep. We read an article about an abduction and we're warning our children not to talk to strangers or go out after dark. We see images of physically fit and beautiful people, then make comments such as, "I shouldn't eat that." Then we are surprised when our children express a fear of getting fat. Fear is contagious. Sensationalized news makes us afraid, so we warn our children to be diligent and to be careful and inevitably, they become afraid. The first step to stopping this unhealthy cycle is to become aware that what we consume becomes part of our mindset and what we fear gets passed on.

An important question to ask yourself is, what do you want your child to be afraid of and what do you not want them to be afraid of? I know it sounds simple, but it might not be. Then you need to consider if you are cultivating any of these fears. Are there any fears that are going to come up in your children's lives on a regular basis? What is your plan for discussing these fears? What are your ideas on how to help them work through these fears?

11.2.2 GATEKEEPING THEIR SMART

Determining the line between teaching and gatekeeping is difficult when it comes to our "smart" value. Firstly, there are so many definitions of "smart," ranging from intelligent to creative to aware, so everything needs to be taken in context. Secondly, as parents, we tend to do a lot of gatekeeping (doing things for our kids instead of letting them go through the process of trial and error) for many reasons. Sometimes, we're trying to protect them and truthfully, most times, it's just easier that way.

Do you recognize yourself and/or your kids in any of the following gatekeeping scenarios?

1. *Lazy Ass or Do-It-For-Me*: They ask for help and what they really want is for me to do something for them. And if I try to teach them how to do something, they will scream their heads off until we reach a boiling point.

2. *Time Saving*: It's easier and quicker for us to do it than it is to teach them how. I see them doing something wrong and decide to solve the problem for them because it will probably save me time.

3. *Huh?*: This is where you are trying to explain something to your kids, but they don't get it AND it still needs to get done.

In order to move away from gatekeeping and into teaching, we need to create room for kids to struggle and fail. This means loosening our control but not to the point where we stand by with our mouths shut while our kids fail on an epic and damaging scale. We're there to provide guidance and guardrails while they learn new skills and try to solve problems using their smart value.

We also need to keep in mind that there is often more than one way to solve a problem or get the job done. Sometimes with kids "good enough" can be good enough—not "good enough but I need to run behind you and do it the way it was SUPPOSED to get done." It's like when my wife "teaches me" to sweep the floor. My version of getting the job done is very different from her version of doing it "properly." She has a masters degree in cleanliness and I am at kindergarten level, but at the end of the day, how clean does a floor really have to be? I mean the dog licks it. (Ok, maybe not a great example.) Just remember when you try to force your kids to learn a certain way, you effectively shut down their critical and creative thinking process and narrow their learning. The result may not be perfect, but that doesn't mean it is wrong.

11.2.3 GATEKEEPING THEIR KIND

The last value is what I consider to be the easiest to teach, and yet is the most difficult one when it comes to forgiving their transgressions. In our family, kindness is non-negotiable. The issues however, aren't like the previous two examples. I have a hard time letting my kids be brave, I have a hard time teaching my girls to be smart, and yet I expect them to be kind... all the time.

There is a great quote from Rebecca Eanes in *A Newbie Guide to Positive Parenting* that says, "So often, children are punished for being human. They are not allowed to have grumpy moods, bad days, disrespectful tones, or bad attitudes. Yet, we adults have them all the time. None of us are perfect. We must stop holding our children to a higher standard of perfection than we can attain ourselves."

I don't know about all of you, but I am guilty of this. Every. Single. Day. Step one of the solution is recognizing the behavior in ourselves so that we are able to change it. I need reminding, so I posted the quote in our kitchen. I tried to move on to the next step of finding a solution, but for the love of all things holy I still catch myself holding them to a standard that I struggle to attain myself. So I thought, there has to be some middle ground here from understanding the concept to changing the behavior. What helps me is to think of parental gatekeeping. It's not my job to solve their bad moods but it IS my job to anticipate their bad moods and help them understand why they feel that way.

Step two is to teach them before they need it. You can't teach someone how to create trust in a relationship when the trust has already been broken. If you want to build trust, build it before you need it. Show your kids how to have healthy relationships so they recognize it when they are in one. Yes you can still teach lessons as they grow, but don't assume that they are just going to know how to be good at making connections and then be surprised when they don't.

Step three is to realize that I have done what I'm able to do when it comes to helping my girls develop healthy relationships AND I know they are going to have some unhealthy relationships. I try to give them positive examples of how people treat each other. It's their job however, to create and nurture their own relationships. Because we have nurtured communication between ourselves, they come to me when they are having problems with friends, and I ask questions to help them come to terms with whatever is going on.

11.3 GATEKEEPING RESILIENCE

Kids who have successfully dealt with loss; death, poverty, their parents' divorce, or those who have overcome some significant hurdles in their lives deal with failure on a different level than those who don't have many hurdles. It's because they have experienced a much more intense feeling of failure, so smaller things in life become more manageable.

My wife brought up a great thought as she was reading the above statement. She asked, "Do you not think that some children who go through a divorce become risk averse to things like relationships and marriage as they get older?" My answer was from a therapist that I spoke with who told me, "Kids handle divorce just fine. They hurt, but they recover from that type of loss. What messes kids up in a divorce isn't the separation, it's how the parents react to the separation." If the parents are hostile towards each other, if they use the children in a custody battle or to manipulate child support, if they witness physical or verbal abuse—those are the types of things that can damage a child.

This is the same when it comes to failure. If children see their mother chastise their father when he makes a mistake, that scars. If they see their father ridicule their mother for any misstep, that scars. This is the "what the bubbles" story transposed into failure. Kids will see your behavior and they will emulate it. We need to understand that how we deal with failure gives our children a roadmap on how to deal with failure.

One evening, Alexandra was struggling with her math and it ended in tears (again). I went back to my personal failure library and pulled out the story of how I lost $7000 on the first event that I organized with my company. It always makes her smile. I tell her why I failed AND how I dealt with it. (By the way, I didn't deal with it well at first. I had to sit with that failure and discuss it and learn from it.) So what do we do with her failure? We sit with it, we discuss it and we learn from it. Does that mean the pain is gone? Of course not, but it does help in being able to continue to overcome even when the pain is there. The remedy for that pain is time and not repeating the same actions to reach that failure again.

The point is that parents have a natural tendency to shield their children from the pain of failure, and just as importantly, shield them from our own failures because we don't want them to see the worst of us. We want them to picture us when they think of success as well as picturing us when they think of integrity. The problem is that if they don't learn how to fail at a young age, then it becomes much easier to feel the shame of that when they get older. Sharing your failures with your children gives them permission to share their failures with you. And because we have changed the language to say that they didn't DO something smart, instead of not BEING smart, they can now see a path to correct. Yes, we need to support them emotionally, but also allow them to be exposed to hurt, struggle and disappointment. If we want to raise resilient children, we need to let them fail safely.

No parent WANTS their kids to hurt so we try to combat that in different ways. Here are some of the things we do:

- Shield them from hurt

- Fix the pain for them instead of having them fix it

- Give quick answers

- Micromanage so they don't fail

- Blame others for mistakes instead of encouraging our kids to take ownership

Some of my best parenting has come when my little ones are hurting. When they have been rejected by their friends at school. When they are scared of telling the truth. When they fail at a task and feel like they aren't enough. When they have had their feelings hurt. It has come when their actions or the situation has been dictated by fear, when someone didn't think about the consequences of their actions, and/or when someone has been unkind.

My absolute best parenting is when I have been able to predict a negative outcome, let it come to pass, and then set up the lesson for them to learn while staying calm and intentional. In these cases, it's not about fixing their problems to make them feel better. It's about preparing them to handle the emotions that they are about to feel. And when I expect those "negative" emotions to flow, then I no longer need to REACT to those emotions. Then I get to be proactive in letting them happen, and I can use any one of my methods to handle the situation.

If I need to react to a negative emotion without being prepared for it, there is a better chance that I will react poorly. If I roll my eyes, or raise my voice, or make snarky comments, I have given them permission to do the same. (Not that they need your permission to react to you like this, they have learned it from MANY other places.) And yet when I prepare myself and get an expected negative outcome, I am not only more prepared to deal with it, but I am even MORE prepared to deal with the ones where I can't predict the outcome because I have already practiced.

With my daughters, I like to facilitate failure in a safe way when no one will be physically or emotionally hurt. There's value in stepping back and letting them figure things out. For example, my daughter wanted to make muffins recently, so I said, "Go for it!" She's never made muffins before and there was no way it was going to go smoothly without my assistance, but I didn't want to force myself into the situation. I wanted to send the message that I trusted her to ask when she needed help. I wanted her to mess up a little, make some mistakes and know that I would be there if she wanted my support. At the end of the day, it's just muffins she could ruin, but the goal is know-how and confidence, not a clean kitchen or tasty muffins.

Our oldest daughter hates getting up in the morning. She always sleeps in and it's a battle to get ready for school, so I gave her full control of her morning routine. For the first couple of days, she was late for school and she didn't like being late. It was a natural consequence of her choices, though, and she learned her lesson. Is she still a sleepyhead? Of course! But now she is the fastest from feet to floor and out the door. She may sleep in more than the others, but she's not late anymore.

Here are some of the situations that you can prepare for to let your kids fail.

They under-prepare for a test, let them fail and don't get mad when it happens.

They get their butts kicked in a sporting activity, let them be disappointed, don't try to fix it.

They are about to get their heart broken by a first crush, don't warn them, let them feel it.

Obviously there are extremes when they are under-preparing for a test to determine if they can pass a grade, or they are flipping out screaming at a soccer referee because they lost. We are talking about mild negative outcomes. If you can recognize the moments when these situations present themselves, you are ten steps ahead of the response and recovery actions, and you are helping build their resiliency at the same time. When I prepare myself ahead of time, I am able to remain calm and ask what they learned from the experience. What went wrong? What would she do differently next time?

CHAPTER 11 TAKE HOME

- Take some time to make a list of what your kids should fight for and what they shouldn't.
- Write down the techniques in which you want to teach them how to fight—like when to stand up for themselves.
- Ask your partner about the moments when you block them from parenting.
- Share with them the moments they block you.
- Think about the fears you have passed down to your kids.
- Consider how you tell your kids to think vs. helping them think through an issue.
- Do you allow your kids to have bad moods and disrespectful tones? What are your limits?
- Think about how you talk to your kids about failure.

CHAPTER 12

FAILURE

12.1 HOW TO BSK FAILURE

I feel like there is an elephant in the room that we need to address. There is a popular idea that has been going around that failure doesn't really exist. Some of the most famous, successful icons of all time have openly supported this notion.

"There is no such thing as failure. There are only results."

TONY ROBBINS

"I have not failed. I have just found 10,000 ways that won't work."

THOMAS EDISON

"There is no such thing as failure. Failure is just life trying to move us in another direction."

OPRAH

I hate to disagree with Oprah, but I take a different angle. The idea that failure doesn't exist is not only bullshit, it's dangerous.

Failure exists. How do we know it exists? Because it hurts. It can cause both physical and emotional pain. For the leaders, speakers and parents that I work with, we talk about failure all the time. Failure to produce results, failure in teamwork, failures in leadership, failure in families, failures in self.

We talk about the consequences of failure. Failure can cost people their jobs. Failure can cost people their relationships. Those are very real circumstances to work with, so to say failure doesn't exist is to negate a very human element, a very human emotion that we need to learn to work through.

When people fail and say to themselves "I'm not good enough, I am not smart enough, I am not worthy enough," that fear of failure can be absolutely paralyzing. You see it when people get up on stage and lose their words, it comes from fear. When leaders suffer from analysis paralysis when they are going through so much information, so much data it's because they are scared to make the wrong choice so they don't make any choice at all.

Here is what I think about failure. Not only does failure exist, but it is unavoidable. Failure is inevitable. And only by coming to terms with the idea that failure is inevitable are we going to be able to move past it.

The only way to get through a fear is to face it. You have to be able to out-brave that fear. You have to be able to out-smart that fear. You have to think about it and come up with strategies to move past it. And, when failure occurs, you have to have self-compassion and extend some kindness to yourself.

I get it when people say that failure doesn't exist. They are focused on what comes next. How are you going to respond and react to that failure? They are saying that you shouldn't get hung up on failures, you should learn from them and keep going. I agree with all of those ideas. But to say that failure doesn't exist removes a huge part of learning about persistence, we have to learn what our next steps are. We have to find that knowledge. We need to get ourselves up, dust ourselves off, and move on to whatever success we are looking for.

So here is the point we are going to work from.

- Failure is real.
- Failure is inevitable.
- Failure is ok.

Now we can look at how to bring brave, smart and kind tactics into our system so we can use it to overcome, learn from, and accept failure.

> Failure is not a consequence of wrong decisions; failure is an inevitability of action. The more actions you take, the greater the number of failures you have. It's math.

It isn't a revelation to say that failure is something that we all go through. "Nobody is perfect" is a go-to statement for good friends who console anyone dealing with the guilt and/or shame of failure. The difficulty is coming to terms with the failure and then figuring out how to fix it, or at least doing your best to fix it so that your consciousness spends less time in the past and starts to look towards the future where success happens. Don't get too excited, it's not only success that happens in the future, failure happens there again as well.

"So many of us choose our path out of fear disguised as practicality. What we really want seems impossibly out of reach and ridiculous to expect so we never ask the universe for it... My father could have been a great comedian, but he didn't believe that that was possible for him, and so he made a conservative choice. Instead, he got a safe job as an accountant, and when I was twelve years old, he was let go from that safe job and our family had to do whatever we could to survive. I learned many great lessons from my father, not the least of which was that you can fail at what you don't want, so you might as well take a chance on doing what you love."

JIM CARREY, 2014

I love the idea of failing at what you love because it helps me, at least in part, to release a certain fear of failure. Think about it. If you make decisions based on fear of failure, your goal is simply "don't fail." In that case, when you fail, it means that you made the "wrong" choice. Accepting that failing is merely a rest stop on the side of EVERY path, means that you are able to seek what you truly love with the courage and knowledge that you'll mess up on the way. "Right" or "wrong" choices no longer apply.

But how do we get through failure without feeling like losers? Well I think there are two answers to that.

First of all, odds are that you have felt and/or will feel like a loser at some point because you failed. And no matter how confident a person says they are with failure; they have either felt like a loser at some point OR have not raised the stakes in their game to fail at something significant. The greater the risk, the bigger the potential success AND the bigger the potential failure.

Secondly, don't forget our job is to lead by GREAT example. Teach our kids that they have a choice—to fail forward or to fail backwards. How do we accept failure, how do we learn from failure, how are we ok with failure, how are we not so ok with failure?

12.2 OWNING YOUR FAILURES

I have already told you about the quote book my mom gave me when I was about to become a father. The first said, "When your children picture integrity, make sure they picture you." The second quote was something along the lines of, "If a child offers you something, accept it every time. Even if it is a rock, it is all they have, and they are choosing to give it to you." This struck me on a deep level. A child offering something to you should fill you with a sense of worthiness. If someone with "nothing" gives you "something" treat it like "everything."

Children learn a sense of ownership early in life—they don't want anyone else hugging their mom, they don't want anyone else playing with their toys. And as parents, we reinforce their claims all the time even without knowing it, that's YOUR pacifier, that is YOUR food, that is YOUR seat in the car, get into YOUR bed. When I find my desk reorganized, food and drinks next to MY laptop, or permanent markers laying open on MY desk, I ask the girls to get out of MY office and not to touch MY work things. I give them all the reasons, but they don't listen. They want to be where I am or where my stuff is because it's cooler than their stuff. And then when they hold on to THEIR stuff, we tell them they need to share—we encourage the crazy.

And if kids can't grasp the nuances of possession, they definitely don't understand the idea of loss in relation to value. If you or I lose a ring we got out of a Cracker Jack Box, or for my European friends a Kinder Egg, we say "no big deal, it wasn't worth anything." If a child loses a plastic spider ring, we cover our eyes and wait for the mushroom cloud.

Adults have a perception of value, and cheap toys with no emotional significance rank on the low end of what we value. If we lose a wedding ring, which typically equates to a high emotional and/or monetary value, it can create a strong feeling of loss and failure, much like a child losing anything. When we lose money on an investment, wreck a car, hurt a friend, lose a job—those can lead to failures that can affect the way we make future decisions. Children don't have our learned understanding of value and they don't have the capacity to mitigate a feeling of failure over what we perceive to be the smallest of issues.

This is why children have such a hard time dealing with their own failures. Children do not deal with grey areas. They exist in a black and white world. Try taking away a pair of sharp scissors from a two-year old and watch the insanity ensue. "Cause and effect" are wasted on them. I try to help them deal with failure by helping them see that something isn't a big deal, but my girls don't have the perspective of what IS a big deal. To them a big deal is that one of their sisters stole their stuffed animal, or that one of them has an extra potato chip in their bowl. Fairness is another concept that only applies in relation to your own experiences.

They understand "have or have not." They understand "success or failure." WHY they failed doesn't matter just as why they shouldn't play with scissors doesn't matter. This doesn't mean you don't need to explain the why to them, it just means that they won't understand. Explaining the "why" is playing the long game.

I first noticed this reaction to failure when Alexandra was five years old and started to jump rope. She saw other kids jumping in a smooth rhythmic motion and it looked so easy. So when she grabbed the rope by the handles, threw her arms around in the air like a wounded pigeon and smacked herself in the face with the rope. She threw the rope down with contempt and tears and decided that "I can't" was the only possible response there was. That was when I knelt down and gave her a nurturing hug, and rubbed her back. I raised her chin up gently to look me right in the eye and with my most inspirational, father-like voice told her, "Sweetheart I know you can do this, you just have to keep trying." She looked up at me, paused for a second and said "NO, I'LL NEVER EVER BE ABLE TO DO IT!" and stomped away in dramatic fashion—leaving me kneeling on the ground looking over at our Golden Retriever before she too walked away with zero sympathy.

Naturally I brought Alex back, gave her a couple of pointers, and she proceeded to hit herself (and me) in the head many times before declaring that she will never jump rope again. Fast forward a couple years and I became the proud father of an extremely talented jump-roping child whose more frequent frustration became that Emmeline would steal the jump rope to use as a leash for Josephine (which she ties around her belt loop to drag her around the living room).

Alexandra's capacity for failure at that time was non-existent, but it does serve as the go-to story I share with her when she gets frustrated because she got her math homework wrong and starts getting angry and uses comments like, "Daddy, I am not smart." I say, "Remember the jump rope. You didn't get that right away either, keep working on it." I tell her that the only not-smart thing to do would be to stop trying. And this is where our definitions come in handy.

Remember how we defined "smart." For our family, it does not have anything to do with getting good grades. Smart is to make good choices.

Smart is intention. Sometimes it takes imagination, sometimes it takes common sense, sometimes it's looking at something from a new angle.

12.3 SHAME AND GUILT IN FAILURE

In her book, *Daring Greatly*, Brené Brown makes an insightful point in the difference between shame and guilt. To her credit, she makes hundreds of insightful points on the topic, but this one has stuck with me through the BSK journey. From Brown's research she concludes that while shame is something that is detrimental to how people function, there is a healthy way that people deal with shortcomings and that is through guilt. Shame involves being disappointed in who you are. Guilt involves being disappointed in what you have done. Who you are isn't changeable. What you do is changeable.

Guilt = healthy

Shame = unhealthy

Because of the way that we define brave, smart and kind, it is much easier for kids to know when they are doing something that is right and when they are doing something that is wrong. What is more difficult is when they struggle, they confuse their DOING with BEING.

"Doing" implies that you made a mistake.

"Being" implies that you ARE the mistake.

I know I am wordsmithing right now, but I believe this distinction is incredibly important. When my girls are doing positive things, I tell them they are "being" brave, smart or kind. When we are talking about the struggles, we talk about what they are "doing." Positive = being. Negative = doing. When my girls hurt someone and say, "Dad, I feel really bad about what I did," I often respond with "Good. If you didn't feel bad about it, then I would worry. Now what are you going to do about it?"

Guilt is easier to correct. If you do something wrong, you recognize it, respond to it, and recover from it. Shame is much more difficult to correct. Shame has deep roots and it comes from a feeling of not BEING enough. What a powerful sentiment when you think about it.

Who you ARE is not something that gets fixed. Guilt, however, is correctable, there is a definitive course of action for someone to fix a problem, or to learn from a mistake. Even if you try to course-correct after you feel shame for who you are, that part of you can linger.

The intense emotional connection between a parent and their child makes it a breeding ground for shame. We need to be so careful of the implicit messages we are sending through our tone of voice, body language and facial expressions. For example, I used to feel a lot of anger as a kid. I remember a day when I was around fourteen years old that I yelled at my mom harshly and made her cry. She sat down on the stairs and asked, "Why are you yelling at me? What did I do that was so wrong?" In truth, I wasn't yelling at her because of something that she did. I was yelling because of what I felt. She wasn't crying because of the things I was saying, but because the angry, aggressive tone I was using made her feel as if she wasn't enough.

Our reactions are indicators of how we feel inside about ourselves—shame, guilt, weakness, selfishness, not being trustworthy, jealousy, contempt. Those feelings often seep out and project onto others, even when we don't mean for them to. Sometimes the language we use accidentally ignites shame. Have you ever said aloud, "I'm so stupid! I can't believe I did that!"? Our kids overhear those words and take that language upon themselves.

It broke my heart when Alex would come to me in tears and say "Daddy, I am not smart." I had to repeatedly define and tell her how smart she is. It wasn't until after I read Brené Brown that I realized that I was part of the problem.

As a father, when I tell my daughters that I want them to BE brave, smart and kind; and then they DO something that isn't brave, smart or kind, it's easy for them to think that they AREN'T brave, that they AREN'T smart, that they AREN'T kind. I had to rework my own language to say, "Alex you ARE smart, you just did something that was dumb." Not to dump on the beloved Forrest Gump quote, "Stupid is as stupid does," but I don't believe that in the least. "Is" and "does" are very separate things. So as I tried to self-correct the unintentional value-shaming in Alex, she kept coming back to me saying, "Daddy I am not smart, I am stupid."

In early 2020, I was having a rough day. I don't remember what it was about, but I was in the kitchen with my wife when I heard pounding steps coming down the stairs. (Alex is more of an elephant when she walks than a gazelle.) She came into the kitchen and said, "Dad, I am so stupid!" I interrupted her story with an annoyed look and tone and said, "Alex! Come on my dear! You can't keep…" then she quickly held her hands up to stop me and jumped in, "No no no, that's not what I mean. It's not that I AM stupid, I just did something stupid."

After she told me about the small, unimportant mistake she made, she walked out of the kitchen and my arms shot up in the air like I was Rocky on the steps of the Philadelphia Museum of Art. "YES!" I exclaimed in a whisper. My wife looked up at me like I was crazy, which isn't an uncommon occurrence in our home. But for this moment in time, it was a simple, yet significant victory. This was the first time Alexandra made the distinction between who she was (smart) and what she had done.

So the trick here is to see our failures more as a consequence of our actions as opposed to a consequence of being ourselves. That isn't to say we don't need to look at what we need or want to improve as people. In listening to a TED speaker who said, "Life will present you with the opportunities to learn the things you need to learn— multiple times if necessary." When you start to see the loops in your life, the repeated mistakes, then it's for you to break the cycle of what you DO so you can continue to be who you ARE. The beautiful part of this concept is that we get to be more comfortable with failure. Now that doesn't mean we get to be apathetic. Becoming complacent with failure is very different from becoming comfortable in that space. Complacency implies a level of satisfaction. Comfortable implies that you are not paralyzed by failure, that you are able to think and act in a safe space.

12.4 CHOICES

You can make all the right choices for all the right reasons and still fail at what you were trying to accomplish. I am going to dive back into my geeky side for a second with a simple analogy of playing blackjack at a casino.

All good blackjack players know the odds of the game. If the dealer is showing a six, and you have a sixteen you are going to stay because the odds are that the dealer is going to bust and you are going to win. (The odds are actually 42% that the dealer will bust but 62% that you will bust.) So you make the right decision to stay, for the right reason given that the odds are against you winning. And then what can happen is that the dealer's other card is a five and then a ten and they get twenty-one, while you get an ulcer and need to take out a loan to pay for your kid's orthodontic work. That example might not be the best, but for the non-blackjack playing readers, it means that you made the right choice for the right reason and still lost.

Granted this example is from a game where we can know the risks before entering the game, but guess what—life has risks, leadership has risks, parenthood is riddled with risks! Do you remember when your kid was ready to ride their bike the first time without training wheels? You were running next to them dodging other people in the park, jumping dogs, getting sticks out of the way. You were trying to minimize the risk that your kid would get hurt. Has anyone NOT fallen off their bike and gotten hurt here? Emmeline got going so fast on her bike that I couldn't keep up. So I had a great idea—I put on my rollerblades so I could be right behind her when she fell. It was genius because I wouldn't have to do a hundred metre sprint to get to her. And it worked great, until I was directly behind her when she saw a squirrel and screeched to a halt to watch it run up a tree. We learned a valuable lesson in how fast a four-year-old on a bike can stop compared to how fast a 210 lbs. man on roller blades can stop. That's called physics and it ended in snot-crying, cut skin, and band-aids—and Emmeline got a little hurt too.

You can make decisions to increase your odds of success.

You can make those decisions for all the right reasons, good intentions, experiences, lessons learned AND you can still fail. The illusion of control is something that gives someone incredible confidence and at the same time can make you crash back into reality. And the higher the confidence you have that you are RIGHT, the harder the crash when you realize that you have failed. However, the higher the confidence you have that you will eventually and inevitably FAIL, the more prepared you are when the failure happens. That doesn't mean that it won't hurt, it just means that those who understand that failure, complete or partial, is inevitable—those are the ones who have the resiliency to bounce back from it.

You essentially have two options in failure:

- Option One: You fail to try, don't even attempt it.

- Option Two: You try and know that you are going to fail along the way.

SO, if you are someone who wants to get off your butt and do something, know that you will fail along the way.

12.5 BSK IT!

Now we need to take what we know about failure and see if our system of values is able to help us through it. Are we able to BSK our failures?

Brave is the ability to stand up to your fears, danger, and difficulty. In failure, people can see fear on both sides. What if I do something and fail? Am I able to accept that failure? What are the consequences of that action? Those are all healthy questions to ask yourself.

The second aspect of failure to come to terms with is what if I DON'T do something and fail? Am I able to accept that failure? What are the consequences of inaction? Also healthy questions to ask.

Here is where BSK can come into play.

Brave is the ability to admit that you are afraid and still be intentional with your decision. You are only able to do that if you face your fear.

Smart is the ability to open your mind. Are you able to reflect? Can you gather information? Can you apply perspective? Can you come up with solutions?

Kind is the ability to open your heart. Can you forgive yourself and others? Can you talk to the people affected by your mistake? Failures can often lead to uncomfortable, necessary conversations. Lean into that kindness.

Like all of our other lessons, this only works if BSK has been defined and if it is discussed. How do you talk about your failures? How do you talk to your children about theirs? Is disapproval the first reaction you show? If so, you don't have to worry about talking to your kids about failure, because they won't come to you when they fail. They will go to the person that they feel safe with.

The bottom line is, if we want to teach our children about BSK through trial and error, we need to create a safe space for them to fail without judgement or massive consequences. We want to talk to our kids about making mistakes and normalize it because a) we want them to feel comfortable sharing with us, b) we want to remove the shame from it, and c) when they fail, we get to teach.

> *"The goal is to create a circle of safety when people trust and share their successes and failures, what they know and what they don't know."*
>
> **SIMON SINEK**

CHAPTER 12 TAKE HOME

- Take a long look at how you deal with failure.
- Think about the strategies you have to move past failure.
- How good are you at apologizing?
- Think about your go-to stories for failure and think of your lessons learned.
- Which stories do your tell your kids?
- Consider if you use shame or guilt when something goes wrong and how your messages are perceived by your kids.
- Pay attention next time your kids mess up and your reaction. If you are really brave, you can ask them to role play you when they mess up. What would they say?

SECTION FIVE

OK
BUT HOW?

CHAPTER 13

MUSCLE MEMORY

In 1996, I took a course at Jamestown Community College in Western New York to get my certification to be an Emergency Medical Technician. I never intended to work as an EMT, I wanted to be a firefighter, and this was a first step. Inevitably I chose a different path, but the EMT course has proven to be invaluable because it taught me how to properly deal with all sorts of emergency situations not just from a medical standpoint but also how to deal with people who are going through immediate mental and physical trauma.

Simply as a passerby of events, I have been able to help everyone from people in car accidents, with neck injuries, concussions, sprained and broken bones, to a random man who turned blue choking on a hotdog, my daughter turning blue choking on a Dorito, to a young lady who had a two-inch wooden splinter in her bum cheek after riding a props crate on a theater stage (yes, true story). Most recently I was able to give CPR to an elderly neighbor who was unconscious in his hallway—while dealing with his wife who was understandably distraught along with another neighbor who was paralyzed by the situation.

None of what I am saying is for bragging purposes. I can point to a handful of my own experiences, but EMTs, firefighters, nurses, doctors, and others handle these issues on a daily basis without hesitation. We deservedly marvel at their poise under pressure, knowing exactly what to do in any given circumstance. And the reason they know exactly what to do in any given circumstance is because they train their butts off in order to handle our emergencies. They are called upon to overcome their own and others' fear, apply their trained knowledge, and help people in need. They are trained to be brave, smart and kind.

The preparation it takes to go into an emergency responder role has been so effective because it makes you understand the importance of quickly reacting to an emergency. For the EMT course, the content was constructed and taught in such a way that it was easy to remember and drilled into us so when we needed it, we could use it. The training is so effective that I could still call on it twenty-seven years later when I saw someone lying on the ground unconscious.

I am giving examples above of the most obvious of careers that need to think on their feet, however there are many others. Athletes need to think and act on their feet, so they learn and train before in order to play instinctively. Pilots need to think and act on their feet, so they learn and train in simulators repeatedly before they apply it to flying. Teachers need to think and act on their feet, so they learn and train before they get into classrooms. (It might be a rumor, but I heard teachers train with feral cats and angry racoons to prepare them for real life situations with our children.)

The model for success isn't complex; learn the concepts and practices, train in simulated/controlled environments to apply those concepts and practices under intense pressure, continue to learn on-the-job and execute to the best of your ability. If we want people to perform in the heat of the moment, these are the steps we take to get them there.

So it amazes me that as parents, we don't prepare for the actual parenting part. It's not to say that there aren't parenting courses out there, but quite frankly, I don't know many people who have taken them. And for those who have, it's typically because they feel something has gone wrong with them as a parent OR they feel something is wrong with their child and THEN they seek guidance. Very rarely do we prepare ourselves as parents before we need to actually parent. Boy does that sound like a recipe for disaster for something where the stakes are so high. How would you like to go to a surgeon who is reading, "How to be a Better Doctor"? What if as you buckle your seatbelt when the airline host says, "Welcome to Flight 478. Our pilots are giving it their best shot today. They haven't flown this particular type of plane before, but don't worry, THEIR parents were pilots too."

As a father, I am responsible for these miniature humans every day. I am not intentionally trying to raise doctors or rocket scientists or professional hockey players, but I am trying to raise good humans who feel like they are able to overcome their challenges, who can think critically and make their own choices, and who can show kindness to others and, just as importantly, show kindness to themselves. I want them to be prepared for life's circumstances and then they can call on their values as they need them either consciously or subconsciously. I'm not naive. I know that they can't possibly be prepared for everything life is going to throw at them, but that doesn't mean I won't give it my best. And hopefully what I am able to do is to give them the mental and physical tools to make the connections when they need them. BSK gives me better guidelines to make me feel like I am doing it right. So what do we need to do now?

- First, make it applicable to adults.

- Second, make it applicable to kids.

If we get ourselves and our children in the conscious habit of making the right choices for the right reasons, then we create the patterns for subconscious action based on the original intent. The starting point for that is to determine what the "right" reasons are. For me that is making the brave, smart, kind connections.

There are three lessons to be learned here:

1. Get in the habit of acting from your positive values.

2. Get your kids in the habit of acting from their positive values.

3. Sign up for an EMT course at your local community college immediately.

13.1 CHIN UP, BRAIN ON, HEART OPEN

The main goal of teaching BSK is to make it actionable so I try to use language that plants that vision into my kids' brains. I've developed catch-phrases with my daughters to serve as a reminder at times when I sense opportunities for them to exercise their BSK values.

When talking about managing your "brave," I use the term, "chin up vs. chin down." When your chin is up, you can see what's coming. You face the fear, danger, and difficulty. When your chin is down, your perspective is limited, you can't face the challenge.

When managing your "smart," we talk about having your "brain on vs. brain off." When your brain is on you are able to process information. There is input and there is output. When your brain is off, there isn't an ability to think critically and output is frozen.

When managing your "kind," we discuss having your "heart open vs. heart closed." When your heart is open you are able to receive others and you are able to give of yourself. When your heart is closed, you are unable to accept what others are able to give, and what is in you can't get out.

In this section, we'll talk about how you can use these cues (or come up with your own) to teach BSK. The more we remind our kids to lead with their values, the more BSK will become ingrained in their muscle memory so that on the occasions when we're not around to offer guidance, our kids will already have a strong sense of where to start.

13.1.1 CHIN UP

When we don't know what's going to happen, sometimes we start to look down because it makes us feel safe and secure, but in reality, the opposite happens. We lose sight of the big picture. When we keep our chins up we pay attention to what is going on around us. We still may be afraid of what is going to happen, but it allows us to be more knowledgeable. And the next time that you find yourself in the same situation you will be able to handle it better, with less fear.

If you keep your chin down, you will still get scared, except the next time something happens, you won't know what you are looking for, you'll keep your head down again and be scared the same way. We often are scared of the unknown. Fear keeps us from taking our next steps. Many fears are overcome (or the process of overcoming fear has begun) after we face our fear the first time. Why is that? Because next time, we know what is coming. Keeping your chin up is one way to be more brave because you get to see what is in front of you. The more you know, the braver you become.

My daughters love to scare each other. Emmeline will hide around a corner and when Alex walks past, Em will jump out at her. And it works, and it's hilarious. Well what happens when Alex KNOWS that Emmeline is hiding around the corner and is going to try to scare her? She prepares herself, she EXPECTS that Emmeline will jump out, and when it happens she isn't as scared. She can now manage her fear and plan a response, which makes her feel empowered.

If we know our kids will feel fear and rely on their bravery, as parents, we need to understand what they fear, what they believe is dangerous, and what is difficult for them. Want to know the best way to do that? Ask them.

Ask your kids to think about what scares them and why. Maybe it's talking to someone they don't know or taking a test when they don't know what it covers. Perhaps it's attending a new school, joining a new sports team, or taking a new class. It's so important to talk about fear with our children. We want to demystify fear, danger, and difficulty for them. Being scared and having hardships is normal and we can prepare for it.

13.1.2 BRAIN ON

In order to manage critical thinking and understand how to keep a brain turned on, we need to consider what it means if a brain is turned off. To help you understand the effects of a turned off brain, I'm going to throw a little biology at you. Bear with me.

Let's imagine your child is in a state of meltdown, either because of sadness, anger, exhaustion, fear, or overstimulation. You know what it looks like—fists clenched, feet stomping, tears flowing, face red, probably yelling or sobbing incoherently. I'm sure you've been there with your child once or twice. As parents, our natural reaction is to either reason with them, "This is not appropriate behavior. Your sister did not mean to hurt you. Calm down." Or to yell back, "This isn't how we act! STOP IT!" How often do these tactics work? Never, right?! Your child goes on to scream and stomp their feet as your frustration rises and your patience disappears.

Maybe your child doesn't tantrum, but goes into withdrawal. They stare at you with a blank look on their face, not even acknowledging you as you question them, "What happened? What's wrong?" As they continue to ignore your attempts to show empathy and support, your frustration rises and your patience wanes.

In both of these cases, your child's reaction isn't personal. Their brain is actually turned off. Biologically!

When your child is in a DEFCON 1 state of stress (cue tantrum or deadpan facial expression), all of the blood in their prefrontal cortex (the area of your brain dedicated to logic and reasoning) rushes to their basal ganglia, which is also known as the reptilian brain (the area responsible for the stress response—flight, flight or freeze). So, here you are trying to reason with your child, when they are biologically not capable of reasoning. All of the blood has literally left that part of the brain! They cannot process what you are saying. And, if you choose to yell at them for not listening or for losing control of their emotions, guess what happens? Your behavior adds more stress and insecurity to the situation and prolongs the process of your child calming down and turning their brain back on.

Knowing this fact has been a life-saver for me. In my earlier parenting years, I would sit with Alex while she was going bat-ass crazy and keep doling out punishments. If she was screaming I would sit there and say, "Ok you've lost your screen time for a day, keep going." And she would keep going. "You have lost it for two days, keep going." And she would keep going. "You have lost it for a week, keep going." And she would... you get the picture.

Now I have learned to disengage from destructive actions. If they have reached that level of "brain off," what I do is sit with them. Recently, one of my kiddos had just lost it, her thinking brain was completely off and she was in fight mode. I calmly asked her to come into my office. Yes, this takes some persuading most of the time. Then I had her sit on the floor, and I sat on the floor with her. It takes a couple minutes, but when her brain turned back on there was a noticeable difference in how she was sitting with me. Her breathing calmed, and she glanced in my direction a couple of times. I was laying on my back waiting for her, and I asked if she wanted to come sit with me. She didn't hesitate. She came and put her head on my chest and cuddled right in. Her brain was on, her heart was open, then we got to talk.

Another tactic I used from when they were babies and crying in my arms was to deliberately slow down my own breathing. While their chests were going in and out at a rapid pace, I would try to slow mine to half their speed. They'd take two breaths, I'd take one. I would slow down my breathing, and they would start to match it. I don't know if this is science or conditioning, but it worked. And it still works. If they are in a panic, I slow my breathing around them until they match it.

Once they are able to turn their brains on again, we get to talk about the needs and the emotions that led to the actions. We get to parent, but that doesn't happen until a brain is on.

To keep brains turned on, here are some other tactics:

- Limit brainless screen time
- Engage them with thought-provoking screen time
- Take care of their bodies (food, exercise, etc.)

- Give them problems to solve

- Let them work with you

- Read their books with them

- Read your books in front of them

- Play games regularly

13.1.3 HEART OPEN

When I first defined what "beautiful" meant to my girls, I was frustrated by the lack of kindness I saw in the world. I wanted them to be able to live a life with an abundance of kindness. The more I thought about my life and the people I've met, the more that frustration seemed unjustified. I know, and have been shaped by, some incredibly kind humans. When I traveled around the world living in host families, every single one of them welcomed me into their homes. And every day, at school, on sports teams, in the community, I meet countless people who are kind to me and my family.

I had to ask myself why I felt so frustrated, and the answer is twofold. Firstly, for all the stories we see of kindness there are many more sensational stories we hear of a lack of kindness. Secondly, kids can be mean.

I work in the field of leadership, that means that I try to keep up with new theories around business leadership, political leadership, and community leadership. For my own part, I also put that into family leadership. When you seek out positive stories, people love to give you negative stories. Not to mention in politics, they are ALL negative stories as people try to break others down to build themselves up. So maybe my frustration in that area is justified.

The second reason, I witnessed the lack of kindness in my family growing up. Don't get me wrong, there was a lot of love, but I witnessed an ugly divorce. I witnessed attacks on my parents from people who they once considered family. I witnessed, and took part in, unkind acts between my sister and I that extended to our parents as well. This was an overwhelming part of my childhood, and I didn't want it to be part of my kids' childhood too. Yes families fight, I get it. And yes it's ok to say we want to do better. I want better for my kids.

So, the words "open heart" are a reminder for me and for my girls to keep noticing acts of kindness, to keep engaging in acts of kindness and make it a priority in our lives. It's also to be able to notice when people have their hearts closed and what that looks like.

When we have an open heart, we are able to both receive and give. Receiving kindness means asking for help, accepting compliments, feeling like you are worthy of love. Giving kindness is based more on what your kindness value looks like to you. Mine is to "take care of others" so an open heart allows me to find ways to do that in a healthy way. Whatever way you define kindness for yourself, keeping your heart open allows you to live in that positive value and extend it to others.

When we have a closed heart, we have a hard time extending our kindness outward. We close circles, are unable to receive kindness, self-protect when there isn't danger, etc. Closed hearts aren't hard to find. It happens when we get hurt, or when we feel we have extended ourselves too far. There are plenty of reasons for it. The best remedy I have found is to surround yourself with others with open hearts. Open hearts are contagious. Unfortunately, closed hearts are contagious too. Be aware of who you surround yourself with AND know that you are that example to your kids as well.

One of my favorite children's books on how we affect others is *How Full is Your Bucket?* by Tom Rath and Mary Reckmeyer. It talks about how we all have buckets that are filled or emptied by what is going on around us and how we are able to use that perspective to lift ourselves and others up. It is worth the read for parents AND it's fantastic language you can use with your kids.

One way I help open my kiddos' hearts is with sticky notes. I'm kind of a sticky note addict. Every time I go on a trip, I leave each of my girls a note on her bed telling them how much they are loved, or how wonderful I think they are. When I get home late some nights, Emmeline leaves me sticky notes on her bed.

Another way we do it is with bead jars. When the girls do something kind, they get a bead. When the bead jar gets full they get a reward. What happens now is that they look for ways to be kind, and they notice the kind things their sisters do too. This is called operant conditioning, or the idea that actions that are followed by a positive response will be repeated in the future. The more we do this, especially with kids at a young age, the more the neural-pathways are formed in their brains. The actions from these neural-pathways are what we call habits. I don't know about you, but if I can get my kids in the habit of being brave, smart and kind, then we are winning the game.

When talking through the concepts of positive reinforcement, I have heard the arguments that some parents want their children to "do the right thing" because it is the right thing, not because they are going to get rewarded for it. And I don't necessarily disagree. I want my kids to be kind because they are genuinely kind. I want them to be smart because they want to put in the effort and they take pride in making good choices. I want my kids to understand their fear and raise their level of consciousness to make brave decisions and take brave actions because they feel empowered to do so. I want them to "do the right thing" for the right reason too AND how will they know what the right thing is? It starts with defining it for them, and then rewarding the positive actions.

Creating muscle memory comes from consistent actions. Positive consistency builds positive habits such as saying thank you, giving of your time and attention, pointing out the wonderful moments, being grateful. Negative consistency builds negative habits like yelling, talking poorly about others, ignoring others while on your phone, and responding with sharp or harsh words, etc.

Which habits are you building and which do you want to build?

- Using caring words
- Observing and acknowledging their kind acts
- Observing and acknowledging the kind acts of others
- Volunteering to help others
- Responding with curiosity
- Writing thank you cards

13.2 CREATING MEMORABLE MOMENTS

Back in chapter five, we talked about how emotions create memories. If it has taken you several weeks or months to read from there to here (yeah it happens to me too), let me remind you. When we are in a moment when we are processing emotion, the brain releases dopamine into our brain. Dopamine helps you bookmark your memories which is why we remember September 11, 2001, and not September 11 of last year.

Now think back to your childhood, to some of those moments that shaped you. Do you remember where you were? Do you remember who you were with? Do you remember what people said or did? Now, some of these things you will remember (and knowing that our long-term memories usually start when we are around four years old), there are going to be many things that have shaped you that you don't remember at all.

Why does this matter as a parent? The strength of our values comes from how we apply our values to ourselves, and to those around us. In *Leadership*, James MacGregor Burns looks at the young lives of some of the world's most influential (positive and negative) leaders. Gandhi, Lenin, Bismark, Hitler, Eleanor Roosevelt. He, and many others like Sigmund Freud and Carl Jung, talk about how personalities are shaped at a very young age. Alexis de Tocqueville says, "The entire of man, so to speak, to be seen in the cradle of the child." Essentially everyone agrees on something that to us now is such a basic statement, that children are shaped by their parents. Did I need to quote those other people for us to understand this point? Of course not, but we aren't to the real point yet. We need to understand how that happens.

The moments of intense emotions are the ones that shape us. "Us" means our children too. Now realize how emotionally charged children can be. I can remember some very influential moments of my childhood. I remember my parents' divorce and my "Uncle" Mike saying that he understood and that it wasn't my fault and that if I ever needed someone to talk to, that he would be there for me. And then I remember him getting divorced from my aunt and never hearing from him again. I remember that when I make promises to kids.

I remember my older cousin Scott always telling me that he loved me—he never said goodbye without saying it. My brain took those emotions and created a bookmark. Now, whether it's my family or my closest male and female friends, we say "I love you" to each other. This isn't for the sake of parenting, it's to make sure the people in our lives know how much we care about them. AND I want my girls to see it.

CHAPTER 13 TAKE HOME

- Think about the positive habits you want your children to have.
- Notice what your kids are struggling with and talk about the courage it takes to overcome.
- Approach their next tantrum with a calm mind and a calm voice. Give them time for their brains to turn back on.
- Identify the times when your kids' hearts close. See if approaching them with an open heart helps.
- Recognize the emotional moments and know your kids are making memories. React in a way you want them to remember you by.

CHAPTER 14

WHAT NEXT?

At this point in the book, we've covered a lot of theory behind BSK—where it fits in the world and why values-based parenting is an intentional way to raise children. I've shared my experience and advice, but you may still be thinking, "Okay PJ. I've learned some things here. We had some laughs and some tears, but what am I supposed to do now? What can I do tomorrow to implement BSK in our lives?"

Well, it's where we started in chapter one and it is going to be the place we end here. There are three areas you need to pay attention to, to make BSK actionable.

14.1 STEP ONE: DEFINE BSK

Some of you might be saying, "For the love of all things holy, you've been telling us we need to define our values for thirteen chapters, but you never tell us how!" Well isn't this your lucky day, that is exactly what I am going to do now. We are going to walk you through the BSK Framework. First we will start with our adults. You can go to www.bravesmartkind.com/workbook and download our "Define your Values" workbook. There are instructions there, but I'll conceptualize them for you here so you know what you are getting into.

On the first page you are going to find six boxes. Use those boxes to answer these six questions.

1. **What are the top five qualities you look for in a leader you would willingly follow?**

    Let me qualify that question a bit. What we are looking for are the top characteristics of your ideal leader. You don't need to name the leader(s) you have in mind. I just want to know what makes you want to follow them. We say "willingly follow" because I am not necessarily looking for a boss or a manager who you were hired to work for. I want to know the leaders you choose to follow, and why.

2. **What are the top five qualities you look for in your closest friends?**

    Again, you don't have to list out the names of your friends, but I do want you to give this some thought. Who are the people that you choose to surround yourself with? Why do you like them? Why do you let them in closer than you let in others? What are your non-negotiables when it comes to friendship?

3. **What are the top five qualities you look for in a teammate?**

    We have teammates in our lives at so many levels—even if we don't notice it. Yes, we could be talking about work. We could be talking about a sports team. These could be people you volunteer with, members of a club, in a religious group, or people you would want to take on a project with. You might think that all of those people would have different qualities, and they might. Think about the qualities that you consistently look for.

4. Why do you fail?

The questions get a bit harder from here. I want to know why you fail, and more importantly, why you fail repeatedly. If you are having trouble with this one, think back at some of your more epic failures. Start telling the story of how you failed. Where we are trying to get to is what qualities in you cause you to fail. Stubbornness? Analysis paralysis? Procrastination? You tell us what those are. Remember from our chapter on failure that failure is real, is inevitable, and it's ok. We just need to talk about it.

5. What makes you angry?

Out of all the questions, this is where I get the most push back. Some people say, "I don't really get angry." And to that I say, bullshit. You may not get aggressive, but those are different things. Anger is an emotion that we feel, and it's completely natural. Call it frustrated if that makes you feel better. There is also a range of anger here. I get angry at injustice in the world, where people are discriminated against for the color of their skin, gender, religion, etc. I also get angry because not a single one of my girls (wife included), puts a toothpaste cap back on and it's a mess! Seriously, how bubbling easy is it to put the cap back on instead of that dried up glob of <breathe>. That's the range. Global issues all the way down to pet peeves.

6. What do you like about you?

I like to end on this positive note. What qualities in yourself do you take pride in? Yes, it's ok to like yourself, and we need to hear a lot more about it. Some people come from families and cultures who have a hard time talking about themselves. We have been taught to be humble—which in many cases is a great characteristic. AND like all of our qualities, any of them taken to an extreme becomes negative. Let's release that inhibition for now and open up. If you have a hard time, close your eyes and think about your best friend, the person who knows you best. What would they tell me are the best qualities in you?

Now we have a little work to do. Let me explain the questions.

For the questions about the leaders, friends and teammates, you probably noticed a lot of the same words coming up. That is not only ok, it's exactly what we are looking for. We want to find the commonalities. This is a simple idea that we choose to surround ourselves with people who are like us. What we need to do is to find and group the similar words. If you have caring, giving, charitable, supportive, group those words together in one bucket. Likewise if you have adventurous, fun-loving, spontaneous, lump those together. This is where we start to make the distinction between our brave, our smart, and our kind values. Start to look for the ways you overcome, how you think critically, and how you treat others and yourself. If you have four or five buckets for now that is ok too. Know that we have hundreds of values inside of us. We are just looking for the top three because when we come to that fork in the road, we want to use our values to make our choices. If we have a top ten values list, it takes a while to make the choice AND we usually rely on our top three anyway.

Note that you may have some words that are outliers. If a word doesn't fit into a group, that is perfectly ok. Especially in teammates we specifically look for qualities we DON'T have. I know that I am a pretty disorganized person. When I have a team, I look for organized people to fill the gaps I am missing. I love those types of people, but I accepted a long time ago that I am not one of them.

For question four regarding failure. Remember that failure doesn't come because we don't have values, it comes because we have taken one value to an extreme. The words you wrote down are your "negative values". If you want to know what you stand for, take those characteristics that caused your failure and reverse engineer them to a positive value when used in moderation. If you wrote "stubborn," your value might be "dedicated." If you wrote "analysis paralysis" then your value might be "diligence." Fit those values in one of your buckets.

For question five regarding anger. When we get angry or frustrated there is a break in one of our values. If global injustice makes me angry, then I know that I value fairness, respect and taking care of others. If not closing the toothpaste cap infuriates me, that comes down to someone's indifference. If I wish people thought about something more, my value is intention. Put those words into buckets.

Lastly, take what you like about you and put those words into buckets as well. Usually at this point, our buckets are starting to come into better focus. One other helpful tip is IF you put the words brave, smart or kind down, challenge yourself to better define what that means to you. If you have any vague words, take the time to flesh them out. What is "kind" to you? I always tell people that the definition of the words matter so much more than the word itself. What kind is to you might be very different from what kind means to me.

There are more instructions in the workbook to help you define your values and understand the framework. As adults, it might be a challenge, but we can answer all of these questions. When it comes to our kids, finding their brave, smart, kind is a bit different. Most of it depends on their age. For my kiddos, I started this when the eldest were four and two years old. If you have older children in their teens, they may be able to answer the questions above. For younger kids they might have some ideas. If you ask your young ones, they will probably just look at you funny and ask you if they can have a popsicle before dinner. (The answer to that is yes by the way.)

What you really need to do is be observant. Find out what they take pride in and keep acknowledging them. See what they sincerely don't care about compared to what they just don't want you to know that they care about. Pay attention to what hurts them. Most importantly, know that they are growing and being shaped every single day. They don't need to fit into a box of the person that you think they are, and definitely not into the core values that you have defined for yourself. Give them time and be open to who they will become. Their brave won't be your brave. Their smart won't be your smart. Their kind won't be your kind. And that is ok.

14.2 STEP TWO: DISPLAY IT

There are debates in marketing circles about how many times a message needs to be seen or heard for it to sink in. Some people say three times. There is a "rule of seven." There are some that say twenty times. I am less concerned about the number of times and more intrigued with "as much as humanly possible without being rendered mute." Funny that right now you are probably thinking this is about how many times a child needs to see brave, smart and kind messages for them to register. Sorry, we aren't talking about kids yet, we are starting with you.

I don't have many pictures on my desk. I have one four by six-inch frame with the girls all sitting on a hammock eating ice cream in Spain. I have another with Violaine holding a tired bare-bottomed Joey as an infant. Then I have a letter-sized frame with my values and their definitions sitting square in front of me. Why would someone who talks about values all day have his values right in front of him? Because it helps me to know what I am focused on. It helps me keep my perspective. It helps me remember my negative values when I go too far.

On the back of that frame I have something else. It is a paper with 4,680 boxes on it. I have fifty-two boxes across, and ninety columns of boxes going down. Each of those boxes represents one week in my life IF I live to the age of ninety—which according to history would be older than any known male has lived in my family. I plan to make it to eighty years old at most. At the end of each week, I check off one of the boxes. I was born in 1977, so at the time of publishing this book, I'd be forty-five years old. The visual representation of your life in boxes is actually terrifying, or was to me when I first did it. I marked down significant dates. I also have marked down the time that I will be lucky enough to have my children living with me. If we want to live a life on purpose, we need to have a very clear idea of what that means. This gives me a bit of a time/reality check. You can find one for yourself on www.bravesmartkind.com/resources. This is an idea I got from Tim Urban who did a fantastic TED talk on The Art of Procrastination.

I don't know about you, but I need visual reminders in my life. I told everyone that we put up the chalk paint in the house for the kids, but the kids were both under the age of four when we did that. We put up the chalk paint for ourselves. I need the reminder that I have written there. "Kids who need the most love ask for it in the most unloving ways," and "Chin up, brain on, heart open." Yes, those are principles I use in raising my girls, but also for all of the firefighting we need to do during the day—with groceries or hockey practice or swim lessons, homework, arguing siblings, it's so difficult to focus on the bigger picture when the smaller pictures are flapping across our brains like a stop-motion film. Displaying them helps me.

For our little ones, yes, it does help for them to see the messages. Even more so it helps when they are able to engage with the messages. I had a custom set of dice made up with brave, smart and kind icons on them. When we are hanging out, we roll the dice and we tell a story from the dice. We have wall art. Alex and I painted our BSK logo on her wall in her room. We have sweatshirts that they cuddle up in when it's cold. We've had other people make BSK magnet boards, pencils, stickers, and more. We are currently developing a line of games that kids can play that helps put BSK right in front of them.

14.3 STEP THREE: DISCUSS IT

There is a reason this is the last part, my friends. This right here is the bread and butter of parenting with purpose. This makes the world of difference in raising kids to be brave, smart and kind. Are you ready for the secret sauce?

Talk to your kids.

TAAAA DAAAA!!!

I know, revolutionary work we are doing here right!?! Well, based on my experience, and what I have seen working with people around the world, talking to your kids is actually pretty revolutionary when we get it right. It can also be disastrous when we either get it wrong or ignore it completely.

The changes that I have seen in the relationships with my girls comes down to our ability to share the hard stuff, the easy stuff, the mundane and the interesting. My ability to have relevant conversations with my kids is make-or-break in my opinion. I get to talk to the girls about fear, danger, and difficulty. We talk about keeping their chin up, being brave. I get to talk to my girls about perspectives, connections, about keeping their brain on, being smart. I get to talk to my girls about how we take care of others and how we take care of ourselves. We talk about keeping our hearts open, being kind.

If you are thinking, "I don't know what to say about those things." Let me help you with that.

I'd like you for a second to imagine your life as a book. Perhaps each chapter is dedicated to an influential period in your life. You'd have a variety of characters you've met, subplots, twists, lessons learned, quotes to live by, values.

Paul Reber, Professor of Psychology at Northwestern University, has theorized that the brain can store two-and-a-half petabytes of data or two-and-a-half million gigabytes. That would loosely equal streaming 5000 years of continuous music on your phone, sixteen billion Facebook photos or thirty years of HD videos. It's estimated that all written works from the beginning of history in all languages is fifty petabytes. If your brain is capable of two-and-a-half petabytes, that equals 5% of all written works in the history of mankind!

If your brain is capable of two-and-a-half petabytes, then your life isn't a book, it's a library. Think back to the epic series of stories, each shaping the person that you are. How many stories do you think you have? Your brain is an ever-expanding library. You have the content to talk to your kids about being brave, smart and kind. You just have to rethink and see it through a new lens.

Think of your stories. If we want to help our kids feel more connected, less alone, then we need to have those types of stories that help them get there. It isn't hard to break down our stories. When we look at it through my BSK lens, we can find relevant questions to answer.

When I did I feel my most courageous? What scares me most? When did I overcome fear? When did I give into fear? When was fear healthy in my actions? Where did my fears come from? Am I afraid of becoming my parents? Why specifically? What examples of courage do I want to show my kids? If they picture the word brave, what do I want them to see? Who do I picture when I picture bravery? When did I need to try again, and again, and again?

When did I not think something through? When did I need to think more about an issue. What happens when I shut my brain off, and why does that happen? Many times those are stories of impatience, stress or anger. When do I feel that I need to breathe? What do I practice so that I can think clearly? When is my brain just not enough, and what do I do in those moments?

What are the relationships that have influenced me the most? Who are the kindest people I know and why do I see them that way? When was a time that someone showed me kindness when I didn't feel I deserved it? When do I ask for help? What do I not want help with? Who have I disappointed? When did I not take care of myself and what were the consequences? When did I let others' opinion of me take me down the wrong path?

If you have that list of conversation starters, where do you think a good place would be to start with those questions? Try your partner, see how that goes. You might learn a lot about each other which only goes even further to raising kids together. Pick the appropriate questions and ask your kids. Kids LOVE to tell stories.

Going back to our first rockstar teacher to implement BSK in her first grade class, Michelle Sabol started a "be brave, be smart, be kind" sharing time. Kids take turns talking about someone they witnessed during the day who lived the values. One day, a little girl named Taylor shared that her lunch box got stuck in the garbage bin and that Felipa was kind enough to get it out for her. Then all the kids started to chime in to say how kind Felipa was and all the good deeds that she does for them. Michelle had to ask around because, quite admittingly, she didn't know any girls at the school named Felipa! After some searching, Michelle found out that Felipa was the name of one of the cleaning staff who she had smiled and waved to hundreds of times. The kids however had a relationship with Felipa, and she was one of their great examples of kindness on a regular basis with all of her wonderful gestures, going above and beyond to make connections with the children. As a thank you, the class made her a poster with all of their names on it and delivered it to Felipa who received it with a beaming smile. This is one of the many stories that the teaching team would have never known about if they didn't do this small, yet significant, exercise to discuss BSK at the end of the day.

Our kids take their cues from us. When we ask them questions, they start to understand what we truly care about. If we ask them questions about their grades, they know that we care about their grades. If we ask them about their interests, they know we care about what they like. If we ask them questions about their friends, they know we care about their relationships. Likewise if we ONLY ask about grades and don't ask about their interests, that also says something to them too.

When we start to talk to our kids about BSK, they start to understand that we care about finding courage, about thoughtful topics, and about how we relate to people. They'll start to find ways to share with you. It is up to us however to start the conversations, to start the process of letting them know that they can come to us. For me, brave, smart and kind have done exactly that.

CHAPTER 14 TAKE HOME

- Follow the steps. Seriously, you didn't come this far only to come this far. Dig in.
- Send us your stories either via bravesmartkind.com or on social media!

CONCLUSION

"We perfect, most dangerously, our children. Let me tell you what we think about children. They're hardwired for struggle when they get here. And when you hold those perfect little babies in your hand, our job is not to say, "Look at her, she's perfect. My job is just to keep her perfect—make sure she makes the tennis team by fifth grade and Yale by seventh grade." That's not our job. Our job is to look and say, "You know what? You're imperfect, and you're wired for struggle, but you are worthy of love and belonging." That's our job. Show me a generation of kids raised like that, and we'll end the problems I think that we see today."

BRENÉ BROWN

"You are imperfect and you are worthy of love and belonging." This is such a wonderful quote. Raising kids to be brave, smart and kind isn't a one-person job. It isn't a two-person job. It takes a village as they say, and you will affect more kids than just your own. Hopefully, what we are doing here will help not only parents to see the wonderful traits and imperfections in their own kids, but help communities see that if we can get everyone on the same page, we can raise generations of kids who will overcome issues that our generations couldn't.

The very first recognition of BSK that I had outside of my family was with *Wizard of Oz* as we discussed in the first part of this book. We know that Dorothy got the instructions from the Good Witch of the North and a bunch of sugar-high little people to follow the yellow brick road to see the Wizard who would be able to get her home. She wanted to get back to Kansas, the Cowardly Lion wanted to get courage, the Scarecrow wanted a brain, and the Tinman wanted a heart. As they followed the path and experienced their journey they arrived in front of the Wizard only to find that they had those qualities inside of them all along. I don't see a more fitting end. Brave, smart and kind aren't simply words to help you raise your children; they are values that are already inside of you to help you on your journey. Even if it doesn't feel like it sometimes, it's true. The trick is to take the time to figure them out. Get specific with your values.

Just like my daughters swearing, your children are going to learn values from you before they learn them from anyone else. They are going to test you. Parenting with purpose means that you are inviting the challenge and stepping forward where many people step back. Please remember that our goal should never be to HAVE brave, smart and kind kids. Parenting has enough pressure and moments where we feel like we have failed. They will show you glimpses of those qualities, and pride is a perfectly normal and healthy emotion to feel. AND they'll fail, and so will you, and that's ok.

The real point of this book, in case you hadn't gotten it by now, is that raising kids to be brave, smart and kind has much less to do with the kids and much more to do with us. It is our understanding of how we act as parents that makes the difference. Like anything else in life, before we teach people a concept, we need to understand the concepts, we need to have some experience. The challenge now is, can you take what you have experienced and teach your kids. No pressure, but there is kinda a lot riding on this part—on you.

If you find ways to live your values, remember you are going to struggle. But I will bet you that when laying on your deathbed (hopefully many, many, many years from now) if you can say that you lived your life with bravery, that you lived your life with thought, and if you lived your life with kindness, you will have lived a purposeful one. And if that is the case, your children will see it and they will mimic it.

Here is my hope for anyone who has managed to get this far in the process. My hope is that this book enables you to go out and make better connections to both yourself and your family. And isn't courage, critical thought, and kindness what connects us as humans anyway? We don't fall in love with what people are wearing or what car they are driving. We don't fall in love with someone for their degree or their titles. What we are attracted to is the soul of someone, how they show up and overcome every single day. We connect with someone's incredible mind, how they think and give us perspective that we don't normally have. What we fall in love with is someone's heart, how they care for us and how they care for others. We look at the world through a lens of brave, smart and kind all the time. Once we understand it better, our view widens. Once we define what those foundational traits mean to us, we get to connect a bit quicker, a bit deeper with our friends, teammates, partners and most importantly, our children— those brave little souls, smart little minds, kind little hearts.

Please be patient, remember it's going to take some time. Parenting with purpose will be an adventure and at the end, the shortest moments are probably going to be the moments you'll want to slow down. You will definitely hit roadblocks, because you are dealing with real life. How you decide to handle those roadblocks will tell you how much you want it, if you need to be tested, and some will just be there for no reason at all. And you will be aiming at moving targets. We don't always know what the destination is, sometimes we just need to take a step in the right direction and trust that we are making the best decision with the information and perspectives that we have. Hopefully, from this book, I have given you a little more information, a different perspective that can help you take those steps towards your destination.

Raising kids to be brave, smart and kind is going to take all you've got. And just as a reminder, what you've got is enough. Remember: keep your chin up, your brain on, and your heart open. You've got this.

ACKNOWLEDGMENTS

First and foremost, to Alexandra, Emmeline, and Josephine. You don't know it yet, but the whole reason to write this book was to have something to pass down to you. I have no idea what will happen on this journey AND I am ok with that because I know the destination, and that is you.

Violaine – As if raising kids wasn't hard enough, I went and shared that experience with the world. Thank you for opening your heart and giving me all the support through this process. Our girls are a beautiful combination of our collective brave, smart and kind; and I am so incredibly thankful for that and for you. I love you.

Mom – I hope you are proud. Not of me, that I already know because you say it so often. I hope you are proud of yourself for doing what you thought was right, even when it was hard. Having the courage to keep trying even when it was a messy, bumpy, bubbled-up road. You were the first to tell me I could do it, and you have never wavered in that. You are amazing. Thank you.

Dad – Rest in Peace, I know you did your best and I love you. For the ways you were able to show up, you were all-in. I know life didn't turn out the way that you wanted it to but that doesn't mean I loved you any less. Thank you for giving everything you had, I miss you.

Chuck – Thank you for being the father who was always present. For the stability and love you gave a son who didn't start out as your own but has grown to become one. I love you.

Candy – This book probably could have been half of your stories. I don't know if I have ever said it to you, but I give a great deal of credit to my capacity to raise little girls to you and Mom. My younger years were completely surrounded by women. Thank you for loving and caring for me, even when it was hard to do.

The Kathman Family – Deke and Debbie, Jason, Jake, Joey and Jon. I loved being around your family growing up and feeling part of it when I would visit. Without any intention, you were showing me an incredible example of how a family could be. Jake, you are a brother to me… a slightly OLDER brother. Deke, thank you for being a father figure to me, as if you didn't have enough sons. PS. I could always take Jake's spot if he turns out to be a terrible disappointment to you.

The Roudebush Family – Bruce and Kate, Michael, Vanessa, Alex and Emily, Cedric, and Olivia. You accepted me and my family as part of yours. That love and togetherness is what I want as our family grows and shapes and spreads. I love all of you. Thank you for… everything.

Scott Strong – Thank you for always saying, "I love you." I don't grow up to be me without you being you. When I picture a man with immense courage, an incredible mind, and a huge capacity for love, I think of you.

Caleb Moore – Some family you are born with, some you choose. Brother, I can't tell you how important you are to me. From instant connection to Best Men to godparents, I know we always have each other's back. I love you and all your girls. I can't wait to do more life with you guys.

Michelle Sabol – This was a parenting idea that you ran with in your classroom. You saw the power of this concept in education before anyone and now it is on its way to becoming an educational movement. I can't possibly express what you have meant to BSK and inspiring me to keep pushing forward.

Ambreen Riyaz – When I was out in the world and talking about public speaking, you told me, "Your best talk is going to be about how you are raising your daughters." I sincerely hadn't thought about that before you said it. Thank you for seeing something in me that I didn't.

Warren Rustand – You are a gift to this world and have impacted countless lives. Thank you for our conversations and for sharing your knowledge and your heart. Both of those things brought me courage. I am fortunate to know you and that you have taken the time to know me.

Rich Mulholland – BSK doesn't exist without your support and guidance. I rarely, if ever, know what I am doing, and yet you always helped me push forward. Thank you for taking the time to tell me that I could do this, being available to talk through some of the hard stuff and opening your family to me. Love you, man.

Steven Shortt – Talk about an amazing example of a man with an open heart. From day one you show people a level of respect and care that is parallel to none. I have sincerely never met anyone like you, and if the world could take even a fraction of that love and spread it around… well, it'd just end in world peace I suppose. For any cloning experts reading this, I'll give you his contact info.

Miten Shah – Thank you for recognizing the real take-home value from our values-based leadership session and showing me other parents could use this.

John Harlan and Sol Feinstone Elementary – For being the first school to adopt a BSK theme and all the work you put in to make sure your students and faculty have the support they need.

Maureen Crawford – I was terrified to show anyone the depth of this brave, smart, kind idea. Not knowing if I was insane or naïve or blind. Thank you for the instant connection and unwavering support. BSK could have died an instant death without the right person in my life at the right time. That person is you and I am so grateful for that.

Krista Clive-Smith and Kelly Cleeve and everyone at the KCS Family of Companies – This book never gets done without you. Your level of knowledge and professionalism mixed with a human connection and empathy for me as a writer and as a father has been next level. Sincerely, thank you for everything.

The Entrepreneurs' Organization – I couldn't begin to list out the people and the lessons here. It was an incredible journey, thank you for letting me be a part of it.

Up with People – To say you changed my life would be the understatement of my lifetime. You taught me incredible lessons of leadership and family. You brought me Timo, Manny, Patrick, Willy, Sean and Angela; brothers and sisters who will always be there with open hearts. You brought me Aly and Mike who are family now. You brought me the Roudebi. You brought me to Belgium the first, second and third time. Not sure why you couldn't have chosen sunnier countries, but I am forever grateful for your impact.

ANNEX

We have spoken so much about values, I thought it might help to share an in-depth explanation of my own to help you develop yours. The process to define my values is much like the one that we walked through in the last chapter except I developed the steps through several years of trial and error. You'll see that my values aren't just words, but phrases. I find that context helps me remember my values more than simply remembering singular characteristics. Please note that I have written and rewritten them. I have changed definitions. I have challenged them and had others challenge them too. I revisit my values once a year to see if they need any polishing. If nothing else, it serves as a reminder for me.

My three values are:

- Take Care of Others
- Be Intentional
- Create Your Own Luck

PERSONAL DEFINITION OF KIND
Take Care of Others

1. Kindness is Badass.

2. Smiles and laughter are contagious. Share yours as often as you can.

3. Appreciate others. Their time and care for you is precious, treat it as such.

4. You can't take care of others if you aren't taking care of yourself once in a while.

5. Be humble. We are all warmed by fires we didn't light, we drink from wells we didn't dig. No one is self-made.

1) Kindness is Badass.

The badass theme may come up a couple of times in this book. I don't know why I admire people who are considered "badass" but I do. I like that word. To me it means that someone still gets to be a rebel, go against the rules, be unique, follow their heart. Chalk this up to some of my favorite childhood characters—Han Solo, Indiana Jones and Robin Hood. (Yes it is a shame that Harrison Ford never played the green-hooded archer, but there are plenty of other characters.) Something always speaks to me when a person walks in with the utmost confidence and is generous, understanding and compassionate. Kindness to me is the ultimate act of a badass. They have all the power in the world to treat someone poorly, yet they choose to be kind. We all have that power and that choice.

2) Smiles and laughter are contagious. Share yours as often as you can.

This may have been one of my earliest values, and yet one that I have to revisit time and time again. It isn't that I forget to smile or laugh, it is that I forget the impact it can have on others. I am reminded often with my daughters because their smiles and laughter are so healing to me. If I have had a bad day or if I am feeling down, I can't see them playing and smiling without it bringing a smile on my face as well. They give me energy when they exude happiness. And we all have that power. Just look at two people smiling at each other, an old man laughing at a joke, or a toddler cracking up on a swing.

3) Appreciate others. Their time and care for you is precious, treat it as such.

I first included this in my personal definition because of how much I sincerely hate being late. I was once told that when you are late, you are saying to people that your time is more valuable than theirs. I don't fully subscribe to that after working and interacting with people who don't prioritize in the same way, but I also feel it rings true if you disregard or are unappreciative of someone's time or attention. Those are gifts that other people give you, and when you get a gift from someone it is precious. I read somewhere that even if a child gives you a stone, treat it as a precious gift because it is all they have and they chose to give it to you.

4) You can't take care of others if you aren't taking care of yourself once in a while.

This is one that I struggled with growing up. When people are infinitely kind, they always put others before themselves. Others before self is a lesson that I believe I first learned in church and it was something that I saw so often in my mother at a young age. And what often happens to people who are infinitely kind to others? They get walked all over. They burn out. They can't say no. They feel guilty when they do something for themselves. "Put your mask on first" is what you hear in the safety presentation before take off on an airplane. I have never been in a situation when the masks drop down, but I bet any amount of money I'll be holding my breath and putting my child's mask on before mine. That is instinct. It doesn't make it the right thing to do, but I am not sure I'll change it. AND when it comes to life, especially with younger kids, it's so easy to get lost in the needs of our kids and the needs of our partners. But I have seen unhealthy versions of parents. Correction, I have been an unhealthy version of that where I can become resentful, exhausted, easily triggered—all because I can't get out and play a sport. Not exercise, I want to compete. I want to fight for a ball, I want some contact, I want the feeling of comradery on a field. Sometimes I need a guys night out, sometimes one-to-one time with my wife, sometimes just to be alone. When I get it, I feel I can give more of myself. Without it, I struggle.

5) Be humble. We are all warmed by fires we didn't light, we drink from wells we didn't dig. No one is self-made.

This is a quote that I first heard used by a good friend and great man, Warren Rustand. Beyond being an amazing father and a successful leader, Warren has a unique ability to inspire others to be so much more than themselves. When I looked up this quote, I found it in the Bible too. Warren is also a religious man. I don't prescribe to any one religion, but the quote helps me define this value better. I can't stand when someone calls themselves, "a self-made man." (Ironically, you never hear a woman calling herself that.) Usually when someone refers to themselves as self-made, they are using it as an excuse to tell someone else that they too should be self-reliant. But here is the catch. That is all a bunch of shit. Unless you were born and left in a forest where all the other animals abandoned you and you foraged for food from birth, you had some help along the way. Maybe it was from parents, or teachers, or friends. Maybe you had food on the table every night and electricity to read by, which also meant someone provided you with books. Not only are there countless scenarios where a "self-made man" was given something, but even if someone else was given the EXACT same "stuff" it doesn't mean your journeys are even comparable. Get off your horse, be humble, recognize that and be grateful without judgement for those who have less or more than you. NO one is self-made.

PERSONAL DEFINITION OF SMART

Be Intentional

1. If you are going to do something, do it with purpose.

2. You've used up more than half of your 29,200 boxes, what's next?

3. Seek knowledge and question everything. There is always another angle to view.

4. Just because happiness is the goal, it doesn't mean that is all you'll find on the path.

5. The worst leader is the one who thinks they've arrived. Keep growing.

Here is how these principles break down.

1) If you are going to do something, do it with purpose.

This was actually my first thought in fathering with values. I can either be the best father I can be and see how my kiddos turn out OR I can do it with more purpose, with greater intention. Purpose implies understanding why you do something, and this is a beautiful and dangerous rabbit hole to explore. The more I can use my critical thought to explore deeper meanings, the more meaningful the specific moments are.

2) You've used up more than half of your 29,200 boxes, what's next?

This might be a bit morbid and has definitely come to a shock to some, but I have a piece of paper on the back of my values with 4,680 boxes on it, or one box for each week if I live to be ninety years old. The boxes up until my current age are checked off. The boxes from my current age until age eighty are blank, and all the boxes past the age of eighty have question marks on them. If you break eighty years into days you get 29,200. That is how many days I hope that I have in my life. Eighty might be ambitious as my father passed away at seventy-one and the three generations of men from his side all passed away before the age of thirty-five. I'll plan for eighty and see where I get. Regardless, I use this exercise as perspective. This is a deathbed exercise. If I know my end is coming, what do I want to say that I did, or that I tried? How do I want to love? How do I want to show up? How do I want to measure my success? Because guess what, I know my end is coming, so why would I wait until I am on my deathbed? So, I don't. I try to make each choice with the best of intentions, and it helps me live with no regrets. This doesn't mean that some days, weeks, months—and yes even years—have gone by where I procrastinated with a choice or in how I have progressed; but I also try to be patient and forgiving with myself. I don't need to be an extremist, I do, however, want to continue to be aware, and this is one way that helps.

3) Seek knowledge and question everything. There is always another angle to view.

Do I believe that ignorance is bliss? Yes I do. I just don't think that bliss is the goal, as you'll notice in the principle just below this one. Knowledge for me is all sorts of input. Some of it is fact, some of it is perspective, some of it is just plain old experience. However you define it, I believe it needs to be sought out. The knowledge that is fed to you shouldn't be blindly trusted. It may be right, but when we start accepting knowledge without questions is where critical thought dies. I was one of the kids that questioned everything. Sometimes I openly questioned people, sometimes I just did it silently.

4) Just because happiness is the goal, it doesn't mean that is all you'll find on the path.

I once wrote a philosophy paper on doing whatever makes you happy as a rule of life. I got a good grade on it, but my professor said that there was a famous philosopher who also wrote on this topic and was beaten and murdered by his students. I put it here in this definition because I get so frustrated with pessimism and negativity. I used to avoid people and situations that would lead me to those negative spaces when I was young. As I got older, I realized the necessity of sitting with your demons, having the hard conversations, and paying attention to the darkness. I don't avoid it—as often.

5) The worst leader is the one who thinks they've arrived. Keep growing.

I have been lucky enough to work with leaders around the world. There are good and bad leaders out there of course, but the worst that I have seen are the ones who are unwilling or unable to continue to improve. Growth and intention go hand in hand in my opinion. For me, I see myself as a leader in all aspects of my life, as a father, husband, friend, teammate, professional. This doesn't mean that people follow me, or that I have any sort of control over others. It means I have control over my own actions, I make choices even if I don't like all my options, and that I am ultimately responsible for my own experiences. There are countless times when my intention was completely thwarted by both outside influence and self-sabotage. Growth, learning, adapting, and "figuring it out on the fly," takes an elastic mind, one that is able to stretch, but also holds thoughts and connections together. That doesn't happen when you think you have all the answers.

PERSONAL DEFINITION OF BRAVE

Create Your Own Luck

1. Luck is when preparation meets opportunity.
2. Keep showing up even when you are scared or tired or unsure. Show up.
3. Don't risk what you aren't willing to lose.
4. Don't be afraid to go with the flow. Miracles sometimes happen in silence.
5. Your privilege comes with responsibility, share your good fortune.

Let's break this one down a bit more.

1) Luck is when preparation meets opportunity.

I like this definition because I believe I have been very lucky in my life. I am lucky for the family I was born into. I was lucky to meet the friends I have along the way. I am lucky, in many parts, to still be alive after some dumb decisions. I have been lucky in my fortunes and misfortunes. I am lucky to be married to my wife and I am lucky to have my kids. That doesn't mean that everything has been a simple coincidence. There is an accountability piece to luck, and that is what my grandmother taught me. She told me that luck is when preparation meets opportunity.

Naturally as a child, I couldn't prepare myself to belong to one family or another, but as I got older and gained that wisdom from my grandma I began to see that indeed I could only blame myself for my bad luck and I had a hand in creating my own luck. How to do that? Prepare as you are able, and keep showing up. No one has ever won the lottery who hasn't bought a ticket. (Side note: lotteries are ridiculous outside of the state collecting a "gullible tax," but the analogy works.) If you don't show up, then good things can't happen. Sometimes showing up gets you kicked in the teeth too. That is where the bravery comes into play. I try to prepare myself well, and I try to keep putting myself out there. If I fail, well we can either look at the preparation or the opportunity. One didn't go right, but that doesn't mean I should stop. It means I need to reassess my planning or how I am showing up.

2) Keep showing up even when you are scared or tired or unsure. Show up.

I suppose you can call this "1) a" but I like to have it separate, and they are my values so I can do what I want to. This is the one that keeps me focused on being present even when it is hard to do so. As negative values go, this one also has gotten me in trouble because I can often show up in places or situations where I am neither wanted or needed. There have been some painful lessons, and some that have needed (and still need) repeating, but I would rather go a bit overboard in this and fail trying, than to live on the cautious side.

3) Don't risk what you aren't willing to lose.

This may be a nod to my father, he was a risk taker too and I feel like he lost more than he won because he didn't have the right limitations. This definition keeps me in check. I enjoy calculated risks. This will overlap with some of my "smart" definitions, but if you are going to keep putting yourself out there, there are consequences. When I am making decisions, I need to be able to assess what the gains and losses are. I have made some of my biggest mistakes when I have miscalculated or simply ignored this rule. There is a quote from influential American journalist Hunter S. Thompson which goes, "Life should not be a journey to the grave with the intention of arriving safely in a pretty and well-preserved body, but rather to skid in broadside in a cloud of smoke, thoroughly used up, totally worn out, and loudly proclaiming *Wow! What a Ride!*" I love that quote AND it also needs to be considered that living that type of life can wear you down. After all, Thompson slid into his grave sideways after battling addiction, depression and committing suicide. Risk the stuff that doesn't matter as much, if you can't live without it… don't risk it.

4) Don't be afraid to go with the flow. Miracles sometimes happen in silence.

I think I added this idea to my definition in my thirties when I was able to create my own team at my company. I was given a list of positions and told to go hire the best. And that is what I did. The problem was that I was so used to having to prove my worth to others so they would give me more responsibility, that I kept meddling in my team's business and didn't allow them to breathe. It wasn't from a place of distrust or micromanaging. I was just showing up so often that it didn't give them enough room to grow. I had to learn that part of creating my own luck was to find situations to still show up AND be quiet. I have found that to be of equal—if not of greater—importance as a father with kids who are growing each and every day. Sometimes what I need to do is to be close enough to be supportive and far enough away that they can succeed and fail on their own accord. I need to be able to go with the flow of parenthood, and sit in silence.

For anyone who knows me, silence isn't easy, but seeing the miracles that are my girls and how they handle their own business is incredible and worthwhile.

5) Your privilege comes with responsibility, share your good fortune.

The last part of creating my own luck goes along with one of my "kind" definitions of realizing that most of it was given to me. I am a white, middle class, man—that alone gave me privilege at birth. I am neither proud nor ashamed of it, that is just who I am and I recognize it. Does that mean it is worse to be born a black, poor, woman? Nope. Does it mean anyone who isn't me is a charity case? Not in the least. It means that If I have been lucky enough, yes even through preparation and opportunity, I have a responsibility in life to share that good fortune with others. Some people have no idea how to prepare themselves and aren't given the same opportunities. I can help with both of those things. This is the concept of servant leadership, it is also an example that I want my girls to understand. Part of me creating my own luck is helping others create theirs.

ABOUT THE AUTHOR

Patrick Jon Brady, or PJ as he is more commonly known, is American by birth, Belgian by marriage and Global by choice. He lives just outside of Brussels with his wife and three daughters. PJ has been entertaining and speaking to audiences since 1998 when he toured with the international musical and leadership organization, Up with People. After three years on the road performing and teaching on stage, and twelve years working with successful entrepreneurs, his true message wasn't discovered until he became a father. He found exceptional similarities between what it takes to be a leader and what it takes to raise children with intention. It all comes down to our fundamental core values of courage, critical thought, and kindness—or for children, how to be brave, smart and kind. Knowing the fundamental values however is not enough. We need to know how to put those values into practice.

In 2017, PJ started The Brave Smart Kind Company, a learning organization that coaches leaders, teachers, parents and organizations to work towards their goals with greater purpose. PJ has spoken to and coached leaders in twenty-seven countries. This is PJ's first book, and hopefully not his last.

CPSIA information can be obtained
at www.ICGtesting.com
Printed in the USA
BVHW080504291022
650556BV00002B/13

9 781957 048758